CHEMISTRY
A Guided Inquiry, Part 2
8th Edition

Richard S. Moog
Professor
Franklin & Marshall College

Gail H. Webster
Professor
Guilford College

John J. Farrell
Professor Emeritus
Franklin & Marshall College

Kendall Hunt
publishing company

The POGIL Project
Director: Richard Moog
Associate Director: Marcy Dubroff
Publications Liaison: Susan Richardson

Cover image © Shutterstock.com
Source for all interior line art: The POGIL Project

www.kendallhunt.com
Send all inquiries to:
4050 Westmark Drive
Dubuque, IA 52004-1840

Published in the United States of America

To the Instructor

The activities in this book are written according to the principles of Process Oriented Guided Inquiry Learning (POGIL), an evidence-based and learner-centered pedagogy. In a POGIL learning environment, students work in structured learning teams using POGIL activities whose design is based on research about how students learn. Materials are available on-line to help instructors use this particular collection of POGIL activities effectively. Please contact Danielle Schlichtmann (dschlichtmann@kendallhunt.com) for information on how to obtain access to these materials.

In addition, The POGIL Project supports the dissemination and implementation of these types of materials for high school chemistry courses at the first-year and AP levels and for most of the undergraduate chemistry curriculum (including introductory, GOB, organic, physical, analytical, and biochemistry). POGIL materials are also available for other STEM disciplines include biology and anatomy and physiology, computer science, and mathematics. Information about The POGIL Project, a not-for-profit 501(c)(3) organization, and its activities (including additional materials, workshops, and other professional development opportunities) can be found at https://pogil.org/.

New for this edition

The most significant and impactful change for this 8th edition of *Chemistry: A Guided Inquiry* is the addition of a new authoring partner, Gail H. Webster. With a fresh set of eyes and extensive experience using the previous editions, she brings new insights and ideas to this effort. As a result, this edition has some of the most substantial changes made to these activities since they were first published twenty-five years ago.

Recently, substantial gains have been made by a variety of colleagues in The POGIL Project – and others – in understanding how to write activities that produce the most learning and the greatest gains in the development of key process skills such as teamwork, critical thinking, problem solving, and metacognition. We have incorporated as many of these new insights into the structure and organization of these materials as we can.

Below we list some of the major changes and highlights for this new edition:

- Each ChemActivity is titled as a question. Typically, the answer to that question embodies one of the important learning goals of the activity - and in most cases a version of that question is included as an Exercise or Problem.

- The number of explicit prompts for students to develop teamwork skills is substantially increased. Students are regularly directed to engage in the practices of working as a team, comparing answers, and reaching consensus.

- Increased attention has been paid to the development of key process skills such as information processing, critical thinking, and problem solving skills within the activities. We have included more prompts that direct students to engage in important learning practices such as explaining their reasoning, identifying the information used as evidence in their analysis, critiquing a suggested analysis, and putting consensus ideas into their own words.

- Several new figures have been added to support student visualization at the molecular level. More opportunities for students to generate molecular-level representations have also been added.

- All of the activities (with two exceptions) now begin with a "Warm-Up" section that students *may* complete before coming to class. In many cases, the activity was reorganized so that much of the text is now in the "Warm-Up" section, enabling students to read introductory material before coming to class and reserving more class time for working on the activities with their teammates. Instructors may choose to use the "Warm-Up" sections in this way, or they may choose to have the students complete the "Warm-Up" sections as part of the team work during class time.

- Several activities were restructured to better incorporate a learning cycle structure of exploration, concept invention, and application.

- Additional exercises and problems were added to many of the activities.

Acknowledgments

This book is the result of innumerable interactions that we have had with a large number of stimulating and thoughtful people.

- We greatly appreciate the support and encouragement of the many members of The POGIL Project. These colleagues continue to provide us with an opportunity to discuss our ideas with interested, stimulating, and dedicated professionals who care deeply about their students and their learning. Over the past several years, our colleagues in The POGIL Project have helped us learn a great deal about how to construct more effective and impactful activities; much of what we have learned from them is reflected in the substantially revised activities in this edition.

- Julie Gemmell is responsible for many of the new images, figures and diagrams in this edition - and also many revised ones! Her ability to take roughly sketched ideas and turn them into beautifully and clearly realized representations is truly remarkable!

- Thanks to the numerous colleagues who used our previous editions in their classrooms. Many provided us with insightful comments and suggestions for which we are grateful.

- Many thanks to our late colleague, Jim Spencer, Professor Emeritus, Franklin & Marshall College, for his helpful and insightful discussions, comments, and corrections.

- A great debt of thanks is due our students in General Chemistry at Franklin & Marshall College and in Chemical Principles at Guilford College. Their enthusiasm for this approach, patience with our errors, and helpful and insightful comments have inspired us to continue to develop as instructors, and have helped us to improve these materials immeasurably.

- Thanks to the National Science Foundation (Grants DUE-0231120, 0618746, 0618758, and 0618800) for its initial support of The POGIL Project, a not-for-profit organization that fosters the development and dissemination of guided-inquiry materials and encourages faculty to develop and use student-centered approaches in their classrooms.

- The participants in the Middle Atlantic Discovery Chemistry Project (MADCP) provided support and encouragement when this work began and for the decades that followed. Their wisdom and feedback was invaluable in shaping these activities.

- Special thanks to Dan Apple, Pacific Crest Software, for starting us on this previously untraveled path. The Pacific Crest Teaching Institute that RSM and JJF attended in 1994 provided us with the initial insights and inspiration to convert our classrooms into fully student-centered learning environments.

Contents

To the Student

Science and engineering have dominated world events and world culture for at least 150 years. The blind and near blind have been made to see. The deaf and near deaf have been made to hear. The ill have been made well. Radio, television and the internet have made the world seem smaller. Computers have played an essential role in all of these developments; they are now ubiquitous. These miraculous events happened by design—not by accident. People set out to accomplish goals. They systematically studied and analyzed the natural world around us. They designed and tested new tools. Human beings have embarked on a journey that cannot be reversed. We hope that you can participate in and contribute to these exciting times.

There is simply too much chemistry—not to mention physics, mathematics, biology, geology, and engineering—for any one person to assimilate. As a result, teams have become essential to identifying, defining, and solving problems in our society. This book was designed for you to use as a working member of a team, actively engaged with the *important basic* concepts of chemistry. Our goals are to have you learn how to examine and process information, to ask good questions, to construct your own understanding, and to build your problem-solving skills.

If ever a book was written for students—this is it. This is *not* a textbook. This is *not* a study guide. This book is "a guided inquiry," in which you will examine data, written descriptions, and figures to develop chemical concepts. Each concept is explored in a *ChemActivity* comprising several sections—one or more **Model** and **Information** sections, **Critical Thinking Questions**, and **Exercises** and **Problems**. You and your team study the Models and Information and systematically work through the Critical Thinking Questions. In doing so, you will discover important chemical principles and relationships. If you understand the answer to a question, but other members of your team do not, it is your responsibility to explain the answer. Explaining concepts to other members of your team not only helps in *their* understanding, it broadens *your* understanding. If you do not understand the answer to a question, you should ask questions to the other members of your team. Learning to ask questions that clearly and concisely describe what you do not understand is an important skill. This book has many Critical Thinking Questions to serve as examples. To reinforce the ideas that are developed, and to practice applying them to new situations, numerous Exercises and Problems are provided; these are important for you to apply your new knowledge to new situations and solidify your understanding. Research has demonstrated that this combination of methods is generally a more effective learning strategy than the traditional lecture, and the vast majority of our students have agreed.

We hope that you will take ownership of your learning and that you will develop skills for lifelong learning. Nobody else can do it for you. We wish you well in this undertaking.

Richard S. Moog   Gail H. Webster   John J. Farrell

Is Energy Released or Used When a Bond Breaks?

WARM-UP

Model 1: Nuclei are Held Together by Coulombic Attraction to Electrons.

Consider two *bare* nuclei, in this case two protons, as shown in Figure 1. From Coulomb's Law we know that these protons will repel each other.

Figure 1.   Coulombic interaction of two protons.

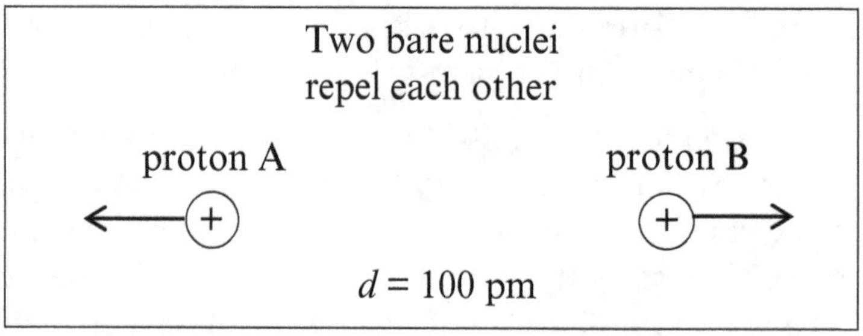

Two bare nuclei
repel each other

proton A   proton B

$\longleftarrow$ (+)   (+) $\longrightarrow$

$d = 100$ pm

The (repulsive) Coulombic potential energy is (see CA 3):

$$V = \frac{k\,q_1\,q_2}{d} = \frac{2.31 \times 10^{-16}\,\text{J} \bullet \text{pm}}{100\ \text{pm}} = 2.31 \times 10^{-18}\,\text{J} \quad \text{(repulsive)} \tag{1}$$

where $k = 2.31 \times 10^{-16}\,\text{J} \bullet \text{pm}$.

Critical Thinking Questions

1. a) Why is "100 pm" in the denominator of equation 1?

    b) Let q_1 = charge on nucleus A and q_2 = charge on nucleus B. What are the values of q_1 and q_2 for equation 1?

    c) Show explicitly how the value for the numerator in equation 1 was obtained from the Coulombic potential energy expression.

Model 2: An Electron Between Two Nuclei.

If an electron is placed halfway between the nuclei, then each nucleus is attracted toward the electron.

Figure 2.   Nuclei are attracted to an electron.

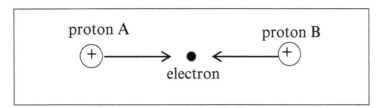

The (attractive) Coulombic potential energy is given by the sum of the interactions of nucleus A with the electron and nucleus B with the electron.

$$V = \frac{-2.31 \times 10^{-16} \text{J} \bullet \text{pm}}{50 \text{ pm}} + \frac{-2.31 \times 10^{-16} \text{J} \bullet \text{pm}}{50 \text{ pm}} = -9.24 \times 10^{-18} \text{ J (attractive)} \quad (2)$$

The net Coulombic potential energy is the sum of the energy of interaction of the two nuclei (given in equation 1) and the energy of interaction of the two nuclei with the electron (given in equation 2):

$$V = 2.31 \times 10^{-18} \text{ J} + (-9.24 \times 10^{-18} \text{ J}) = -6.93 \times 10^{-18} \text{ J} \qquad \text{(attractive)}$$

Critical Thinking Questions

2.   a)   Why is "50 pm" in the denominator of each term in equation 2?

     b)   Show explicitly how the value for the numerator in both terms of equation 2 was obtained from the Coulombic potential energy expression.

3.   Explain why the numerator in equation 1 is positive, but the numerator in equation 2 is negative.

4. The net attractive potential energy in Figure 2 is -6.93×10^{-18} J. Will energy be required to separate the nuclei or will energy be released upon separation? Explain.

Information

This model, of course, only approximates reality. One cannot simply place a stationary electron between two nuclei. Electrons move (have kinetic energy) and occupy certain regions of space (domains or orbitals). Nonetheless, the model above demonstrates that nuclei can be held together by electron sharing between nuclei.

As we have seen previously, typically there are two electrons (or multiples of two) being shared between atoms to form a bond in real molecules. Based on the concepts developed in Models 1 and 2, we expect that energy will be required to break a bond.

END OF WARM-UP

Model 3: Endothermic and Exothermic Processes.

When chemical processes occur, energy (typically as heat) is either released—an **exothermic** process, or absorbed—an **endothermic** process. The breaking of bonds requires energy to pull the atoms apart; bond-breaking is thus an endothermic process. When bonds are formed, energy is released—precisely the same amount of energy which would be required to break those bonds. Thus, the making of bonds is an exothermic process.

The quantity of energy released or absorbed in a chemical process can be designated by an enthalpy (energy) change, ΔH, for that process. If there is a release of energy when the reaction occurs, the value of ΔH is negative, and the reaction is exothermic. If the reaction results in a net consumption of energy, then ΔH is positive, and the reaction is endothermic.

Figure 3.   A simple chemical process.

$$H_2 \longrightarrow H + H$$

Critical Thinking Questions

Answer CTQs 5 – 7 as a team.

5. Is the chemical reaction represented in Figure 3 exothermic or endothermic?

6. Is ΔH for the chemical reaction represented in Figure 3 positive or negative?

7. Provide a chemical equation for a reaction with a value of ΔH that has the same magnitude of ΔH as the reaction in Figure 3, but has the opposite sign.

Model 4: Enthalpy of Atom Combination.

Figure 4.   The enthalpy of atom combination of $CH_4(g)$ at 25 °C.

$$\underline{1 \text{ mole C(g)} + 4 \text{ mole H(g)}} \longleftarrow \begin{array}{c}\text{enthalpy of}\\ \text{one mole C(g) and}\\ \text{four moles H(g)}\end{array}$$

$H \uparrow$
increasing
enthalpy

$$\Delta H^{\circ}_{ac} = -1662.09 \text{ kJ}$$

$$\underline{1 \text{ mole } CH_4 \text{ (g)}} \longleftarrow \begin{array}{c}\text{enthalpy of}\\ \text{one mole } CH_4 \text{ (g)}\end{array}$$

When a mole of a compound is produced from its constituent atoms in the gas phase at 1 atmosphere pressure and 25 °C, energy is released as bonds are formed. The standard state heat (or enthalpy) of atom combination, ΔH°_{ac}, is the difference in enthalpy of product and reactants ($H^{\circ}_{product} - H^{\circ}_{reactants}$) when this occurs. Equation 3 is the (hypothetical) chemical equation for this process for $CH_4(g)$, and Figure 4 provides a visual representation of this process.

$$C(g) + 4H (g) \longrightarrow CH_4(g) \tag{3}$$

Critical Thinking Questions

Answer CTQs 8 – 12 as a team.

8. Based on the information in Model 4, what is the value of ΔH° for reaction 3?

9. Is the enthalpy of atom combination for $CH_4(g)$ exothermic or endothermic?

Table 1.   Standard state enthalpies of atom combination, ΔH°_{ac}.

Substance	ΔH°_{ac} (kJ/mol)	Substance	ΔH°_{ac} (kJ/mol)
H(g)	0	CH_4(g)	−1662.09
C(g)	0		
N(g)	0	H_2O(g)	−926.29
O(g)	0	H_2O(ℓ)	−970.30
H_2(g)	−435.30	NH_3(g)	−1171.76
N_2(g)	−945.408	NO_2(g)	−937.86
O_2(g)	−498.340	N_2O_4(g)	−1932.93

10. Based on the data in Table 1, what is ΔH° for the reaction represented by

$$H(g) + H(g) \longrightarrow H_2(g)?$$

11. Why is ΔH°_{ac} of C(g) = 0? Why is ΔH°_{ac} of H(g) = 0?

12. For molecules, why are all of the values for enthalpies of atom combination negative?

13. a) Individually, draw the Lewis structures for N_2 and O_2. Once all team members are done, compare answers and make any needed changes.

   b) Individually, explain how these Lewis structures are consistent with the relative enthalpies of atom combination for N_2(g) and O_2(g). Once all team members are done, compare your answers and reach consensus on a team best answer.

Model 5: Breaking One Mole of $CH_4(g)$ into its Constituent Atoms.

1 mole C(g) + 4 mole H(g)

$H \uparrow$ $\Delta H° = 1662.09$ kJ

1 mole $CH_4(g)$

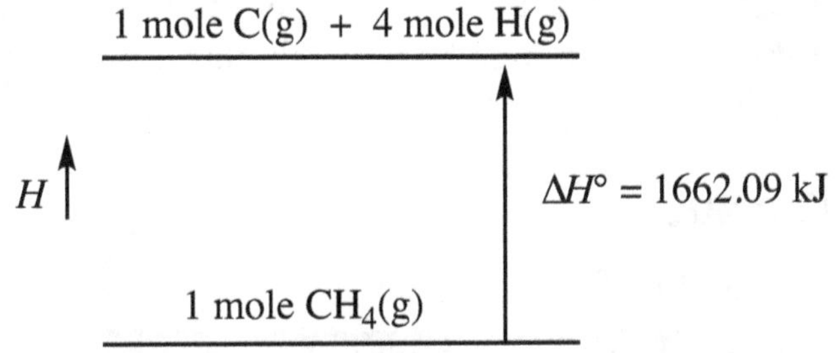

One can also imagine the process in which a mole of a substance is broken apart into its constituent gas phase atoms. This is precisely the reverse of an "enthalpy of atom combination reaction," and, in this case, energy will be consumed. For example, the value of $\Delta H°$ for the reaction represented by

$$CH_4 (g) \longrightarrow C(g) + 4H(g)$$

is 1662.09 kJ/mole, as shown in Model 4.

Critical Thinking Questions

Answer CTQs 14 and 15 as a team.

14. What is the value of $\Delta H°$ for the overall process of separating one mole of CH_4 into its constituent atoms, and then reforming one mole of CH_4?

15. a) Calculate the amount of energy released (always a positive number) when exactly 2 moles of CH_4 are formed from the appropriate constituent atoms (as opposed to forming *one* mole of CH_4).

 b) Calculate the change in enthalpy when 1.5 moles of C(g) combines with 6 moles of H(g) to form 1.5 moles of CH_4 (g).

Model 6: Bond Strength and Enthalpies of Atom Combination.

Recall that for bonds between pairs of atoms, "the stronger the bond, the shorter the bond length." That is, a C–O double bond is stronger than a C–O single bond, and the double bond is also shorter. For bonds between similar atoms, we also find that "the shorter the bond length, the stronger the bond."

Critical Thinking Questions

16. Consider H–F, H–Cl, and H–Br.

a)   Individually, rank the three molecules in order of increasing bond length and explain your reasoning. Check your answer with your teammates before continuing to part b.

b)   Based on the answer to part a, list the three molecules in order of increasing bond strength.

c)   Examine the ΔH_{ac}° data for these species [see Table A.3 in the Appendix]. As a team, discuss and explain how the answer to part b is (or is not) consistent with these values.

For CTQ 17, discuss and answer each part as a team.

17.   a)   Which bond is longer: C-H or C-Cl? Explain your reasoning.

b)   Based on your answer to part a, which do you expect to be the stronger bond, C–H or C–Cl?

c)   Examine the ΔH_{ac}° data for $CH_4(g)$ and $CH_3Cl(g)$ and explain how your answer to part b is (or is not) consistent with these values.

d)   Based on the ΔH_{ac}° values for $CH_4(g)$ and $CH_3Cl(g)$, predict ΔH_{ac}° for $CH_3F(g)$ and $CH_3Br(g)$. Explain your reasoning.

Exercises

1. When a bond breaks, is energy released or consumed? Provide an explanation that would convince someone who thinks that your answer is not correct.

2. Predict whether the reactions represented by each of the following equations is exothermic or endothermic:

    a) $CO(g) \longrightarrow C(g) + O(g)$

    b) $2 H(g) + O(g) \longrightarrow H_2O(g)$

    c) $Na^+(g) + Cl^-(g) \longrightarrow NaCl(s)$

3. What is the sign for ΔH in each of the reactions in Exercise 1?

4. Which of the following enthalpies of atom combination is obviously incorrect?

    i) $CHCl_3(g)$ $\Delta H_{ac}^\circ = -1433.84$ kJ/mole

    ii) $Cr(g)$ $\Delta H_{ac}^\circ = 0$

    iii) $I_2(s)$ $\Delta H_{ac}^\circ = 213.68$ kJ/mole

    iv)   none of these is obviously incorrect

5. The ΔH_{ac}° of C(graphite) is -716.682 kJ/mole and the ΔH_{ac}° of C(diamond) is -714.787 kJ/mole. Overall, are the bonds stronger in diamond or graphite? Explain your reasoning.

6. Based on their values of ΔH_{ac}° (see Table A.3 in Appendix), indicate whether the following statement is true or false and explain your reasoning.

    The bonds in $SiCl_4(g)$ are stronger than the bonds in $SnCl_4(g)$.

7. Potentially useful information:

Substance	ΔH_{ac}° (kJ/mole)
$H_2O(g)$	-926.29
$H_2S(g)$	-734.74

    a)   Determine the O-H bond energy in H_2O and the S–H bond energy in H_2S.

    b)   Based on your answer to part a, which is the stronger bond, O-H or S-H?

    c)   Give a rationale based on the structures of the molecules for the relative bond strengths of O-H and S-H found above.

8. For each of the following groups of compounds, draw the Lewis structures, predict which molecule will have the most negative ΔH_{ac}°, and explain your reasoning.

    a) Cl_2, Br_2, I_2

    b) N_2, P_2, As_2

9.a)   Which do you predict has the stronger bond, C–H or C–Cl?

   b)   Calculate the average C–H bond energy in CH_4 from ΔH°_{ac}.

   c)   Calculate the average C–Cl bond energy in CCl_4 from ΔH°_{ac}.

   d)   Compare the two bond energies. Is this the result you predicted?

10.   The O–H bond energy in H_2O is 464 kJ/mole.

   a)   Do you expect the C–H bond energy in CH_4 to be less than or greater than the O–H bond energy? Explain.

   b)   Is your prediction consistent with the ΔH°_{ac} data? Explain your reasoning.

ChemActivity 33

Is Energy Released or Consumed When a Chemical Reaction Occurs?

WARM-UP

Model 1: An Atom Combination Reaction.

$$3 \text{ H(g)} + \text{N(g)} \longrightarrow \text{NH}_3\text{(g)}$$

Critical Thinking Questions

1. Consider the reaction represented by the chemical equation in Model 1.

   a) Are bonds formed when this reaction occurs?

   b) Are bonds broken when this reaction occurs?

   c) Is this reaction exothermic or endothermic?

   d) Is $\Delta H°$ for this reaction a positive number or a negative number?

2. A student says "Whenever a bond is broken, energy is released. So, breaking a bond can provide energy that can be used to make other things happen."

   Explain using one or two sentences why this student is *incorrect*.

END OF WARM-UP

Model 2: Using Enthalpies of Atom Combination to Calculate Enthalpies of Reaction.

In most chemical reactions, bonds are both broken and made. Whether the overall reaction is endothermic or exothermic depends on the energy required to perform the needed changes in bonding. To determine the overall value of $\Delta H°$ for a chemical reaction, one can consider the reaction to take place by breaking apart all of the reactant molecules into their constituent atoms, and then reassembling those atoms into the product molecules. Although (in general) this is not the actual process that takes place when chemical reactions occur, thinking about the reaction in this manner is a valid way to determine the value of $\Delta H°$ for the reaction.

Figure 1.   The enthalpy diagram for a chemical reaction.

$$N_2O_4(g) \longrightarrow 2\, NO_2(g)$$

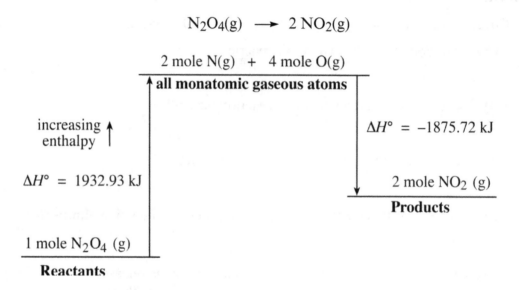

Table 1.   Standard state enthalpies of atom combination, ΔH°_{ac}.

Substance	ΔH°_{ac} (kJ/mol)	Substance	ΔH°_{ac} (kJ/mol)
H(g)	0		
N(g)	0		
O(g)	0		
$H_2(g)$	–435.30	$NH_3(g)$	–1171.76
$N_2(g)$	–945.408	$NO_2(g)$	–937.86
$O_2(g)$	–498.340	$N_2O_4(g)$	–1932.93

Critical Thinking Questions

Answer CTQs 3 – 8 as a team.

3. a) How much energy is required to break one mole of $N_2O_4(g)$, the reactants, into gaseous atoms?

    b) Provide two separate ways that you could find the answer to part a from information in Model 2 (including the previous page).

4. Circle all of the terms below that apply to the process described in CTQ 3.

bonds breaking	exothermic	$\Delta H° = 0$
bonds forming	endothermic	$\Delta H° > 0$
energy released	energy consumed	$\Delta H° < 0$

5. a) How much energy is released when two moles of $NO_2(g)$, the products, are formed from gaseous atoms?

    b) Describe how you could obtain an answer to part a from information provided in Table 1.

6. Circle all of the terms below that apply to the process described in CTQ 5.

bonds breaking	exothermic	$\Delta H° = 0$
bonds forming	endothermic	$\Delta H° > 0$
energy released	energy consumed	$\Delta H° < 0$

7. For the overall reaction:
    a) is energy released or consumed?
    b) is the reaction endothermic or exothermic?

8. Based on the information in Figure 1, what is $\Delta H°$ for the following reaction?

$$N_2O_4(g) \longrightarrow 2\,NO_2(g)$$

9. For the reaction represented by the chemical equation:

$$N_2(g) + 3 H_2(g) \longrightarrow 2 NH_3(g)$$

a) Individually, make a diagram similar to that in Figure 1. Compare diagrams with your teammates before proceeding to part b.

b) As a team, calculate $\Delta H°$ based on the diagram.

10. Use one or two sentences to write a consensus description of how to calculate the $\Delta H°$ for the reaction in CTQ 9 given the $\Delta H°_{ac}$ of the three species.

11. For any given chemical reaction, if the sum of the enthalpies of atom combination for all of the reactants is more negative than the sum of the enthalpies of atom combination for all of the products, will the value of ΔH for the reaction be positive or negative? Discuss and explain your team's reasoning.

Exercises

1. Calculate $\Delta H°$ for each of the following reactions:

    a) $MgO(s) + H_2O(\ell) \longrightarrow Mg(OH)_2(s)$

    b) $2\,Zn(s) + O_2(g) \longrightarrow 2\,ZnO(s)$

    c) $TiCl_4(g) + 2\,H_2O(g) \longrightarrow TiO_2(s) + 4\,HCl(g)$

2. Given a balanced chemical equation, describe how to determine if energy is released or consumed when that chemical reaction occurs.

Problem

1. As mentioned previously, molecules attract each other. The forces of attraction between molecules are called intermolecular forces. Consider the following transformations:

    $$CH_3OH(\ell) \longrightarrow CH_3OH(g)$$
    $$H_2O(\ell) \longrightarrow H_2O(g)$$
    $$SO_3(s) \longrightarrow SO_3(\ell)$$
    $$SO_3(s) \longrightarrow SO_3(g)$$

    a)   Calculate the value of $\Delta H°$ for each of these reactions.

    b)   Based on these results, in which phase (gas, liquid, solid) are the intermolecular forces the weakest? The strongest? Explain your reasoning.

What is the Rate of a Chemical Reaction?

WARM-UP

Information

The Greek letter Δ is often used to represent a change from an initial condition or state to a final condition or state. For example, a change in temperature from an initial temperature, T_i, to a final temperature, T_f, can be written as $\Delta T = T_f - T_i$.

Model 1: The Rate of Consumption of a Reactant

$$\text{Reactants} \longrightarrow \text{Products}$$

The rate of a chemical reaction depends on how quickly reactants are consumed or how quickly products are formed. By convention, rates of reaction, rates of consumption, and rates of production are always reported as positive numbers.

$$\begin{array}{c} \text{rate of consumption} \\ \text{of reactant} \end{array} = -\frac{\text{change in molarity of a reactant}}{\text{change in time}} = -\frac{\Delta(\text{reactant})}{\Delta\text{time}} \quad (1)$$

Critical Thinking Questions

1. If time is measured in seconds, what are the units for a rate of consumption?

2. What words do the symbols Δ and ( ) replace in equation 1?

   Δ replaces: ( ) replaces:

3. a) Why is Δ(reactant) a negative value in equation 1?

   b) What is the purpose of the negative signs in equation 1?

4. Provide an expression for the rate of production of a product that looks like equation 1.

END OF WARM-UP

Model 2: The Rate of a Chemical Reaction.

$$3\ ClO^-(aq) \longrightarrow 2\ Cl^-(aq) + ClO_3^-(aq) \tag{2}$$

The reaction described in equation 2 was carried out in an aqueous solution with a volume of 2.00 liters. Table 1 displays some data relating to that experiment.

Table 1.   Experimental data for Equation 2 in a 2.00-liter flask.

Time (s)	Moles of ClO^-	Moles of Cl^-	Moles of ClO_3^-
0	2.40	0	0
1.00×10^2	1.80		

Critical Thinking Questions

Answer CTQs 5 and 6 individually; then check your answers with your teammates.

5.   a)   According to equation 2, how many moles of Cl^- are produced when 3 moles of ClO^- are consumed?

b)   How many moles of ClO^- are consumed during the first 1.00×10^2 seconds of reaction?

c)   Fill in the missing entries in Table 1.

(Hint: The number "1.20" is not a correct value.)

6.   Based on the data in Table 1, calculate each of the following. Your answer must include appropriate units.

a)   rate of consumption of ClO^-

b)   rate of production of Cl^-

c)   rate of production of ClO_3^-

7.   As a team, discuss and provide one or two sentences to explain why the rate of production of Cl^- is twice the rate of production of ClO_3^-.

Information

The rate of a reaction is defined to be the rate of consumption of a reactant (or the rate of production of a product) whose stoichiometric coefficient is 1 in the balanced chemical equation describing the process. The rate of a reaction can be expressed in terms of the rate of change of concentration of any of the reactants or products.

Critical Thinking Questions

Answer CTQs 8 – 11 as a team.

8. Based on the answers to CTQ 6, what is the rate of the reaction in the model?

9. Note that for the data in Table 1,

$$\text{rate of reaction} = \frac{1}{2} \text{ rate of production of } Cl^- = \frac{1}{2} \frac{\Delta(Cl^-)}{\Delta t}$$

Write a similar equation to describe the relationship between the rate of reaction and:

a)   the rate of production of ClO_3^-.

b)   the rate of consumption of ClO^-.

10. How is the rate of reaction related to the rate of production of a product and its stoichiometric coefficient? Provide your answer in the form of an equation.

11. How is the rate of reaction related to the rate of consumption of a reactant and its stoichiometric coefficient? Provide your answer using a sentence.

Exercises

1. Indicate whether each of the following statements is true or false and explain your reasoning:

    a) The rate of a reaction is equal to the rate at which each of the products is formed.

    b) When PCl_5 decomposes according to the reaction $PCl_5(g) \longrightarrow PCl_3(g) + Cl_2(g)$, the rate of consumption of PCl_5 is twice the rate of production of Cl_2.

2. For the reaction $N_2(g) + 3 H_2(g) \longrightarrow 2 NH_3(g)$, the rate of consumption of H_2 was observed to be 3.50×10^{-4} M/s under certain conditions.

    a) Determine the rate of production of ammonia.

    b) Determine the rate of this reaction.

3. For the reaction $2 O_3(g) \longrightarrow 3 O_2(g)$, the rate of production of O_2 was observed to be 1.35×10^{-4} M/s under certain conditions. Determine the rate of consumption of ozone and the rate of this reaction.

4. For the reaction $3 I^-(aq) + IO_2^-(aq) + 4 H^+(aq) \longrightarrow 2 I_2(aq) + 2 H_2O$, the rate of production of H_2O was observed to be 5.0×10^{-2} M/s under certain conditions.

    a) Determine the rate of consumption of I^-, IO_2^-, and H^+.

    b) Determine the rate of production of I_2.

    c) What is the rate of this reaction?

5. Consider the information given in the table below for the reaction:

    $$3 F_2(g) + Cl_2(g) \longrightarrow 2 ClF_3(g)$$

Time (seconds)	Conc. of $F_2(g)$ (mol/L)	Conc. of $Cl_2(g)$ (mol/L)	Conc. of $ClF_3(g)$ (mol/L)
0	0.125	0.250	0
2.50	0.074	0.233	0.034

    Determine the rate of this reaction from the information given. Explain your reasoning clearly.

6. Describe what is meant by the "rate of a chemical reaction."

Do Reactions Ever Really Stop?

WARM-UP

Model 1: The Conversion of *cis*-2-butene to *trans*-2-butene.

Consider a simple chemical reaction where the forward reaction occurs in a single step and the reverse reaction occurs in a single step:

$$A \rightleftharpoons B$$

The following chemical reaction, where *cis*-2-butene is converted into *trans*-2-butene, is an example.

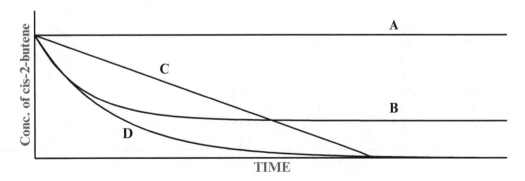

In this example, one end of a *cis*-2-butene molecule rotates 180° to form a *trans*-2-butene molecule. Rotation around a double bond rarely happens at room temperature because the collisions are not sufficiently energetic to weaken the double bond.

At higher temperatures, around 400 °C for *cis*-2-butene, collisions are sufficiently energetic and an appreciable reaction rate is detected.

Critical Thinking Question

1. Predict which line in the graph shown (A, B, C, D) would best describe each situation below:

    i)   a large number of *cis*-2-butene molecules is placed in a container and allowed to stand at room temperature for a long time.

    ii) a large number of *cis*-2-butene molecules is placed in a container and allowed to stand at 400 °C for a long time.

Model 2: The Number of Molecules as a Function of Time.

Consider the simple reaction:

$$A \rightleftharpoons B$$

The system is said to be at **equilibrium** when the concentrations of reactants and products stops changing.

Imagine a hypothetical system in which 1.0000×10^{22} A molecules are placed in a container maintained at 800 °C. We have the ability to monitor the number of A molecules and the number of B molecules in the container at all times. We collect the data at various times and compile Table 1.

Table 1.   Number of A and B molecules as a function of time.

Time (seconds)	Number of A Molecules ($\times 10^{20}$)	Number of B Molecules ($\times 10^{20}$)	Number of A Molecules that React in Next Second ($\times 10^{20}$)	Number of B Molecules that React in Next Second ($\times 10^{20}$)	Number of A Molecules Formed in Next Second ($\times 10^{20}$)	Number of B Molecules Formed in Next Second ($\times 10^{20}$)
0	100.00	0	25.00	0	0	25.00
1	75.00	25.00	18.75	2.50	2.50	18.75
2	58.75	41.25	14.69	4.13	4.13	14.69
3	48.19	51.81	12.05	5.18	5.18	12.05
4	41.32	58.68	10.33	5.87	5.87	10.33
5	36.86	63.14	9.21	6.31	6.31	9.21
6	33.96	66.04	8.49	6.60	6.60	8.49
7	32.07	67.93	8.02	6.79	6.79	8.02
8	30.85	69.15	7.71	6.92	6.92	7.71
9	30.05	69.95	7.51	6.99	6.99	7.51
10	29.53	70.47	7.38	7.05	7.05	7.38
11	29.20	70.80	7.30	7.08	7.08	7.30
12	28.98	71.02	7.24	7.10	7.10	7.24
13	28.84	71.16	7.21	7.12	7.12	7.21
14	28.74	71.26	7.19	7.13	7.13	7.19
15	28.68	71.32	7.17	7.13	7.13	7.17
16	28.64	71.36	7.16	7.14	7.14	7.16
17	28.62	71.38	7.15	7.14	7.14	7.15
18	28.60	71.40	7.15	7.14	7.14	7.15
19	28.59	71.41	7.15	7.14	7.14	7.15
20	28.58	71.42	7.15	7.14	7.14	7.15
21	28.58	71.42	7.14	7.14	7.14	7.14
22	28.58	71.42	7.14	7.14	7.14	7.14
23	28.57	71.43	7.14	7.14	7.14	7.14
24	28.57	71.43	7.14	7.14	7.14	7.14
25	28.57	71.43	7.14	7.14	7.14	7.14
30	28.57	71.43	7.14	7.14	7.14	7.14
40	28.57	71.43	7.14	7.14	7.14	7.14
50	28.57	71.43	7.14	7.14	7.14	7.14

Critical Thinking Questions

2. Circle the number of A molecules present at time = 1 second.

   75.00   75.00 × 10^{-20}   75.00 × 10^{20}   75.00 × 10^{21}   75.00 × 10^{22}

END OF WARM-UP

3. As a team, decide which line from the graph in CTQ 1 best describes the data in Table 1 assuming that molecule A is *cis*-2-butene. Explain how your team reached your conclusion by explicitly referring to information in Table 1.

As a team, carefully examine Table 1 and answer CTQs 4 – 12.

4. During the time interval 0 – 1 s:

   a)   How many A molecules react?

   b)   How many B molecules are formed?

   c)   Why are these two numbers equal?

5.   During the time interval 10 – 11 s:

   a)   How many B molecules react?

   b)   How many A molecules are formed?

   c)   Why are these two numbers equal?

6.   a)   During the time interval 0 – 1 s, what fraction of A molecules react?

   b)   During the time interval 10 – 11 s, what fraction of A molecules react?

   c)   During the time interval 24 – 25 s, what fraction of A molecules react?

   d)   During the time interval 40 – 41 s, what fraction of A molecules react?

7. Using the pattern seen in your team answers to CTQ 6, show that 1.033×10^{21} molecules of A react during the time interval 4 – 5 s.

8. During the time interval 100 – 101 s, how many molecules of A react? Explain your reasoning.

9. a) During the time interval 1 – 2 s, what fraction of B molecules react?

    b) During the time interval 10 – 11 s, what fraction of B molecules react?

    c) During the time interval 24 – 25 s, what fraction of B molecules react?

    d) During the time interval 40 – 41 s, what fraction of B molecules react?

10. Using the pattern seen in your team answers to CTQ 8, show that 5.87×10^{20} molecules of B react during the time interval 4 – 5 s.

11. During the time interval 100 – 101 s, how many molecules of B react? Explain your reasoning.

12. For the reaction described in Table 1:
    a) How long did it take for the reaction to come to equilibrium?

    b) Are A molecules still reacting to form B molecules at $t = 500$ seconds?

    c) Are B molecules still reacting to form A molecules at $t = 500$ seconds?

Information

For the process in Model 2,

$$\frac{\text{rate of conversion}}{\text{of B to A}} = \frac{\text{number of B molecules}}{\text{that react per second}} = \frac{\Delta \text{ number of B molecules}}{\Delta t}$$

The relationship between the rate of conversion of B to A and the number of B molecules is given by equation 1:

$$\text{rate of conversion of B to A} = k_B \times \text{number of B molecules} \qquad (1)$$

where k_B is a constant.

Critical Thinking Questions

Answer CTQs 13 and 14 as a team.

13. What is the value of k_B in equation 1? Be sure to include units in your answer.

14. a) Write a mathematical equation (analogous to equation 1) that relates the rate of conversion of A molecules into B molecules to the number of A molecules present. This equation should include a constant k_A.

    b) What is the value of k_A (include units)?

Exercises

1. Describe, in one or two sentences, what is meant by the phrase "at equilibrium" as it refers to the chemical process:

$$A \rightleftharpoons B$$

2. The chemical system $2A \rightleftharpoons B$ is at equilibrium. In the next second 3.44×10^{21} molecules of A will react to form B molecules.

    a) How many B molecules will be produced in the next second?
    b) How many B molecules will react in the next second?
    c) How many A molecules will be produced in the next second?

3. Indicate whether this statement is true or false and explain your reasoning.

    When a chemical reaction reaches equilibrium, the reactant molecules stop being transformed into product molecules.

What Happens When a Reaction Reaches Equilibrium?

WARM-UP

Information

In ChemActivity **35,** we saw that:

rate of conversion of B to A $= 0.10\ \text{s}^{-1} \times$ number of B molecules

rate of conversion of A to B $= 0.25\ \text{s}^{-1} \times$ number of A molecules.

We can easily change equation 1 from units of molecules/s to the units $\dfrac{\text{moles}}{\text{L s}}$:

$$\text{number of A molecules} \times \frac{\text{mol}}{6.022 \times 10^{23}\,\text{molecules}} \times \frac{1}{V(\text{in Liters})} = (A)$$

Thus, equation 1 can be rewritten as

$$\text{rate of conversion of A to B} = 0.25\ \text{s}^{-1}\ (A) = k_A\ (A)$$

We can now write for the reaction of A to B:

$$A \rightleftharpoons B$$

$$A \longrightarrow B \qquad \text{rate} = k_A\ (A) \quad = 0.25\ \text{s}^{-1}\ (A)$$

$$B \longrightarrow A \qquad \text{rate} = k_B\ (B) \quad = 0.10\ \text{s}^{-1}\ (B)$$

or

$$\text{rate}_{\text{forward}} = k_A\ (A) = 0.25\ \text{s}^{-1}\ (A) \tag{1}$$

$$\text{rate}_{\text{reverse}} = k_B\ (B) = 0.10\ \text{s}^{-1}\ (B) \tag{2}$$

where k_A and k_B are called the **rate constants** for the forward and reverse reactions.

Model: The Concentration of Molecules as a Function of Time.

Consider the reaction A $\rightleftharpoons$ B in ChemActivity 35. If the volume of the container is 1.0000 L, we can calculate the concentrations of A and B as a function of time.

Table 1. The concentrations of A and B as a function of time.

		Volume of container = 0.1661 L				
		$k_A = 0.25$ s^{-1}		$k_B = 0.10$ s^{-1}		
Time (seconds)	Number of A Molecules ($\times 10^{20}$)	Number of B Molecules ($\times 10^{20}$)	(A) (M)	(B) (M)	Forward Rate (10^{-2} M s^{-1})	Reverse Rate (10^{-2} M s^{-1})
0	100.00	0	0.1000	0.0000	2.50	0.00
1	75.00	25.00	0.0750	0.0250	1.88	0.25
2	58.75	41.25	0.0588	0.0413	1.47	0.41
3	48.19	51.81	0.0482	0.0518	1.20	0.52
4	41.32	58.68	0.0413	0.0587	1.03	0.59
5	36.86	63.14	0.0369	0.0631		
6	33.96	66.04	0.0340	0.0660	0.85	0.66
7	32.07	67.93	0.0321	0.0679	0.80	0.68
8	30.85	69.15	0.0308	0.0692	0.77	0.69
9	30.05	69.95	0.0301	0.0699	0.75	0.70
10	29.53	70.47	0.0295	0.0705	0.74	0.70
11	29.20	70.80	0.0292	0.0708	0.73	0.71
12	28.98	71.02	0.0290	0.0710	0.72	0.71
13	28.84	71.16	0.0288	0.0712	0.72	0.71
14	28.74	71.26	0.0287	0.0713	0.72	0.71
15	28.68	71.32	0.0287	0.0713	0.72	0.71
16	28.64	71.36	0.0286	0.0714	0.72	0.71
17	28.62	71.38	0.0286	0.0714	0.72	0.71
18	28.60	71.40	0.0286	0.0714	0.72	0.71
19	28.59	71.41	0.0286	0.0714	0.71	0.71
20	28.58	71.42	0.0286	0.0714	0.71	0.71
25	28.58	71.42	0.0286	0.0714	0.71	0.71
30	28.58	71.42	0.0286	0.0714	0.71	0.71
40	28.57	71.43	0.0286	0.0714	0.71	0.71
50	28.57	71.43	0.0286	0.0714	0.71	0.71

Critical Thinking Questions

1. Calculate and confirm that the concentration of A at $t = 5$ s is correct (given that the number of A molecules is 36.86×10^{20}).

2. Solve for the forward rate in each situation. Use equation 1 and the given rate constant. Confirm that your answers are correct by comparing your calculated values to those shown in Table 1.

   a) (A) = (A)$_o$ (the initial concentration of A; $t = 0$ s)

   b) (A) = (A)$_e$ = [A] (the equilibrium concentration of A)

3. Solve for the reverse rate in each situation. Use equation 2 and the given rate constant. Confirm that your answers are correct by comparing your calculated values to those shown in Table 1.

   a) (B) = (B)$_o$ (the initial concentration of B; $t = 0$ s)

   b) (B) = (B)$_e$ = [B] (the equilibrium concentration of B)

END OF WARM-UP

4. Individually, use equation 1 to calculate the value of the "Forward Rate" (column 6) at (A) = (A)$_5$ (at $t = 5$ s). Then, reach consensus with your teammates and enter this value into Table 1.

5. Individually, use equation 2 to calculate the value of the "Reverse Rate" (column 7) at (B) = (B)$_5$ (at $t = 5$ s). Then, reach consensus with your teammates and enter this value into Table 1.

6. As a team, discuss and then write a consensus statement describing the relationship between the forward rate and reverse rate at equilibrium.

Information

Figure 1.   The concentrations of A and B as a function of time.

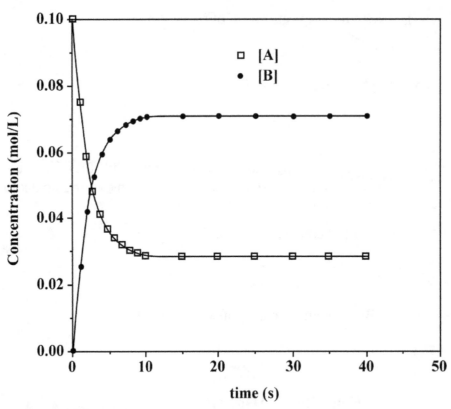

Critical Thinking Questions

7. The data in Figure 1 can be divided into two regions—the kinetic region and the equilibrium region. As a team:

    a)   Indicate these regions (time intervals) on the figure.

    b)   Write a consensus sentence to describe the kinetic region.

8. As a team, and *using Figure 1 only*, discuss and estimate the value of $\frac{(B)}{(A)}$ at:

    a) $t = 1\,s$

    b) $t = 4\,s$

    c) $t = 15\,s$

    d) $t = 20\,s$

    e) $t = 40\,s$

9. In what region (kinetic or equilibrium) is the quantity $\frac{(B)}{(A)}$ a constant?

Exercises

1. Use Table 1 to calculate the value of $\dfrac{(B)}{(A)}$ at:

   a) $t = 1$ s   b) $t = 4$ s   c) $t = 15$ s   d) $t = 20$ s   e) $t = 40$ s

   Why is there a small difference between these values and your values in CTQ 8?

2. Suppose that the container and initial concentrations of A and B are identical to those in Table 1 but the values of the two rate constants were changed to $k_A = 0.10$ s^{-1} and $k_B = 0.25$ s^{-1}. What would be the equilibrium concentrations [A] and [B]?

3. Indicate whether this statement is true or false and explain your reasoning.

   > The rate of a chemical reaction remains the same over the course of the reaction.

4. Describe what happens at equilibrium to the rates of the forward and reverse reactions and also the concentrations of the products and reactants.

Problem

1. Examine this graph, which describes a chemical reaction involving A, B, and C.

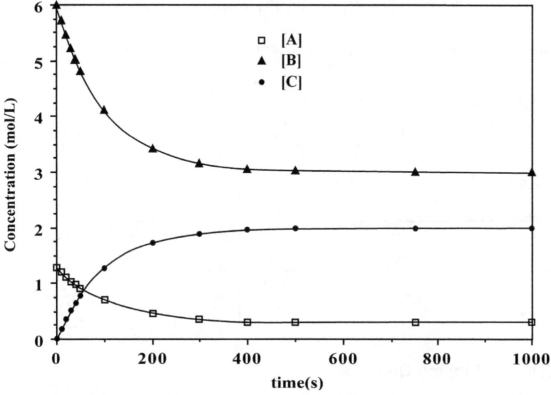

   a) Indicate the kinetic region and the equilibrium region on the graph.
   b) Estimate $(A)_o$, $(B)_o$, $(C)_o$.
   c) Estimate [A], [B], [C].
   d) Write a chemical equation for this reaction.

What Describes the Amounts at Equilibrium?

WARM-UP

Model 1: A Simple Gas Phase Reaction, Y(g) $\rightleftharpoons$ Z(g).

Consider a simple reaction:

$$Y(g) \rightleftharpoons Z(g)$$

$$\text{rate}_{\text{forward}} = k_Y (Y) \tag{1}$$

$$\text{rate}_{\text{reverse}} = k_Z (Z) \tag{2}$$

The system is said to be at equilibrium when the concentrations of reactants and products stop changing. At equilibrium,

$$(Y) = (Y)_e = [Y] \quad \text{and} \quad (Z) = (Z)_e = [Z]$$

Table 1. Results of various experiments on the system Y $\rightleftharpoons$ Z at some temperature.

(Note that Molecules "Y" and "Z" are different for each set.)

Set	Trial	$(Y)_o$ (mol/L)	$(Z)_o$ (mol/L)	k_Y (s^{-1})	k_Z (s^{-1})	[Y] (mol/L)	[Z] (mol/L)
M	1	1.00	0	0.20	0.30	0.60	0.40
	2	0.50	0.50	0.20	0.30	0.60	0.40
	3	2.00	0	0.20	0.30		
N	1	2.00	0	0.60	0.20	0.50	1.50
	2	0.50	1.50	0.60	0.20	0.50	1.50
O	1	1.00	0	0.50	0.50	0.50	0.50
P	1	0.80	0.20	0.20	0.60	0.75	0.25
	2	0.59	0.41	0.20	0.60	0.75	0.25

Critical Thinking Questions

1. What is the distinction between $(Y)_o$ and [Y] in the column heading of Table 1?

END OF WARM-UP

For CTQs 2 and 3, perform the calculation individually and then compare the answers among team members and reach consensus.

2. For Trial M2, calculate the rate of the forward reaction (Y ⟶ Z) at equilibrium and the rate of the reverse reaction (Z ⟶ Y) at equilibrium. How do these values compare?

3. For Trial P2, calculate the rate of the forward reaction (Y ⟶ Z) at equilibrium and the rate of the reverse reaction (Z ⟶ Y) at equilibrium. How do these values compare?

4. In general, how does the rate of the forward reaction (Y ⟶ Z) at equilibrium compare to the rate of the reverse reaction (Z ⟶ Y) at equilibrium?

5. As a team, examine Table 1 and then answer:

    a)   If $k_Y < k_Z$, which is greater at equilibrium, [Y] or [Z]?

    b)   If $k_Y > k_Z$, which is greater at equilibrium, [Y] or [Z]?

6. Use the general result from CTQ 4, along with equations 1 and 2 (where k_Y and k_Z are constants):

    a)   to show that $\dfrac{[Z]}{[Y]}$ is a constant.

    b)   to answer CTQs 5a and 5b without using Table 1.

Model 2: The Law of Mass Action.

The Law of Mass Action states that for a chemical system described by the balanced chemical equation

$$a\,A + b\,B \rightleftharpoons c\,C + d\,D$$

the ratio $\dfrac{[C]^c\,[D]^d}{[A]^a\,[B]^b}$ is a constant at a given temperature. This ratio is referred to as the **equilibrium constant expression**, and the numerical value of the ratio is called the **equilibrium constant**, K_c.

$$K_c = \frac{[C]^c\,[D]^d}{[A]^a\,[B]^b}$$

Note that a, b, c, and d are the **stoichiometric coefficients** in the chemical equation. By convention, equilibrium constant values are given without units.

For example:

the reaction: $2\,H_2(g) + O_2(g) \rightleftharpoons 2\,H_2O(g)$

the equilibrium constant expression: $K_c = \dfrac{[H_2O]^2}{[H_2]^2[O_2]}$ (3)

the equilibrium constant (25 °C): $K_c = 10^{83}$ (experimental number)

Critical Thinking Questions

Answer CTQs 7 – 9 as a team.

7. Circle the statement below that best describes the equilibrium constant expression:

    i)   The equilibrium constant expression is a ratio of the concentrations of **reactants** raised to their stoichiometric coefficients divided by the concentration of the **products** raised to their stoichiometric coefficients.

    ii) The equilibrium constant expression is a ratio of the concentrations of **products** raised to their stoichiometric coefficients divided by the concentration of the **reactants** raised to their stoichiometric coefficients.

8. When a mixture of $H_2(g)$, $O_2(g)$, and $H_2O(g)$ reaches equilibrium, what species is present in the largest amount? Explain your team's reasoning.

9. a) Write the equilibrium constant expression for the reaction in Model 1.

$$K_c \ =$$

   b) Find the value of the equilibrium constant K_c for data set M.

   c) Find the values of [Y] and [Z] for trial 3 of data set M.

Model 3: Two Related Chemical Reactions.

$$PCl_3(g) \ + \ Cl_2(g) \ \rightleftharpoons \ PCl_5(g) \tag{4}$$

$$PCl_5(g) \ \rightleftharpoons \ PCl_3(g) \ + \ Cl_2(g) \tag{5}$$

Critical Thinking Questions

Answer CTQs 10 and 11 as a team.

10. a) Provide the equilibrium constant expression for the K_c of reaction 4.

    b) Provide the equilibrium constant expression for the K_c of reaction 5.

    c) What is the relationship between reactions 4 and 5?

    d) What is the relationship between the equilibrium constant expression for reaction 4 and the equilibrium constant expression for reaction 5?

11. If the value of K_c for reaction 4 is 1.27×10^3, what is the value of K_c for reaction 5?

Exercises

1. Explain why, if $k_Y > k_Z$, then $[Z] > [Y]$.

2. The equilibrium state is often described as being "dynamic equilibrium." What does the word "dynamic" refer to?

3. Calculate the value of K_c for each of the sets of trials in Table 1. For each data set, does K_c depend on the initial concentrations of Y and Z?

4. Write the equilibrium constant expression, K_c, for each of the following reactions:

   a) $2 HI(g) \rightleftharpoons H_2(g) + I_2(g)$

   b) $3 H_2(g) + N_2(g) \rightleftharpoons 2 NH_3(g)$

   c) $\frac{3}{2} H_2(g) + \frac{1}{2} N_2(g) \rightleftharpoons NH_3(g)$

   d) cis-2-butene(g) $\rightleftharpoons$ trans-2-butene(g)

   e) $O_3(g) \rightleftharpoons O_2(g) + O(g)$

   f) $Xe(g) + 2 F_2(g) \rightleftharpoons XeF_4(g)$

5. Find the mathematical relationship between the equilibrium constant expressions of reaction b and reaction c in Exercise 4.

6. When the following reaction reaches equilibrium,

$$A(g) + 2 B(g) \rightleftharpoons C(g)$$

   the following concentrations are measured: $[A] = 0.60$ M; $[B] = 0.20$ M; $[C] = 0.55$ M. What is the value of K_c for this reaction?

7. An equilibrium mixture of PCl_5, PCl_3, and Cl_2, at a certain temperature in a 5.0 L container consists of 0.80 mole PCl_5, 0.55 mole PCl_3, and 1.2 mole Cl_2. Calculate K_c for the reaction:

$$PCl_3(g) + Cl_2(g) \rightleftharpoons PCl_5(g)$$

8. Calculate K_c for the reaction:

$$3 H_2(g) + N_2(g) \rightleftharpoons 2 NH_3(g)$$

   given that the equilibrium concentrations are: $[H_2] = 1.5$ M; $[NH_3] = 0.24$ M; $[N_2] = 2.5$ M.

9. $K_c = 150.0$ at a certain temperature for the reaction:

$$2\,NO(g)\ +\ O_2(g)\ \rightleftharpoons\ 2\,NO_2(g)$$

What is the concentration of NO_2 if the equilibrium concentration of NO and O_2 are 1.00×10^{-3} and 5.00×10^{-2}, respectively?

10. Two gases are added to an otherwise empty 1.00-L container: 2.0 moles of A; 4.0 moles of B. These gases react as follows:

$$A(g)\ +\ 3\,B(g)\ \rightleftharpoons\ C(g)\ +\ 2\,D(g)$$

At equilibrium, the container contains 0.4 moles of D.

a) Calculate the moles of A, B, and C in the container at equilibrium.

b) Calculate the concentrations of A, B, C, and D at equilibrium.

c) Calculate the value of the equilibrium constant, K_c, for this reaction.

11. A 1.00-L flask contains an equilibrium mixture of 24.9 g of N_2, 1.35 g of H_2, and 2.15 g of NH_3 at some temperature. Calculate the equilibrium constant for the given reaction at this temperature.

$$3\,H_2(g)\ +\ N_2(g)\ \rightleftharpoons\ 2\,NH_3(g)$$

12. The reaction $2\,NO(g)\ +\ O_2(g)\ \rightleftharpoons\ 2\,NO_2(g)$ has $K_c = 100.0$.

What is the value for K_c for the reaction: $2\,NO_2(g)\ \rightleftharpoons\ 2\,NO(g)\ +\ O_2(g)$?

13. Write the equilibrium constant expressions, K_c, for

$$3\,H_2(g)\ +\ N_2(g)\ \rightleftharpoons\ 2\,NH_3(g)$$

$$\frac{3}{2}\,H_2(g)\ +\ \frac{1}{2}\,N_2(g)\ \rightleftharpoons\ NH_3(g)$$

a) If $K_c = 0.78$ for the first reaction, what is K_c for the second reaction (at the same temperature)?

b) What is the value of K_c for the reaction (at the same temperature)?

$$NH_3(g)\ \rightleftharpoons\ \frac{3}{2}\,H_2(g)\ +\ \frac{1}{2}\,N_2(g)$$

14. Consider the chemical reaction: $2\,NOCl(g)\ \rightleftharpoons 2\,NO(g) + Cl_2(g)$.

When the reaction has reached equilibrium at some temperature in a 5.0-liter container, the following amounts are present: 0.113 moles of NO, 0.0567 moles of Cl_2 and 4.87 moles of NOCl. Calculate K_c for the given reaction at this temperature.

15. The equilibrium constants at a particular temperature are given for the following reactions:

$$2 \, NO(g) \rightleftharpoons N_2(g) + O_2(g) \qquad\qquad K_c = 2.4 \times 10^{-18}$$

$$NO(g) + \tfrac{1}{2} \, Br_2(g) \rightleftharpoons NOBr(g) \qquad K_c = 1.4$$

Using this information, determine the value of the equilibrium constant for the following reaction at the same temperature:

$$\tfrac{1}{2} \, N_2(g) + \tfrac{1}{2} \, O_2(g) + \tfrac{1}{2} \, Br_2(g) \rightleftharpoons NOBr(g)$$

Problems

1. Indicate whether the following statement is true or false and explain your reasoning.

   The value of K_c for the reaction $2 \, AB(g) + B_2(g) \rightleftharpoons 2 \, AB_2(g)$ must be less than the value of K_c for the reaction $2 \, AB_2(g) \rightleftharpoons 2 \, AB(g) + B_2(g)$.

2. Consider the following reaction:

$$2 \, A(g) \rightleftharpoons B(g)$$

   One mole of A was placed in a 1.0 L flask and the reaction was followed as a function of time. The data are shown in the figure below:

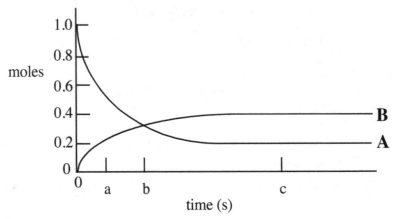

   a) Determine the *value* of the equilibrium constant, K_c.

   b) Which is larger at time "a", the forward rate or the reverse rate? Briefly explain.

   c) Which is larger at time "b", the forward rate or the reverse rate? Briefly explain.

   d) Which is larger at time "c", the forward rate or the reverse rate? Briefly explain.

If We're Not at Equilibrium, Which Way Do We Go?

WARM-UP

Model 1: A Chemical System at Equilibrium.

$$PCl_3(g) \; + \; Cl_2(g) \; \rightleftarrows \; PCl_5(g)$$

A 5.00-liter box at 25 °C has 0.0500 moles of $PCl_3(g)$, 0.0200 moles of $Cl_2(g)$, and 0.200 moles of $PCl_5(g)$. It is known that:

$$K_c \; = 1.00 \times 10^3 \; = \; \frac{[PCl_5]}{[PCl_3]\,[Cl_2]} \tag{1}$$

Critical Thinking Questions

1. What is the concentration of $PCl_3(g)$ in the system described in Model 1?

2. Verify that the reaction occurring in the box described above is at equilibrium.

END OF WARM-UP

Model 2: More Reactant Is Added.

A needle is inserted into the box described in Model 1. An additional 0.0600 moles of PCl_3 are injected into the reaction mixture.

Critical Thinking Questions

Answer CTQs 3 and 4 as a team.

3. At the instant of injection (before any chemical reaction takes place):

   a)   What is the total number of moles of PCl_3 in the box?

   b)   What is the new concentration of PCl_3 in the box?

   c)   Is the system now at equilibrium? Explain.

4. Predict which of the following will happen to the moles of PCl_5 after injection of the 0.0600 moles of PCl_3.

    i)   No change in the moles of PCl_5 because the system is at equilibrium.

    ii) PCl_3 and Cl_2 will be consumed to form more PCl_5.

    iii) PCl_5 will be consumed to form more PCl_3 and Cl_2.

    Explain your team's reasoning.

Model 3: The Reaction Quotient.

The **reaction quotient**, Q_c, for the reaction

$$a\,A + b\,B \;\rightleftharpoons\; c\,C + d\,D$$

is defined as follows:

$$Q_c = \frac{(C)^c\,(D)^d}{(A)^a\,(B)^b}$$

Note that the reaction quotient expression *looks* similar to the equilibrium constant expression. The difference is that the reaction quotient can be calculated at any time during the reaction—at equilibrium or not at equilibrium. For reactions involving liquids or solids, the corresponding reaction quotient, Q, omits those species (the same species that are not included in the equilibrium constant expression).

Critical Thinking Questions

Answer CTQs 5 – 8 as a team.

5. a) Provide the expression for Q_c for the reaction in Model 1.

    b) Use your answer to part a to verify that $Q_c = 4.55 \times 10^2$ in Model 2 after the 0.600 moles of PCl_3 has been added.

6. Is the reaction mixture at equilibrium? If not, what will happen?

    i)   No change because the system is at equilibrium.

    ii) PCl_3 and Cl_2 must be consumed to form more PCl_5.

    iii) PCl_5 must be consumed to form more PCl_3 and Cl_2.

    Explain your team's reasoning.

7.   Consider a situation in which the reaction quotient, Q_c, for a given reaction is larger than the equilibrium constant, K_c.

    a)   How must the value of Q_c change to reach equilibrium?

    b)   Describe how the concentrations of reactants and/or the concentration of products must change to reach equilibrium.

8.   Provide a consensus description of why the reaction quotient is useful.

A Return to Models 1 and 2.

Consider the following reaction:

$$PCl_3(g) + Cl_2(g) \rightleftharpoons PCl_5(g)$$

A 5.00-liter box at 25 °C has 0.0500 moles of $PCl_3(g)$, 0.0200 moles of $Cl_2(g)$, and 0.200 moles of $PCl_5(g)$. A needle is inserted into this box and an additional 0.0600 moles of PCl_3 are injected into the reaction mixture. (This is the same scenario as in Models 1 and 2.)

Critical Thinking Questions

Answer CTQs 9 – 12 as a team.

9.   At the instant of injection (before any chemical reaction takes place), the total number of moles of PCl_3 in the box is 0.1100 (see CTQ 3).

    a)   How many moles of Cl_2 are present (before any chemical reaction takes place)?

    b)   How many moles of PCl_5 are present (before any chemical reaction takes place)?

10.   Assume that x moles of PCl_3 react in order to reach equilibrium.

    a)   How many moles of Cl_2 react?

    b)   How many moles of PCl_5 are formed?

c)   Complete the following table:

Reaction:	$PCl_3(g)$ +	$Cl_2(g) \rightleftharpoons$	$PCl_5(g)$
initial moles	0.1100		
change in moles	$-x$		x

11. How many moles of each species are present at equilibrium? Fill in the appropriate expression for each species in the row "equilibrium moles." (The first two rows are identical to the first two rows in CTQ 10c.)

Reaction:	$PCl_3(g)$ +	$Cl_2(g) \rightleftharpoons$	$PCl_5(g)$
initial moles	0.1100		
change in moles	$-x$		x
equilibrium moles	$0.1100 - x$		

12. For the reaction in the model, recall that the total volume is 5.00 L and fill in the appropriate concentrations in the row "equilibrium concentration." (The first three rows are identical to the first three rows in CTQ 11.)

Reaction:	$PCl_3(g)$ +	$Cl_2(g) \rightleftharpoons$	$PCl_5(g)$
initial moles	0.1100		
change in moles	$-x$		x
equilibrium moles	$0.1100 - x$		
equilibrium concentration	$\dfrac{0.1100 - x}{5.00}$		

Information

The expressions from the bottom line of the table in CTQ 12 can be substituted into the equilibrium constant expression relationship (Equation 1) to give:

$$K_c = 1.00 \times 10^3 = \frac{[PCl_5]}{[PCl_3][Cl_2]} = \frac{\left(\frac{0.200+x}{5.00}\right)}{\left(\frac{0.1100-x}{5.00}\right)\left(\frac{0.0200-x}{5.00}\right)}$$

After some algebraic manipulation, this equation can be rearranged to give:

$$1.00 \times 10^3 x^2 - 1.35 \times 10^2 x + 1.20 = 0 \quad .$$

This is a quadratic equation that can be solved using the quadratic formula.

Critical Thinking Questions

For CTQ 13, answer parts a and b individually. Once all team members are done, compare answers and reach consensus before moving to CTQ 14.

13. When the quadratic formula is used to solve the equation in the Information section above, two values of x are obtained: 0.125 and 9.55×10^{-3}.

      a. Explain why one of the values of x cannot be correct.
         [Hint: Think about what x represents.]

      b. Use the valid value of x to calculate the equilibrium concentrations of PCl_3, Cl_2, and PCl_5.

14. For the reaction in Model 1, write the equilibrium constant expression and enter the values found in CTQ 13b. Verify that the appropriate multiplication and division yields the value of the equilibrium constant. This is a method to verify your answer. If you do not get the value of K_c (to at least two significant figures), you made a mistake somewhere! Make sure that all team members have completed this question before continuing to CTQ 15.

Answer CTQs 15 and 16 as a team.

15. Assume that the system is at equilibrium as determined in CTQ 13. What will happen to the number of moles of PCl_3 present if some Cl_2 gas is suddenly injected into the box? Explain your reasoning.

16. Assume that the system is at equilibrium as determined in CTQ 13. What will happen to the number of moles of PCl_3 present if some PCl_5 gas is suddenly injected into the box? Explain your reasoning.

Model 4: Equilibrium Calculations at Constant Volume

The approach to finding the equilibrium amounts for a chemical reaction that was developed in this activity can be used to address any situation that involves equilibrium states. As seen for the reaction that we just considered, this can result in some relatively "messy" algebra. Frequently, however, chemical reactions take place at constant volume – as was the case for the process in this activity. When that is the case, the algebra can be simplified by assigning x to be the *concentration* of one of the components, rather than the number of moles.

As an example, we will reconsider the problem described in Models 1 and 2:

$$PCl_3(g) + Cl_2(g) \rightleftharpoons PCl_5(g)$$

Immediately after 0.0600 moles of PCl_3 are injected into the box, this is the situation:

Volume of box = 5.00 liters

| 0.1100 moles of $PCl_3(g)$ |
| 0.0200 moles of $Cl_2(g)$ |
| 0.200 moles of $PCl_5(g)$. |

Critical Thinking Questions

17. As a team, calculate the concentration of each species in the box in Model 4.

   a)   concentration of $PCl_3(g)$:

   b)   concentration of $Cl_2(g)$:

   c)   concentration of $PCl_5(g)$:

18. Let x represent the decrease in *concentration* for PCl_3 when the reaction proceeds to reach equilibrium. As a team, use this definition for x and your answers to CTQ 17 to fill in the rest of the table below.

Reaction: $PCl_3(g) + Cl_2(g) \rightleftharpoons PCl_5(g)$

	$PCl_3(g)$	$Cl_2(g)$	$PCl_5(g)$
initial concentration (moles/L)	0.0220		
change in concentration (moles/L)	$-x$		
equilibrium concentration (moles/L)	$0.0220 - x$		

19. Substitute the expressions from the bottom line of the table in CTQ 18 into the equilibrium constant expression

$$K_c = 1.00 \times 10^3 = \frac{[PCl_5]}{[PCl_3]\,[Cl_2]}$$

and rearrange the algebraic expression into the form $ax^2 + bx + c = 0$.

[Note that the correct expression has b = –27.0]

20. When the quadratic formula is used to solve the equation from CTQ 19, two values of x are obtained: 2.51×10^{-2} and 1.91×10^{-3}.

a) Explain why one of the values of x cannot be correct.

[Hint: Think about what x represents.]

b) Use the valid value of x to calculate the equilibrium concentrations of PCl_3, Cl_2, and PCl_5 and then compare these values to those obtained from CTQ 13b.

Exercises

1. How is the reaction quotient used to determine if a reaction proceeds to form more products or reactants? Provide an explanation in on e or two sentences.

2. Calculate the value of x (in CTQ 13) using equation 1, the entries in the table in CTQ 12, and the quadratic formula.

3. Consider the following reaction in a 5.0 L reaction vessel and at some temperature:

$$CO_2(g) + H_2(g) \rightleftharpoons CO(g) + H_2O(g)$$

$K_c = 0.20$ at this temperature.

Complete the following table (use x where appropriate):

Reaction:	$CO_2(g)$ +	$H_2(g) \rightleftharpoons CO$	+	H_2Og)
initial moles	1.00	2.00	0	0
change in moles				
equilibrium moles				
equilibrium conc.				
equilibrium conc. value (no "x")				

Verify that your equilibrium concentrations are correct!

4. The following reaction does not proceed at room temperature (the equilibrium constant is exceedingly low, $K_c \approx 10^{-31}$), but NO is produced at higher temperatures (such as found in automobile engines).

$$N_2(g) + O_2(g) \rightleftharpoons 2 NO(g) \quad .$$

Suppose that 5.00 moles of N_2 and 10.00 moles of O_2 are added to a fixed-volume reaction chamber at room temperature. The temperature is increased to 1000 °C. If x moles of N_2 react:

a) How many moles of O_2 react?

b) How many moles of NO are formed?

5. Complete the following table for the reaction $N_2(g) + O_2(g) \rightleftharpoons 2 NO(g)$.

Reaction:	$N_2(g)$ +	$O_2(g) \rightleftharpoons 2NO(g)$	
initial moles	5.00	10.00	0
change in moles	$-x$		
equilibrium moles	$5.00 - x$		

6. Consider the following reaction in a 1.00-L reaction vessel and at some temperature:

$$N_2(g) + 2 H_2(g) \rightleftharpoons N_2H_4(g)$$

$K_c = 5.0 \times 10^{-3}$ at this temperature.

Complete the following table:

Reaction:	$N_2(g)$	+ $2 H_2(g)$	$\rightleftharpoons N_2H_4 (g)$
initial conc. (mol/L)	1.00	1.50	0
change in conc. (mol/L)			
equilibrium conc. (mol/L)			

a)   Which is the correct concentration of N_2H_4 at equilibrium?

   i)   0.11 M

   ii) 1.1×10^{-3} M

   iii) 1.1×10^{-5} M.

b)   What is the concentration of N_2 at equilibrium?

c)   What is the concentration of H_2 at equilibrium?

7. $K_c = 1.60$ at 986 °C for the following reaction:

$$CO_2(g) + H_2(g) \rightleftharpoons CO(g) + H_2O(g)$$

Complete the following table for a 1.00-L vessel:

Reaction:	$CO_2(g)$	+ $H_2(g)$	$\rightleftharpoons CO(g)$ +	$H_2O(g)$
initial moles	1.00	2.00	1.00	2.00
change in moles				
equilibrium moles				
equilibrium conc. expression				
equilibrium conc. value				

Verify that your equilibrium concentrations are correct!

8. Consider the equilibrium process

$$2 NH_3(g) \rightleftharpoons N_2(g) + 3 H_2(g)$$

An otherwise empty 2.0-liter container is filled with 2.65 moles of $NH_3(g)$ and the system is allowed to come to equilibrium at some temperature. At equilibrium, there are 1.26 moles of $H_2(g)$ present. Complete the table (note that x is not required here, all numerical values can be used).

Reaction:	$2NH_3(g) \rightleftharpoons$	$N_2(g)$	$+$	$3H_2(g)$
initial moles	2.65			
change in moles				
equilibrium moles				1.26
equilibrium conc. value				

What is the equilibrium constant K_c for the reaction at this temperature?

9. Consider the reaction:

$$3 H_2(g) + N_2(g) \rightleftharpoons 2 NH_3(g)$$

At 500 °C, the equilibrium constant for this reaction is 6.0×10^{-2}. For each of the following situations, indicate whether or not the system is at equilibrium. If the system is not at equilibrium, indicate whether the system will shift to the right (produce more ammonia) or shift to the left (produce more hydrogen and nitrogen).

a) $(NH_3) = 2.00 \times 10^{-4} M$ $(N_2) = 1.50 \times 10^{-5} M$ $(H_2) = 0.354 M$

b) $(NH_3) = 0.0010 M$ $(N_2) = 1.0 \times 10^{-5} M$ $(H_2) = 0.0020 M$

c) $(NH_3) = 1.0 \times 10^{-4} M$ $(N_2) = 5.0 M$ $(H_2) = 0.010 M$

10. Consider the chemical reaction:

$$CO(g) + H_2O(g) \rightleftharpoons CO_2(g) + H_2(g) \qquad K_c = 0.72 \text{ (at 800 °C)}$$

At 800 °C, 1.0 mole each of CO, H_2O, CO_2, and H_2 are placed into a 1.0-liter box.

Predict what will happen to the moles of CO_2 beginning from the above situation:

i) No change in moles of CO_2 because the system is at equilibrium.

ii) The number of moles of CO_2 will increase in order to reach equilibrium.

iii) The number of moles of CO_2 will decrease in order to reach equilibrium.

Explain your reasoning.

Problems

1. Indicate whether each of the following statements is true or false and explain your reasoning. All three statements refer to the reaction:

$$2\,SO_3(g) \rightleftharpoons 2\,SO_2(g) + O_2(g)$$

   a)   The rate of production of O_2 is equal to the rate of consumption of SO_3.

   b)   When the above reaction reaches equilibrium, $[SO_2] = 2 \times [O_2]$.

   c)   When $Q_c > K_c$, the rate of the forward reaction is greater than the rate of the reverse reaction.

2. When solutions containing $Fe^{3+}(aq)$ ions and SCN^- (aq) ions are mixed together, the following equilibrium is established:

$$Fe^{3+}(aq) + SCN^-\,(aq) \rightleftharpoons FeSCN^{2+}(aq)$$

   At equilibrium at some temperature, in 3.0 liters of total solution, there are 0.653 moles of $FeSCN^{2+}(aq)$, 0.0385 moles of $Fe^{3+}(aq)$, and 0.0465 moles of SCN^- (aq).

   a)   Calculate the value of the equilibrium constant, K_c, for the reaction at this temperature.

   b)   An inquiring student pours another liter of water into the beaker holding the solution described above. She notices that the number of moles of Fe^{3+} and SCN^- are then seen to increase, and the number of moles of $FeSCN^{2+}$ decreases. Explain this observation.

3. A chemist examining the conversion of methane to other fuels was investigating the following reaction describing the reaction of methane with steam at 1200 K:

$$CH_4(g) + H_2O(g) \rightleftharpoons CO(g) + 3\,H_2(g) \qquad K_c = 0.26 \text{ at } 1200 \text{ K}$$

   The chemist simultaneously injected 1.8 moles of each gas (CH_4, H_2O, CO, and H_2) into a 2.00-liter flask held at 1200 K.

   a)   In which direction will the reaction proceed in order to reach equilibrium? Explain your reasoning.

   b)   The chemist is interested in the concentration of H_2 produced at equilibrium. Provide an algebraic expression whose solution would enable this concentration to be determined. Explicitly describe how the $[H_2]$ could be determined from the solution of this equation. DO NOT SOLVE THE EQUATION.

4. Sulfur dioxide reacts with molecular oxygen to form sulfur trioxide.

$$2\ SO_2(g)\ +\ O_2(g)\ \rightleftharpoons\ 2\ SO_3(g)$$

At some temperature the equilibrium constant, K_c, for this reaction is 16. If 1.0 mole of SO_2, 1.8 mole of O_2, and 4.0 mole of SO_3 are placed in a 2.0-liter flask at this temperature:

a) will the reaction proceed to the left or to the right?

b) set up the equation that will enable you to determine the concentrations of SO_3, O_2, and SO_3 at equilibrium (use "x"). Do *not* attempt to solve the equation.

c) Estimate a value for x, in moles, without doing any further calculation. Briefly explain.

How Soluble Are Ionic Salts?

WARM-UP

Model 1: The Dissolution of Magnesium Hydroxide in Water.

When solid $Mg(OH)_2$ dissolves in water the chemical reaction is:

$$Mg(OH)_2(s) \rightleftharpoons Mg^{2+}(aq) + 2\,OH^-(aq) \tag{1}$$

where $Mg^{2+}(aq)$ represents magnesium ions surrounded by water molecules.

Table 1. The results (after equilibrium has been established) of adding solid $Mg(OH)_2$ to 10.0 L of water at 25 °C.

Total amount of $Mg(OH)_2$ added		Mg^{2+} concentration in the resulting solution	OH^- concentration in the resulting solution	Mass of $Mg(OH)_2$ that does not dissolve
(g)	(moles)	$[Mg^{2+}]$, (M)	$[OH^-]$, (M)	(g)
0.00963	1.65×10^{-4}	1.65×10^{-5}	3.30×10^{-5}	0.00000
0.01604	2.75×10^{-4}	2.75×10^{-5}	5.50×10^{-5}	0.00000
0.09590	1.64×10^{-3}	1.64×10^{-4}	3.29×10^{-4}	0.00000
0.09630	1.65×10^{-3}	1.65×10^{-4}	3.30×10^{-4}	0.00000
0.09700	1.66×10^{-3}	1.65×10^{-4}	3.30×10^{-4}	0.00070
0.10000	1.71×10^{-3}	1.65×10^{-4}	3.30×10^{-4}	0.00370
0.14445	2.48×10^{-3}	1.65×10^{-4}	3.30×10^{-4}	0.04815
0.19260	3.30×10^{-3}	1.65×10^{-4}	3.30×10^{-4}	0.09630

Critical Thinking Questions

1. Choose one of the masses of $Mg(OH)_2$ in the left-hand column of Table 1 and verify that the corresponding number of moles of $Mg(OH)_2$ is correct.

2. When 2.75×10^{-4} moles of $Mg(OH)_2$ are added:

    a)   why is $[Mg^{2+}] = 2.75 \times 10^{-5}$ M?

    b)   why is $[OH^-] = 5.50 \times 10^{-5}$ M?

3. Each beaker shown below corresponds to one of the rows in Table 1.

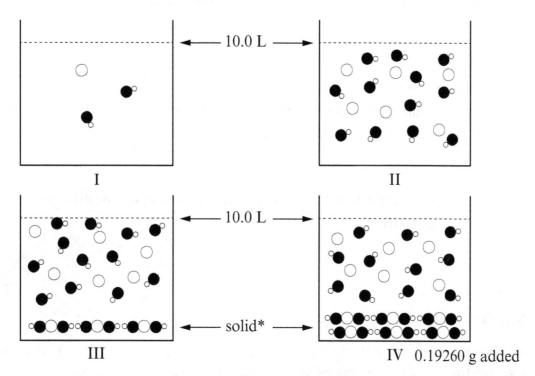

I

II

10.0 L

III

IV   0.19260 g added

solid*

H_2O molecules not shown

*solid $Mg(OH_2)$ that remains undissolved

    a)   What chemical species does "◯" represent?

    b)   What chemical species does "●o" represent?

    c)   For each of the remaining beakers (I, II, III), determine which line in
         Table 1 best corresponds to the representation in that beaker and then
         write the total mass of $Mg(OH)_2(s)$ added next to the label.

         For example, beaker IV corresponds to the bottom row in the table –
         after a total mass of 0.19260 g of $Mg(OH)_2$ has been added as indicated.

END OF WARM-UP

Answer CTQs 4 – 6 as a team.

4.   a)   When 0.14445 grams of $Mg(OH)_2$ are added, how many grams dissolve?

      b)   When 0.09700 grams of $Mg(OH)_2$ are added, how many grams dissolve?

5.   According to Table 1, what is the maximum number of moles of $Mg(OH)_2$ that can be dissolved in 10.0 L of water?

6.   Based on your answer to CTQ 5:

      a)   what is the maximum number of moles of $Mg(OH)_2$ that can be dissolved in 1.00 L of water?

      b)   what is the maximum mass of $Mg(OH)_2$ that can be dissolved in 1.00 L of water?

Information

We have seen that there is a maximum amount of solid $Mg(OH)_2$ that can be dissolved in a given amount of water. This is a general phenomenon – at a given temperature there is a maximum amount of any solid that can be dissolved per liter of water. This amount is known as the **solubility** of the solute. For $Mg(OH)_2$, we say that the solubility of magnesium hydroxide is 9.63×10^{-3} grams/liter or the solubility of magnesium hydroxide is 1.65×10^{-4} moles/liter. The latter value is often referred to as the **molar solubility**.

Once equilibrium is established between a solid material and the associated aqueous species, the solution is **saturated**. By convention, if a saturated solution of an ionic compound has a molar solubility that is greater than about 0.1 M, we say that the compound is **soluble**. If the molar solubility of the saturated solution is less than about 1×10^{-3} M, the compound is said to be **insoluble**. Intermediate cases are said to be **moderately soluble**. Experimental evidence shows that essentially all compounds containing the nitrate ion, NO_3^-, and also all those containing the Group I metal ions (such as sodium ion, Na^+ or potassium ion, K^+) are soluble in water.

Critical Thinking Questions

7. a) What is the molar solubility of $Mg(OH)_2$? After answering individually, reach consensus with your teammates before continuing to part b.

    b) Is $Mg(OH)_2$ considered to be a soluble or insoluble compound? Explain how you reached this conclusion.

8. As a team, determine which (one or more) of the beakers in CTQ 3 represents a saturated solution. Explain in one or two sentences how your team reached this conclusion.

9. At room temperature, a saturated solution of lead(II) chloride, $PbCl_2$, is obtained after 0.032 moles of the solid have dissolved in 2.00 liters of water.

    Is lead(II) chloride considered to be soluble, insoluble, or moderately soluble? Discuss as a team and then individually present the consensus analysis.

10. A student adds 0.07 moles of an ionic compound to 500 mL of water and all of the material dissolves. Is the ionic compound soluble, insoluble, moderately soluble, or is it impossible to tell? Individually, explain your reasoning and include at least one calculation in your analysis. When all teammates are done, compare answers and make any needed changes before moving to Model 2.

Model 2: The Solubility Product.

As shown in Model 1, the dissolution of $Mg(OH)_2$ is an equilibrium process. So, there is an equilibrium constant expression associated with the chemical equation shown in Equation 1. The equilibrium constant expression for the dissolution of solid $Mg(OH)_2$ as given in equation 1 is:

$$K_c \ = \ \frac{[Mg^{2+}(aq)][OH^-(aq)]^2}{[Mg(OH)_2(s)]} = 4.44 \times 10^{-13} \quad (at\ 25\ °C) \qquad (2)$$

Because the concentration of the solid is always constant (at a particular temperature), the concentration of the solid can be combined with K_c as follows:

$$K_c \times [Mg(OH)_2(s)] \ = \ [Mg^{2+}(aq)][OH^-(aq)]^2 = K \equiv K_{sp}$$

This new equilibrium constant, K, is called the **solubility product** and is given the symbol K_{sp}. The subscript "sp" is used only with the equilibrium constant, K, that describes the dissolution of an ionic solid in water. Thus, for the dissolution of $Mg(OH)_2(s)$:

$$Mg(OH)_2(s) \ \rightleftharpoons \ Mg^{2+}(aq) \ + \ 2\ OH^-(aq)$$

$$K_{sp} \ = \ [Mg^{2+}(aq)][OH^-(aq)]^2 \ = \ 1.80 \times 10^{-11} \quad (at\ 25\ °C) \qquad (3)$$

Critical Thinking Question

Answer CTQs 11 – 13 as a team.

11.   Use the data in Table 1 to verify the value of K_{sp} (at 25 °C) for $Mg(OH)_2$.

12.   Write the solubility constant expression, K_{sp}, for each reaction below.

a) $AgCl(s) \ \rightleftharpoons \ Ag^+(aq) + Cl^-(aq)$

b) $Cu_3(PO_4)_2(s) \ \rightleftharpoons \ 3\ Cu^{2+}(aq) + 2\ PO_4{}^{3-}(aq)$

c) $Li_2CO_3(s) \ \rightleftharpoons \ 2\ Li^+(aq) + CO_3{}^{2-}(aq)$

13.   The molar solubility of lithium carbonate, Li_2CO_3, is 0.0742 M. A student suggests that the value of K_{sp} for lithium carbonate is $(0.0742)^2(0.0742)$.

Explain why the student is *not correct* and then calculate the correct value of K_{sp} for lithium carbonate.

Model 3a: Two Beakers Before Mixing.

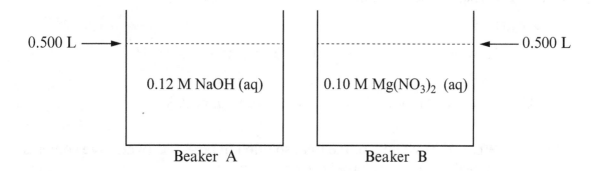

0.500 L →   ← 0.500 L

0.12 M NaOH (aq)   0.10 M Mg(NO₃)₂ (aq)

Beaker A   Beaker B

Critical Thinking Question

14.   A representation of the contents of Beaker A is shown below. OH⁻ is represented by ●○ and Na+ is represented by ▢.

Create an analogous representation for the contents of Beaker B. Each symbol should represent 0.01 moles of that substance.

Reach consensus with the entire team before proceeding to Model 3b.

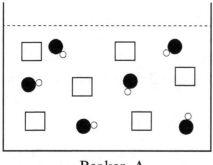

Beaker A   Beaker B

Model 3b: Mixing the Solutions Together: What Happens?

At 25 °C, the contents of Beakers A and B are combined into Beaker C, which was previously empty.

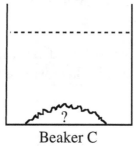

Beaker C

If a solid material forms when two solutions are mixed together, the solid is said to **precipitate** out of solution. The solid is referred to as the **precipitate.**

Critical Thinking Questions

Answer CTQs 15and 16 as a team.

15. In Model 3,

  a)   How many moles of $Mg^{2+}(aq)$ are present in beaker B?

  b)   How many moles of $OH^-(aq)$ are present in beaker A?

  c)   What is the volume of the final solution in beaker C (where the contents of beakers A and B have been combined)?

  d)   Assuming that no reaction occurs, what would be (Mg^{2+}) in beaker C?

  e)   Assuming that no reaction occurs, what would be (OH^-) in beaker C?

  f)   Write the expression for the reaction quotient, Q_{sp}, for this reaction:

$$Mg(OH)_2(s) \rightleftharpoons Mg^{2+}(aq) + 2\,OH^-(aq)$$

Using your answers to parts d and e, calculate the value of the reaction quotient, Q_{sp}, in beaker C.

  g)   Given the K_{sp} for $Mg(OH)_2$ at 25 °C is 1.80×10^{-11}, is the system in beaker C at equilibrium upon mixing? If not, in what direction will it shift?

  h)   Does a precipitate of $Mg(OH)_2(s)$ form?

16. Using data from Model 3 and ideas from the Information section on page 258, explain why we can expect that there will be no $NaNO_3(s)$ precipitate formed.

Information

When an equilibrium expression is written for a chemical equation, pure solids and liquids are normally omitted from the expression (because they are constants), and the value of the equilibrium constant, K, is assumed to apply to the remaining species. However, whenever the equilibrium constant is denoted as K_c, all substances must be included in the equilibrium constant expression. For example:

$$PbCl_2(s) \rightleftharpoons Pb^{2+}(aq) + 2\,Cl^-(aq) \quad K_c \;=\; \frac{[Pb^{2+}(aq)]\,[Cl^-\,aq)]^2}{[PbCl_2(s)]} \tag{4}$$

$$PbCl_2(s) \rightleftharpoons Pb^{2+}(aq) + 2\,Cl^-(aq) \quad K_{sp} \;=\; [Pb^{2+}(aq)]\,[Cl^-(aq)]^2 \tag{5}$$

$$2\,Mg(s) + O_2(g) \rightleftharpoons 2\,MgO(s) \qquad K_c \;=\; \frac{[MgO(s)]^2}{[Mg(s)]^2\,[O_2(g)]} \tag{6}$$

$$2\,Mg(s) + O_2(g) \rightleftharpoons 2\,MgO(s) \qquad K \;=\; \frac{1}{[O_2(g)]} \tag{7}$$

Critical Thinking Question

17. Write the equilibrium constant expression, K, for each of the following reactions. Where appropriate, designate the K as K_{sp}.

    a) $BaCO_3(s) \rightleftharpoons BaO(s) + CO_2(g)$

    b) $NH_4HS(s) \rightleftharpoons NH_3(g) + H_2S(g)$

    c) $Ag_2SO_4(s) \rightleftharpoons 2\,Ag^+(aq) + SO_4^{2-}(aq)$

Exercises

1. Write the equilibrium constant expression, K, for each of the following reactions. Where appropriate, designate the K as K_{sp}.

   a) $2 H_2(g) + O_2(g) \rightleftharpoons 2 H_2O(g)$

   b) $2 Hg(\ell) + Cl_2(g) \rightleftharpoons Hg_2Cl_2(s)$

   c) $BaSO_4(s) \rightleftharpoons Ba^{2+}(aq) + SO_4^{2-}(aq)$

   d) $NH_4Cl(s) \rightleftharpoons NH_3(g) + HCl(g)$

   e) $2 Ag^+(aq) + SO_4^{2-}(aq) \rightleftharpoons Ag_2SO_4(s)$

2. Indicate whether this statement is true or false, and explain your reasoning.

   For the reaction $CaCO_3(s) \rightleftharpoons CaO(s) + CO_2(g)$, the amount of CO_2 present at equilibrium in a 2.00 liter box is greater if 10.0 g of $CaCO_3$ are originally placed in the box than if only 5.00 g of $CaCO_3$ are originally present. (Hint: write the equilibrium constant expression, K, for the reaction.)

3. What mass of CuI will dissolve in 1.00 liter of water if $K_{sp} = 1.1 \times 10^{-12}$?

4. What mass of MgF_2 will dissolve in 125 mL of water if $K_{sp} = 6.5 \times 10^{-9}$?

5. When 1.0 g of AgCl is placed in a beaker containing 2.00 liters of water at room temperature, only a small amount of AgCl(s) is observed to dissolve. In fact, only 8.0×10^{-5} moles of AgCl are found to dissolve.

   Calculate the equilibrium constant, K_{sp}, for the reaction:

   $$AgCl(s) \rightleftharpoons Ag^+(aq) + Cl^-(aq)$$

6. A saturated solution of SrF_2 is produced when 0.11 grams of the ionic solid dissolves in 1.00 L of water. Calculate the value of K_{sp} for SrF_2.

7. The molar solubility of $MnCO_3$ is 4.24×10^{-6} M. What is the K_{sp} for $MnCO_3$?

8. Determine which has a greater molar solubility and explain your reasoning.

   $CaCO_3 (K_{sp} = 2.8 \times 10^{-9})$ or $MgCO_3 (K_{sp} = 3.5 \times 10^{-8})$

9. $PbCl_2(s)$ is not very soluble in water.

   $$PbCl_2(s) \rightleftharpoons Pb^{2+}(aq) + 2 Cl^-(aq)$$

   a)   If x moles of $PbCl_2(s)$ dissolve in 1.00 L of water, how many moles of $Pb^{2+}(aq)$ are produced? How many moles of $Cl^-(aq)$ are produced?

   b)   The equilibrium constant, K_{sp}, for the dissolution of $PbCl_2(s)$ in water is 1.6×10^{-5}. What is the concentration of $Pb^{2+}(aq)$ at equilibrium? What is the concentration of $Cl^-(aq)$ at equilibrium?

10. For each of the following situations, determine whether or not a precipitate of MgF_2 is expected to form. K_{sp} for MgF_2 is given in Exercise 4.

    a)   500.0 mL of 0.050M $Mg(NO_3)_2$ is mixed with 500.0 mL of 0.010 M NaF.

    b)   500.0 mL of 0.050M $Mg(NO_3)_2$ is mixed with 500.0 mL of 0.0010 M NaF.

11. Is a precipitate of $Cd(CN)_2$ expected to form when 500.0 mL of 0.010 M $Cd(NO_3)_2$ is mixed with 500.0 mL of 0.0025 M NaCN? Both cadmium(II) nitrate and sodium cyanide are completely dissociated in the original solutions. The K_{sp} of $Cd(CN)_2$ is 1.0×10^{-8}.

12. Show that $[Mg(OH)_2(s)] = 40.5$ mole/L. Hint: for $Mg(OH)_2(s)$, MW = 58.32 g/mole and the density of $Mg(OH)_2(s)$ is 2.36 g/mL.

13. In CTQ 3, each symbol ($\bigcirc$ and $\bullet\circ$) represents the same number of ions.

    a)   How many moles does each symbol represent (to three significant figures)?

    b)   Confirm that your answer to part a is correct by using it to determine the concentration of Mg^{2+} ions in each beaker in CTQ 3.

14. How does K_{sp} allow chemists to determine the molar solubility of an ionic salt? Describe the steps necessary in a few sentences given a particular salt and the value of K_{sp}.

Problems

1. The K_{sp} of Ag_2SO_4 is 1.4×10^{-5}. Will a precipitate form when 250 mL of 0.12 M $AgNO_3$ is mixed with 500 mL of 0.0050 M Na_2SO_4?

2.   a)   Write a chemical equation that describes the dissolution of solid AuCl to Au^{3+} and Cl^- ions found in water.

    b)   Write the expression for the K_{sp} of $AuCl_3$.

    c)   Calculate how many grams of Au^{3+} would be found in one liter of a saturated solution of $AuCl_3$. The K_{sp} for $AuCl_3$ is 3.2×10^{-23}.

3. Five hundred (500.) mL of a $Pb(NO_3)_2$ solution and 500. mL of a NaCl solution are added to a large beaker. At equilibrium the result is depicted below:

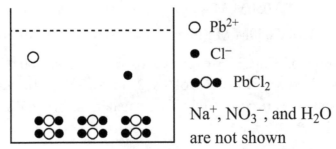

○ Pb^{2+}

● Cl^-

●○● $PbCl_2$

Na^+, NO_3^-, and H_2O are not shown

a) Which solution prior to mixture, $Pb(NO_3)_2$ or NaCl, had the higher concentration in moles/liter? Explain your reasoning.

b) Explain how you know from the diagram that the solution was not prepared by dissolving $PbCl_2$ in water.

c) Given that each symbol, ○ and ●, represents 2.5×10^{-2} moles, calculate the K_{sp} of $PbCl_2$ at this temperature.

4. For $PbBr_2$, $K_{sp} = 6.3 \times 10^{-6}$.

a) What is the molar solubility of $PbBr_2$ in pure water?

b) Instead of dissolving the $PbBr_2$ in pure water, a student adds solid $PbBr_2$ to a 2.0-liter solution of 0.10 M KBr. How much $PbBr_2$ will dissolve in this case compared to the amount that would dissolve in 2.0 liters of pure water?

i) more than in pure water

ii) less than in pure water

iii) the same amount as in pure water

iv) impossible to tell from the information given

Clearly explain your analysis.

What are Acids and Bases?

WARM-UP

Model 1: Two Definitions of Acids and Bases.

Arrhenius Definitions

- An **acid** is a substance that produces hydronium ions, $H_3O^+(aq)$, when it is added to water.
- A **base** is a substance that produces hydroxide ions, $OH^-(aq)$, when it is added to water.

Bronsted-Lowry Definitions

- An **acid** is a substance that donates a proton, H^+, to another species.
- A **base** is a substance that accepts a proton, H^+, from another species.

Acid-base reactions are one of the most important types of chemical reactions.

Table 1. Equilibrium constants for some acid-base reactions.

Reaction	K_c	
$HCl(g) + H_2O(\ell) \rightleftharpoons H_3O^+(aq) + Cl^-(aq)$	$2. \times 10^4$	(1)
$NH_3(aq) + H_2O(\ell) \rightleftharpoons NH_4^+(aq) + OH^-(aq)$	3.3×10^{-7}	(2)
$HCN(aq) + H_2O(\ell) \rightleftharpoons H_3O^+(aq) + CN^-(aq)$	1.1×10^{-11}	(3)

Critical Thinking Questions

1. a) Each of the three forward reactions in Table 1 contains *either* an Arrhenius acid *or* an Arrhenius base. Complete the appropriate columns in the table below by indicating which is present for each reaction.

    b) Each of the three forward reactions contains both a Bronsted-Lowry acid and a Bronsted-Lowry base. Complete the appropriate columns in the table below.

Rxn	Arrhenius Acid	Arrhenius Base	Bronsted-Lowry Acid	Bronsted-Lowry Base
1				
2				
3				

2. Find the chemical species in Table 1 that acts as both an acid and a base. Indicate whether you have used the Arrhenius definition or the Bronsted-Lowry definition to find your answer.

3. Based on the data in Table 1, which do you think is considered the stronger acid, HCl or HCN? Explain your reasoning.

END OF WARM-UP

4. As a team, consider reaction 1 in Table 1.

    a) What species results from the loss of a proton from the Bronsted-Lowry acid in the forward reaction?

    b) Does the species indicated in part a (the answer that you gave) act as an acid or a base when the reverse of reaction 1 occurs?

    c) What species results from the gain of a proton by the Bronsted-Lowry base in the forward reaction?

    d) Does the species indicated in part c act as an acid or a base when the reverse of reaction 1 occurs?

    e) Answer parts a – d for reactions 2 and 3 also. Use a sentence to describe any general relationship that you observe.

Model 2: Conjugate Acid-Base Pairs.

Within the Bronsted-Lowry model, certain pairs of molecules are described as **conjugate acid-base pairs**. The two species in a conjugate acid-base pair differ by a proton *only*. For a conjugate acid-base pair, we say that that the base has a conjugate acid and the acid has a conjugate base.

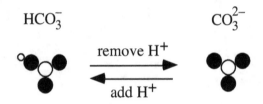

$$HCO_3^- \qquad CO_3^{2-}$$

Table 2.   Examples of conjugate acid-base pairs.

Acid	Base
H_2CO_3	HCO_3^-
HCO_3^-	CO_3^{2-}
H_3O^+	H_2O
H_2S	HS^-

A conjugate acid-base pair differs by a proton, H^+.
The species with more protons is the acid.

Critical Thinking Questions

5. Individually, write the chemical equation for the reaction of H_2S, as an acid, with water. Make sure that your response is properly charge balanced.

6. Individually, write the chemical equation for CO_3^{2-}, as a base, with water. Make sure that your response is properly charge balanced.

Check your answers to CTQs 5 and 6 with your team members and reach consensus before continuing to CTQ 7.

7. As a team, answer and explain each of the following:

    a) What is the conjugate acid of NH_3?

    b) What is the conjugate base of H_2O?

Exercises

1. What are the defining characteristics of acids and bases?

2. Give the conjugate base of each species:

    a) HSO_4^- b) HCO_3^- c) H_2O d) OH^- e) H_3O^+

    f) NH_4^+ g) $CH_3NH_3^+$ h) HF i) CH_3COOH

3. Give the conjugate acid of each species:

    a) SO_4^{2-} b) CO_3^{2-} c) H_2O d) OH^- e) O^{2-}

    f) NH_3 g) CH_3NH_2 h) CN^- i) CH_3COO^-

    j) F^- k) HCO_3^- l) NH_2^-

4. For each of the following reactions:

    i) $H_2SO_4(aq) + H_2O \rightleftharpoons H_3O^+(aq) + HSO_4^-(aq)$

    ii) $HSO_4^-(aq) + H_2O \rightleftharpoons SO_4^{2-}(aq) + H_3O^+(aq)$

    iii) $H_2O + H_2O \rightleftharpoons H_3O^+(aq) + OH^-(aq)$

    iv) $HCN(aq) + CO_{2-}^3(aq) \rightleftharpoons HCO_3^-(aq) + CN^-(aq)$

    v) $H_2S(g) + NH_3(\ell) \rightleftharpoons HS^-(am) + NH_4^+(am)$
            (am) = dissolved in liquid ammonia

    a)   Which reactant is the acid?
    b)   Which reactant is the base?
    c)   Find the two conjugate pairs present in the reaction.

5. Complete the following table of conjugate acids and bases:

Acid	Base
H_2S	
	S^{2-}
	NO_2^-
H_3PO_4	
	OCN^-
H_3O^+	
OH^-	
	F^-
	HPO_4^{2-}
$HOCl$	

6. Ammonia can react as an acid or a base.

   a) What is the conjugate acid of ammonia?

   b) What is the conjugate base of ammonia?

   c) Complete the following acid-base reaction in which $NH_3(\ell)$ acts as both an acid and a base:

   $$NH_3(\ell) + NH_3(\ell) \rightleftharpoons$$

How Strong is an Acid?

WARM-UP

Model 1: K_c and K_a for Acids.

When an acid HA is placed in water, hydronium ions and the conjugate base A^- are produced:

$$HA(aq) + H_2O(\ell) \rightleftharpoons H_3O^+(aq) + A^-(aq) \qquad (1)$$

Given that this reaction produces hydronium ions, chemists often refer to these types of reactions as **acid ionization reactions**. (They are also known as *acid dissociation reactions*.) The equilibrium constant, K_c, for this type of process is:

$$K_c = \frac{[H_3O^+]\,[A^-]}{[HA]\,[H_2O]} \qquad (2)$$

Most solutions are sufficiently dilute that the concentration of water is the same before and after reaction with the acid. The concentration of the water is incorporated into the value of K_c and the equilibrium expression is given a special name and symbol — the acid ionization constant, K_a.

$$[H_2O] \approx \frac{1000 \text{ g/L}}{18 \text{ g/mol}} \approx 55 \text{ M}$$

$$K_c = \frac{[H_3O^+]\,[A^-]}{[HA]\,[55]}$$

$$K_a = K_c \times 55 = \frac{[H_3O^+][A^-]}{[HA][55]} \times 55$$

$$K_a = \frac{[H_3O^+][A^-]}{[HA]} \qquad (3)$$

Critical Thinking Question

1. For each acid below, use equation (1) as a guide to provide a balanced chemical equation. Then, in each case, circle the conjugate base and write the K_a expression as shown in equation 3:

    a) acetic acid, CH_3COOH (the last H is the proton that is lost).

    b) nitrous acid, HNO_2

    c) hydrofluoric acid, HF

Table 1.   The names and formulas of acids commonly encountered in general chemistry courses and the values of K_c and K_a for each.

Acid Name	Molecular Formula	K_c	K_a
acetic acid	CH_3COOH	3.2×10^{-7}	1.75×10^{-5}
carbonic acid	H_2CO_3	8.2×10^{-9}	4.5×10^{-7}
hydrobromic acid	HBr	2×10^7	1×10^9
hydrochloric acid	HCl	2×10^4	1×10^6
hydrofluoric acid	HF	1.3×10^{-5}	7.2×10^{-4}
hydroiodic acid	HI	5×10^7	3×10^9
hydrosulfuric acid	H_2S	1.8×10^{-9}	1.0×10^{-7}
nitric acid	HNO_3	≈ 0.5	28
nitrous acid	HNO_2	9.2×10^{-6}	5.1×10^{-4}
perchloric acid	$HOClO_3$	2×10^6	1×10^8
phosphoric acid	H_3PO_4	1.3×10^{-4}	7.1×10^{-3}
sulfuric acid	H_2SO_4	2×10^1	1×10^3

Critical Thinking Questions

2.   a)   In a solution of nitrous acid: $[HNO_2] = 1.33$ M; $[H_3O^+] = 0.026$ M; $[NO_2^-] = 0.026$ M. Show that K_a is correct in Table 1.

b)   When a certain amount of HBr is dissolved in water, $[Br^-] = 1.2 \times 10^{-3}$ M. What is $[H_3O^+]$?

END OF WARM-UP

3.   As a team, examine the information in Table 1 and decide:

a)   which acid will produce the highest $[H_3O^+]$ in solutions that are all the same molarity? Explain your choice. (You should answer this question without doing extensive equilibrium calculations.)

b)   which acid will produce the lowest $[H_3O^+]$ in solutions that are all the same molarity? Explain your choice. (You should answer this question without doing extensive equilibrium calculations.)

Answer CTQ 4 as a team.

4.   For a 1.00 M HNO_3 solution, $[H_3O^+]$ = $[NO_3^-]$ = 0.967 M.
   a)   Write the K_a expression for HNO_3.

   b)   Without using the value for K_a, determine $[HNO_3]$ in this solution. Describe how your team determined your answer.

   c)   Use the answers to parts a and b to show that K_a = 28 for HNO_3.

Information

The **relative strength** of an acid is determined by the relative concentration of H_3O^+ produced at equilibrium for a given molarity of the acid. For example, if a 0.5 M solution of HA has $[H_3O^+]$ = 1×10^{-4} M and a 0.5 M solution of HX has $[H_3O^+]$ = 1×10^{-3} M, then HX is a *stronger* acid than HA.

Critical Thinking Questions

5.   Individually, rank the six acids in Table 1 with $K_a < 1$ in order from weakest to strongest. Once everyone is done, reach consensus with your teammates before continuing.

6.   As a team, use the data about HNO_3 in CTQ 4 to calculate the percentage of HNO_3 that has reacted in a 1.00 M HNO_3 solution.

7. As a team, consider two acids, HA and HQ. If HA is a stronger acid than HQ, how would the percentage of HA that reacts compare to the percentage of HQ that reacts for equal molarities of the two acids. Explain your team's reasoning.

Model 2: Percent Ionization of Acids

Percent ionization is the percentage of the original acid molecules that have reacted to produce the conjugate base and H_3O^+.

Table 2.   The acids in Table 1 arranged by K_a.

Acid Name	Molecular Formula	K_c	K_a	% Ionization in a 1.00 M solution
hydroiodic acid	HI	5×10^7	3×10^9	100.
hydrobromic acid	HBr	2×10^7	1×10^9	100.
perchloric acid	$HOClO_3$	2×10^6	1×10^8	100.
hydrochloric acid	HCl	2×10^4	1×10^6	100.
sulfuric acid	H_2SO_4	2×10^1	1×10^3	100.
nitric acid	HNO_3	≈ 0.5	28	96.7
phosphoric acid	H_3PO_4	1.3×10^{-4}	7.1×10^{-3}	8.4
hydrofluoric acid	HF	1.3×10^{-5}	7.2×10^{-4}	2.7
nitrous acid	HNO_2	9.2×10^{-6}	5.1×10^{-4}	2.3
acetic acid	CH_3COOH	3.2×10^{-7}	1.75×10^{-5}	0.42
carbonic acid	H_2CO_3	8.2×10^{-9}	4.5×10^{-7}	0.07
hydrosulfuric acid	H_2S	1.8×10^{-9}	1.0×10^{-7}	0.03

Critical Thinking Questions

Answers CTQs 8 and 9 as a team.

8. a) Use the information in Table 2 to calculate $[H_3O^+]$, $[NO_2^-]$, and $[HNO_2]$ for a 1.000 M solution of HNO_2. [Hint: see CTQs 4 and 6.]

    b) Write a sentence that describes the qualitative relationship between K_a and the percent ionization of the acids in Table 2.

9. The acids in Table 2 are divided into two groups: those with $K_a > 1$ and those with $K_a < 1$. Describe each of these two groups in terms of percent ionization.

Model 3: Strong and Weak Acids.

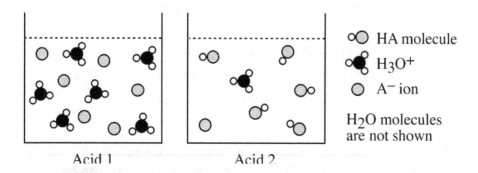

Acid 1   Acid 2

A **strong acid** is one that is more than 95% ionized in water.

A **weak acid** is one that is only slightly ionized in water, generally less than 20% ionized and often less than 10% ionized.

Critical Thinking Questions

Discuss and answer CTQs 10 – 13 as a team.

10. In Model 2, one acid is a strong acid and the other is a weak acid. Circle the correct term for each acid below and explain how you reached that conclusion.

    Acid 1: strong   weak   Acid 2: strong   weak

11. In Table 2, label each acid as strong or weak.

12. For the group of strong acids in Table 2:

    a)   which is the strongest strong acid?

    b)   which is the weakest strong acid?

13. For the group of weak acids in Table 2:

    a)   which is the weakest weak acid?

    b)   which is the strongest weak acid?

Model 4: Neutral, Acidic, and Basic Solutions.

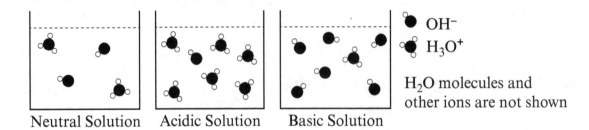

Neutral Solution   Acidic Solution   Basic Solution

Aqueous solutions in which $[H_3O^+] > [OH^-]$ are said to be **acidic**.

Solutions in which $[OH^-] > [H_3O^+]$ are said to be **basic**.

Solutions in which $[H_3O^+] = [OH^-]$ are said to be **neutral**.

Table 3.   Characteristics of solutions of various amounts of hypochlorous acid, HOCl, dissolved in water to make 1.00 L of solution at 25 °C.

Moles of HOCl added	$[H_3O^+]$ (M)	$[OH^-]$ (M)
0.00	1.0×10^{-7}	1.0×10^{-7}
0.30	9.3×10^{-5}	1.1×10^{-10}
0.75	1.5×10^{-4}	6.8×10^{-11}
1.00	1.7×10^{-4}	5.9×10^{-11}

Critical Thinking Questions

For CTQ 14, answer individually. Once all team members are done, compare your answers and resolve any differences.

14.   a)   Label each solution in Table 3 as acidic, basic or neutral.

b)   According to the data in Table 3, is HOCl an acid or a base? Explain your answer.

15. As a team, use Table 3 to answer both parts of this question.

    a) Which of these expressions is a constant?

       i) $[H_3O^+] + [OH^-]$

       ii) $\dfrac{[H_3O^+]}{[OH^-]}$

       iii) $[H_3O^+] - [OH^-]$

       iv) $[H_3O^+] \times [OH^-]$

    b) What is the value of the constant for the expression that your team chose in part a?

Information

Water is capable of acting as both an acid and a base; it is possible for water to react with itself in an acid-base reaction.

$$H_2O(\ell) + H_2O(\ell) \rightleftharpoons H_3O^+(aq) + OH^-(aq) \qquad (5)$$

Critical Thinking Questions

16. Based on equation 5, is water considered to be acidic, basic, or neutral? Discuss with your team and provide a consensus explanation.

17. As a team, write the expressions for the K_c and K_a of water (see equations 1-3).

18. The value of the K_a of water is 1.8×10^{-16}. Recall that $[H_2O] \approx 55$ M.

    a) As a team, use this information and the expression for the K_a of water from CTQ 17 to calculate the value of $[H_3O^+] \times [OH^-]$.

b)   As a team, compare the value $[H_3O^+] \times [OH^-]$ calculated in part a with the value determined in CTQ 15b. How well do they agree?

Information

The value of $[H_3O^+] \times [OH^-]$ is given a special name and symbol—the **water-dissociation equilibrium constant**, K_w. The value of K_w at 25 °C is 1.0×10^{-14}.

Critical Thinking Question

19.   Individually, use the value of K_w to calculate the hydronium ion concentration and the hydroxide ion concentration in pure water. Check to make sure that everyone in the team obtained the same value and showed their work.

Exercises

1.   Provide the names and the chemical formulas for the conjugate bases of the acids listed in Table 1.

2.   Rank the weak acids in Table 1 in order from strongest to weakest.

3.   For each of these acids, write the balanced equation for the reaction of the acid with water and the corresponding K_a expression.

     a) HF   b) H_2S c) H_2CO_3 d) HOBr

4.   Indicate whether the following statement is true or false and explain your reasoning:

     A 0.25 M solution of acetic acid has a higher $[H_3O^+]$ than does a 0.25 M solution of nitrous acid.

5.   The hydronium ion concentration of a sample of lemon juice at 25 °C is 6.3×10^{-3} M. What is the hydroxide ion concentration?

6.   The hydroxide ion concentration of a sample of vinegar at 25 °C is 3.3×10^{-12} M. What is the hydronium ion concentration?

7.   For each of the following $[H_3O^+]$, what is $[OH^-]$?

     a) 3.5×10^{-5} M   b) 7.1×10^{-1} M   c) 4.5×10^{-10} M   d) 2.1×10^{-7} M.

8.   For each of the following $[OH^-]$, what is $[H_3O^+]$?

     a) 3.5×10^{-5} M   b) 7.1×10^{-10} M   c) 5.7×10^{-12} M   d) 1.1×10^{-7} M.

9. Which of the solutions in Exercise 7 are acidic? Which are basic?

10. Which of the solutions in Exercise 8 are acidic? Which are basic?

11. Indicate whether the following statements are true or false and explain your reasoning:

    a)   All acidic solutions have $[OH^-] < 10^{-7}$ M.

    b)   A solution is considered to be acidic whenever $[H_3O^+] > 0$.

12. Consider solutions of acetic acid (CH_3COOH, $K_a = 1.75 \times 10^{-5}$) and carbonic acid ($H_2CO_3$, $K_a = 4.5 \times 10^{-7}$), each of which has the same – but unknown – concentration (x M). Which statement below is correct?

    i)   The x M carbonic acid solution has a higher $[H_3O^+]$ than the x M acetic acid solution.

    ii)   The x M acetic acid solution has a higher $[H_3O^+]$ than the x M carbonic acid solution.

    iii) Both solutions have the same $[H_3O^+]$.

    iv)   It is not possible to determine which solution will have a higher $[H_3O^+]$ from the information given.

    Explain your reasoning.

Problems

1. Describe how to determine whether an acid is a strong acid or a weak acid from an experimental measurement.

2. A student says: "A solution with $[H_3O^+] = 0.10$ M must contain an acid that is stronger than the acid in a solution with $[H_3O^+] = 0.050$ M." Explain why the student is incorrect.

3. The equation for dissolving metal hydroxides in water, such as $Mg(OH)_2$, is:

    $$Mg(OH)_2(s) \rightleftharpoons Mg^{+2} (aq) + 2\ OH^- (aq)$$

    A student examines two beakers containing solutions of metal hydroxides in water. One beaker contains $Mg(OH)_2$ and the other contains $Cu(OH)_2$. Both solutions are saturated and there is solid remaining in the bottom of each beaker. Thus, both systems are at equilibrium.

    The $[OH^-]$ in the $Mg(OH)_2$ solution is greater than the $[OH^-]$ in the $Cu(OH)_2$ solution.

    Which solid, $Mg(OH)_2$ or $Cu(OH)_2$ has a larger value of K_{sp}? Explain your reasoning clearly.

ChemActivity 42

How Much Acid or Base Reacts?

WARM-UP

Model 1: A Weak Acid Increases the Hydronium Concentration of a Solution, but the Amount of Ionization is Small.

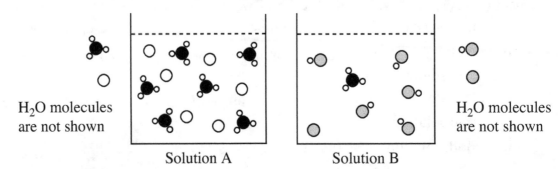

H₂O molecules
are not shown   H₂O molecules
                                                                                 are not shown

Solution A   Solution B

Table 1.   Characteristics of two 1.00-L acid solutions at 25 °C.

Acid	Moles of acid added	$[H_3O^+]$ (M)	$[OH^-]$ (M)
HCl	0.10	0.10	1.0×10^{-13}
HF	0.10	8.5×10^{-3}	1.2×10^{-12}

Critical Thinking Questions

1.   Based on the data in Table 1:

   a)   What is the percent ionization of HCl in a 0.10 M HCl solution?

   b)   Based on your answer to part a, determine if HCl(aq) is a strong acid or weak acid and explain your reasoning.

   c)   What is the percent ionization of HF in a 0.10 M HF solution?

   d)   Based on your answer to part c, determine if HCl(aq) is a strong acid or weak acid and explain your reasoning.

2. Solution A and Solution B in Model 1 represent the two acids in Table 1.

    a) Assign each of the two acids in Table 1 to the solution that is a better representation.

    b) Complete the legend in Model 1 by identifying the chemical species for

    , O , oO , O .

3. Identify the species, other than water, that is not shown in the model. Provide a reason for why it is not shown.

4. Complete and balance the following equation for the weak acid HOCl:

    $$HOCl(aq) + H_2O(\ell) \rightleftharpoons$$

    Write the equilibrium expression for the K_a of HOCl.

END OF WARM-UP

For CTQs 5 – 9, answer each question individually and then reach consensus as a team before moving on to the next question or question part.

5. Complete the balanced equation from CTQ 4 above the following table and then complete the table assuming that 0.30 moles of HOCl are added to sufficient water to make 1.0 L of solution at 25 °C. Because the volume remains constant in this process, the analysis can be done in terms of concentrations.

    Balanced equation: $H_2O(\ell)$ + $\rightleftharpoons$ +

initial concentration (moles/L)	0.30	0	0
change in concentration (moles/L)	$-x$		
equilibrium concentration (moles/L)	$0.30 - x$		

6. Describe in words what "x" represents in this table with respect to:

    a) HOCl

    b) H_3O^+

    c) OCl^-

7.   At 25 °C, the K_a for HOCl is 2.9×10^{-8}.

   a)   Provide the equilibrium constant expression K_a for HOCl.

   b)   Substitute the appropriate expressions from the table in CTQ 5 into the expression from part a and set it equal to the value of K_a of HOCl.

   c)   Rearrange the equation in part b and then use the quadratic formula to solve for x.

   (Note: you should get these two values for x: -9.4×10^{-5} and 9.3×10^{-5}.)

   d)   Determine which value of x above is correct and use it to determine the equilibrium concentration values for HOCl, H_3O^+, and OCl^-.

   HOCl:

   H_3O^+:

   OCl^-:

   e)   Use the answer to part b to verify that your equilibrium concentrations are correct.

   f)   Add the missing values for 0.30 M HOCl to Table 2 on the next page.

Table 2.   Characteristics of solutions of various amounts of hypochlorous acid, HOCl, dissolved in water to make 1.00 L of solution at 25 °C.

Moles of HOCl added	$[H_3O^+]$ (M)	$[OH^-]$ (M)	$[HOCl]$ (M)	$[OCl^-]$ (M)
0.00	1.0×10^{-7}	1.0×10^{-7}	0	0
0.30		1.1×10^{-10}		
0.75	1.5×10^{-4}	6.8×10^{-11}	0.75	1.5×10^{-4}
1.00	1.7×10^{-4}	5.9×10^{-11}	1.0	1.7×10^{-4}

8.   Determine the value of K_W from the data given in Table 2. Does this value agree with your value calculated from Table 3 of CA 41?

9.   For the three acidic solutions:

a)   Explain why the equilibrium concentration of H_3O^+ is equal to the equilibrium concentration of OCl^-.

b)   Based on information from Table 2, calculate the number of moles of HOCl(aq) present at equilibrium for each of the three acidic solutions.

c)   Explain why the number of moles of HOCl added is equal to the number of moles of HOCl at equilibrium in spite of the fact that some of the HOCl reacts!

Model 2: An Approximation for a Solution of a Weak Acid.

The results that we have obtained for the weak acid HOCl are generally valid for any weak acid. That is, for any weak acid dissolved in water, hydronium ions are produced according to the reaction

$$HA(aq) + H_2O(\ell) \rightleftharpoons H_3O^+(aq) + A^-(aq)$$

The acid-ionization constant expression for the reaction is

$$K_a = \frac{[H_3O^+] \, [A^-]}{[HA]}$$

If $(HA)_o$ is the initial concentration of the weak acid (before equilibrium is reached), then at equilibrium we generally find that $[HA] = (HA)_o$. (For the HOCl example from CTQs 5 – 7, $(HA)_o = 0.30$ M $= [HA]$.) This relationship holds because the value of "x" (the amount of weak acid that reacts) is so small compared to the initial amount of HA that the equilibrium concentration of HA is essentially the same as the initial concentration.

This approximation, that $[HA] = (HA)_o - x \approx (HA)_o$ greatly simplifies the analysis of solutions of weak acids, and avoids the use of the quadratic formula in calculating the equilibrium concentrations.

Read in your textbook, or other materials assigned by your instructor, for more information about when these approximations are valid.

Critical Thinking Questions

Complete CTQs 10 – 13 as a team.

10. Use the approximation described in Model 2 to complete the table for a 0.75 M solution of HOCl, using x to represent the concentration of HOCl that reacts.

Balanced equation: $H_2O + HOCl(aq) \rightleftharpoons H_3O^+(aq) + OCl^-(aq)$

	HOCl	H_3O^+	OCl^-
initial concentration (moles/L)			
change in concentration (moles/L)			
equilibrium concentration (moles/L)			

11. Substitute the equilibrium concentration expressions from the last line of the above table into the K_a expression for HOCl and then calculate the equilibrium concentration of H_3O^+.

12. Confirm that your answer to CTQ 11 is correct by comparing it to the data in Table 2.

13. Acetic acid, CH_3COOH, is a weak acid. A student prepares a 0.50 M solution of acetic acid and determines that at equilibrium $[CH_3COO^-] = 3.0 \times 10^{-3}$ M. Use the approximation suggested in Model 2 to complete the table below and then determine the value of K_a for acetic acid.

Balanced equation: $H_2O + CH_3COOH$ (aq) $\rightleftharpoons H_3O^+$(aq) $+ CH_3COO^-$ (aq)

	CH_3COOH	H_3O^+	CH_3COO^-
initial concentration (moles/L)	0.50		
change in concentration (moles/L)			
equilibrium concentration (moles/L)			3.0×10^{-3}

Model 3: A Weak Base Increases the Hydroxide Concentration of a Solution, but the Amount of Reaction Is Small.

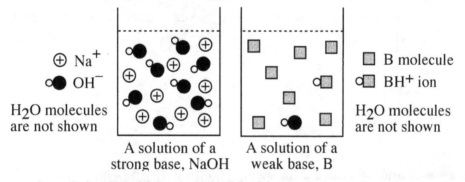

$\oplus$ Na^+
$\circ\!\bullet$ OH^-
H_2O molecules are not shown

A solution of a strong base, NaOH

A solution of a weak base, B

$\blacksquare$ B molecule
$\circ\!\blacksquare$ BH^+ ion
H_2O molecules are not shown

When a base B is placed in water, hydroxide ions are produced according to the reaction

$$B(aq) + H_2O(\ell) \rightleftharpoons BH^+(aq) + OH^-(aq) \qquad (1)$$

The equilibrium constant, K_c, for this type of reaction is:

$$K_c = \frac{[BH^+]\,[OH^-]}{[B]\,[H_2O]}$$

As with acids, the concentration of the water is incorporated into the value of K_c and the equilibrium expression is given a special name and symbol—the base-dissociation constant, K_b.

$$K_c \times [H_3O^+] = K_b = \frac{[BH^+]\,[OH^-]}{[B]}$$

Table 3. **Characteristics of solutions of various amounts of the base pyridine, C_5H_5N, dissolved in water to make 1.00 L of solution at 25 °C.**

Moles of C_5H_5N added	$[H_3O^+]$ (M)	$[OH^-]$ (M)
0.00	1.0×10^{-7}	1.0×10^{-7}
0.30	4.4×10^{-10}	2.3×10^{-5}
0.75	2.8×10^{-10}	3.6×10^{-5}
1.00	2.4×10^{-10}	4.1×10^{-5}

Critical Thinking Questions

Answer CTQs 14 – 24 as a team.

14. What species acts as an acid in the forward process in reaction 1?

15. For a base, why is $[BH^+] = [OH^-]$?

16. Analogous to weak acids, the values of K_b for weak bases are very small. Use this fact to explain why for a weak acid, we can generally use the approximation that $[B] = (B)_0$.

17. Complete and balance the following equation for the weak base pyridine:

$$C_5H_5N(aq) + H_2O(\ell) \rightleftharpoons$$

Write the equilibrium expression for the K_b of C_5H_5N.

18. Complete the following table assuming that 0.30 moles of C_5H_5N are added to sufficient water to make 1.0 L of solution at 25 °C:

    Balanced equation:

	C_5H_5N	OH^-	$C_5H_5NH^+$
initial concentration (moles/liter)	0.30	0	0
change in concentration (moles/liter)	$-x$		
equilibrium concentration (moles/liter)			

19. a) What does the x in the table represent?

    b) Why is it appropriate to analyze this reaction in terms of concentrations rather than moles?

20. The K_b of C_5H_5N, at 25 °C, is 1.7×10^{-9}.

    a) Use the approximation described in Model 2 to determine the equilibrium concentrations of C_5H_5N, $C_5H_5NH^+$, and OH^-.
    (Hint: Look at CTQ 7 if you need some guidance.)

    b) Verify that your equilibrium concentrations are correct by substituting them back into the K_b expression.

    c) Calculate the $[H_3O^+]$ in a 0.30 M pyridine solution.

21. Add the missing values to Table 4 on the next page.

Table 4.   Characteristics of solutions of various amounts of pyridine, C_5H_5N, dissolved in water to make 1.00 L of solution at 25 °C.

Moles of C_5H_5N added	$[H_3O^+]$ (M)	$[OH^-]$ (M)	$[C_5H_5N]$ (M)	$[C_5H_5NH^+]$ (M)
0.00	1.0×10^{-7}	1.0×10^{-7}	0	0
0.30				
0.75	2.8×10^{-10}	3.6×10^{-5}	0.75	3.6×10^{-5}
1.00	2.4×10^{-10}	4.1×10^{-5}	1.00	4.1×10^{-5}

22.   a)   Based on information in Table 4, calculate the number of moles of C_5H_5N present at equilibrium for each of the three basic solutions in Table 4.

        b)   Explain why the moles of C_5H_5N added are equal to the moles of C_5H_5N at equilibrium in spite of the fact that some of the C_5H_5N reacts!

23.   Explain why the equilibrium concentration of OH^- is equal to the equilibrium concentration of $C_5H_5NH^+$.

24.   A 0.50 M solution of a base B contains 3.1×10^{-3} M OH^-. Determine the value of K_b for this base B. (Hint: compare to CTQ 13.)

Exercises

1.   In a 0.30 M solution of a weak acid, $[H_3O^+] = 5.7 \times 10^{-4}$ M. What is the value of K_a for this acid?

2. In a 0.200 M solution of a weak acid, $[OH^-] = 7.0 \times 10^{-10}$ M. What is the value of K_a for this acid?

3. a) HONO is a weak acid. What is the equilibrium concentration of HONO in a 0.80 M solution of HONO?

   b) Write the chemical reaction of HONO with water.

   c) Write the expression for K_a.

   d) What is the numerical value of the hydronium ion concentration in a 0.80 M solution of HONO, given that K_a for HONO is 5.1×10^{-4}?

4. a) What is the equilibrium concentration of the weak base CH_3NH_2 in a 1.5 M solution of CH_3NH_2?

   b) Write the chemical reaction of CH_3NH_2 with water.

   c) Write the expression for K_b.

   d) What is the numerical value of $[OH^-]$?

5. When a weak acid or weak base reacts with pure water, why is it often reasonable to assume that the amount of the acid or base reacting does not change the equilibrium concentration of the weak acid or weak base? Explain

Problem

1. The sting from some ant bites is due to formic acid, HCOOH. When 0.10 moles of formic acid are dissolved in enough water to make 1.00 liter of solution, the resulting $[H_3O^+] = 0.0042$ M. The reaction that occurs is

$$HCOOH(aq) + H_2O(\ell) \rightleftharpoons HCOO^-(aq) + H_3O^+(aq)$$

   a) What is $[OH^-]$ in this solution?

   b) Draw the Lewis structure of formic acid.

   c) Draw the Lewis structure of the conjugate base of formic acid.

   d) What is the value for K_a for formic acid? Show all of your work.

2. Typically,[1] for a weak acid HA:

$$[H_3O^+] \approx [A^-] \quad \text{and} \quad [HA] = (HA)_o - [A^-] \approx [HA]_o$$

   Substitute these relationships into the K_a expression for HA to show that when these approximations are valid, $K_a \approx \dfrac{[H_3O^+]^2}{(HA)_o}$.

---

[1]These relationships will not be true for a solution of an extremely dilute acid. This situation will rarely be encountered in this course.

What is pH?

WARM-UP

Information: Logarithms and Exponents.

$$\log 10^x = x \tag{1}$$

$$\log(A \times B) = \log A + \log B \tag{2}$$

$$10^a \times 10^b = 10^{a+b} \tag{3}$$

$$\log A/B = \log A - \log B \tag{4}$$

Critical Thinking Questions

1. What is the value of each of the following expressions?

    a) $\log (2.5 \times 10^{-5})$

    b) $\log (2.5 \times 10^{5})$

    c) $\log (5.0 \times 10^{-4})$

2. a) Show that $\log (10^5 \times 10^{-5}) = 0$ without actually calculating a value for $10^5 \times 10^{-5}$.

    b) Identify which relationship you used from the Information to perform part a.

Information

The water-dissociation equilibrium constant, K_w, is (at 25 °C)

$$K_w = [H_3O^+][OH^-] = 1.0 \times 10^{-14}$$

Several definitions have been found to be useful:

$$pH \equiv -\log [H_3O^+]$$

$$pOH \equiv -\log [OH^-]$$

$$pK_w \equiv -\log K_w$$

In general, $pX \equiv -\log X$

For pX expressions involving concentrations, the concentration units are always mole/liter, but they are omitted in the calculation. Thus, for example, values for pH are unitless.

Note on significant figures. **For logarithms, the number of significant figures is determined by the number of digits to the right of the decimal point.** The value to the left of the decimal point indicates only the power of ten by which the number is to be multiplied. For example, if pH = 2.15, then the corresponding value for [H_3O^+] has only 2 significant figures (7.1×10^{-3}). The "2" in the value "2.15" is not considered a significant figure in the conversion to concentration.

Critical Thinking Question

3. Which of the following is the correct value for the answer to CTQ 1c?

  i)   –3.3

  ii) –3.30

  iii) –3.301

END OF WARM-UP

Model 1: pH of a Solution.

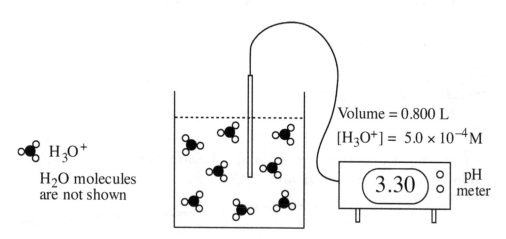

Volume = 0.800 L

[H_3O^+] = 5.0×10^{-4} M

H$_3$O$^+$

H$_2$O molecules are not shown

3.30   pH meter

Critical Thinking Questions

4. a) Show that the pH reading in the model is correct – given that the hydronium ion concentration is 5.0×10^{-4} M.

  b) As a team, construct an explanation about why the value is *not* 3.3. Write your team's explanation in a way that another person or team in class can clearly understand your reasoning.

5. a) Assume that the acid in Model 1 is HCl, c⊘. Add the appropriate number of Cl⁻, ⊘, to the model.

    b) Assuming that each symbol, ⊘ or 🔴 represents the same number of particles, how many particles does each symbol represent?

    c) Given your answer to 5b, explain why it is reasonable that the hydroxide ions are not represented in the model.

Answer CTQs 6 – 8 as a team.

6. Consider a neutral aqueous solution.

    a) What is $[H_3O^+]$ in a neutral aqueous solution?

    b) What is the pH of a neutral aqueous solution?

    c) What is the pOH of a neutral aqueous solution?

7. What is the numerical value of pK_w?

8. Based on the relationships given in the Information sections, what is the relationship between pH, pOH, and pK_w?

9. Individually, calculate the pH of each these solutions:

    a) 2.0 M HCl (recall that HCl is a strong acid)

    b) 5.0 M NaOH (recall that Na^+ salts are very soluble in water)

Once all team members are done with CTQ 9, compare answers and reach consensus before continuing to the next question.

10. A student is asked to describe the values of pH that characterize an acidic solution and a basic solution. The student says:

> "An acidic solution has a pH above 0 and less than 7 and a basic solution has a pH above 7 and less than 14. A solution with a pH of exactly 7 is actually neither acidic nor basic – it is neutral."

As a team, discuss these two sentences and then write a consensus statement in one or two sentences that explains why one of them is incorrect. Then provide a correct replacement statement for the incorrect one.

Exercises

1. Determine the pH and pOH of each of the following solutions, and indicate whether each is acidic, basic, or neutral:

    a)   Milk, $[H_3O^+] = 3.2 \times 10^{-7}$ M

    b)   Pickle juice, $[H_3O^+] = 2.0 \times 10^{-4}$ M

    c)   Beer, $[H_3O^+] = 3.2 \times 10^{-5}$ M

    d)   Blood, $[H_3O^+] = 4.0 \times 10^{-8}$ M

2. Determine the $[H_3O^+]$ and $[OH^-]$ of each of the following solutions, and indicate whether each is acidic, basic, or neutral:

    a)   Lime juice, pH = 1.9   b)   Tomato juice, pH = 4.2
    c)   Saliva, pH = 7.0   d)   Kitchen cleanser, pH = 9.3

3. Rank the following aqueous solutions in order of increasing pH without referring to a table of acid/base constants. Explain your reasoning.

    a)   pure H_2O b) x molar NaOH

    c) x molar HCl   d) x molar acetic acid

4. Rank the following aqueous solutions in order of increasing pH (you will need to refer to a table of acid/base constants). Explain your reasoning.

    i)   pure H_2O ii) x molar NaOH
    iii) x molar C_5H_5N iv) x molar NH_3

5. What is pH? Describe how it is related to $[H_3O^+]$ and how its value is related to the acidic or basic nature of an aqueous solution.

6. The pH of a 0.040 M solution of HOBr is 5.01. Determine K_a for the weak acid HOBr.

7. The pH of 0.300 M formic acid is 2.13. What is the K_a of formic acid?

8. The pH of a 0.15 M hydrazine (H_2NNH_2; a weak base) is 10.68. What is the K_b of hydrazine ?

For the following problems, you will need to refer to a table of acid/base constants.

9. How many moles of NH_3 must be dissolved in 1.00 liters of aqueous solution to produce a solution with a pH of 11.47?

10. What are the pH and the pOH of 0.125 M $HClO_4$?

11. What are the pH and the pOH of 0.125 M HCl?

12. What are the H_3O^+ and OH^- concentrations in a 125 mL solution prepared with 0.100 mol of HI and water?

13. What are the H_3O^+ and OH^- concentrations in a 125 mL solution prepared with 0.100 mol of NaOH and water?

14. What is the pH of a solution prepared from 6.50 g of benzoic acid (a weak acid), C_6H_5COOH, and 500 mL of water?

15. What is the pH of a solution prepared from 3.52 g of aniline (a weak base), $C_6H_5NH_2$, and 200 mL of water?

16. Calculate the pH for each of the following solutions:

    a)   0.45 M NaOH   b)   0.45 M HCl
    c)   0.45 M CH_3COOH d)   0.45 M CH_3NH_2

Problem

1. When 500.0 mL of 0.10 M NaOH solution (containing Na^+ and OH^- ions) is mixed with 500.0 mL of 0.10 M $Mg(NO_3)_2$ solution (containing Mg^{2+} and NO_3^- ions) a precipitate of solid $Mg(OH)_2$ forms, and the resulting aqueous solution has pH = 9.43. n0Based on this information, determine the value of K_{sp} for $Mg(OH)_2$. Show your reasoning clearly.

2. For a weak acid, HA: $HA(aq) + H_2O(\ell) \rightleftharpoons H_3O^+(aq) + A^-(aq)$

    a)   Write the equilibrium expression for K_a.

    b)   Show that: $pH = pK_a + \log([A^-]/[HA])$

         Note: The relationship in part b is known as the Henderson-Hasselbalch equation.

What Makes an Acid Strong?

WARM-UP

Model 1: Bond Strengths of Two Acids with Related Structure.

$$H—\overset{..}{\underset{..}{O}}—H \qquad\qquad H—\overset{..}{\underset{..}{S}}—H$$

O–H bond enthalpy = 463 kJ/mol   S–H bond enthalpy = 367 kJ/mol

Critical Thinking Questions

1. The H–X bond strength decreases in the series HF, HCl, HBr, HI. Explain this trend in terms of the bond types and lengths in the molecules.

2. Based on the data in Model 1, which bond is easier to break: O–H or S–H? Explain how you can reach this conclusion using information from Model 1.

3. Explain the relative bond strengths from CTQ 2 in terms of the bond types and lengths of the two molecules in Model 1.

4. Recall that acid strength increases in the series HF, HCl, HBr, HI. Based on this trend and your answers to CTQ 1- 3, predict which is most likely to be the stronger acid: H_2O or H_2S. Explain your reasoning by referring to the information in Model 1 and the trends observed in the H-X acids.

5. Based on your analysis above, which do you expect to be the stronger acid, NH_4^+ or PH_4^+? Explain your reasoning.

END OF WARM-UP

Model 2: Relative Acid Strength for Molecules with Similar Structures but Very Different H-Q Bond Strengths.

Table 1.   Characteristics of some acids. Acids within each group have similar structures.

Similar Structures	Acid	Bond	Bond Enthalpy (kJ/mole)	K_a
A	H_2O	H–O	463	1.8×10^{-16}
A	H_2S	H–S	367	1.0×10^{-7}
B	NH_4^+	H–N	390	5.6×10^{-10}
B	PH_4^+	H–P	325	$\approx 10^{14}$
C	HF	H–F	568	7.2×10^{-4}
C	HCl	H–Cl	432	1×10^6
C	HBr	H–Br	366	1×10^9
C	HI	H–I	298	3×10^9

Critical Thinking Questions

Answer CTQs 6 and 7 as a team.

6. a)   Select one acid from each group in Table 1 (A, B, C), write the reaction of that acid with H_2O, and identify the conjugate base.

    b)   Decide which acid in Table 1 is the strongest acid. Explain how your team was able to identify it.

7. Based on the data in in Table 1, discuss the following statements and decide which one best describes relative acid strength. Explain your team's reasoning.

    •   When the bond strengths between the acidic hydrogen and the atom to which it is attached are *not* comparable, the acid strength increases as the bond strength increases.

    •   When the bond strengths between the acidic hydrogen and the atom to which it is attached are *not* comparable, the acid strength decreases as the bond strength increases.

Model 3: Acidity of Molecules with More Than One Hydrogen Atom.

For molecules with more than one hydrogen atom, the hydrogen atom with the largest partial positive charge tends to be the acidic hydrogen.

Figure 1.   Partial charges on the atoms in acetic acid and trichloroacetic acid.

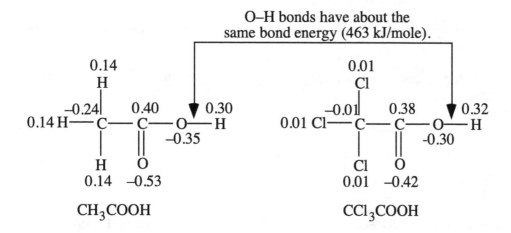

Critical Thinking Questions

8.   a)   Individually, circle the most acidic hydrogen in CH_3COOH in Figure 1.

    b)   Individually, circle the most acidic hydrogen in CCl_3COOH in Figure 1.

    c)   When all team members have completed parts a and b, compare answers and then develop (and write) a team explanation for your consensus answers.

9.   As a team, use information from Figure 1 to predict which is more likely to be the stronger acid: CH_3COOH or CCl_3COOH. Explain your team's reasoning.

Model 4: The Acidity of Molecules that Contain O-H Bonds.

> For molecules that contain one or more oxygen atoms, the most acidic hydrogen atom is one that is bonded to an oxygen atom.

Critical Thinking Questions

Answer CTQs 10 – 12 as a team.

10.   Which hydrogen atom is the most acidic hydrogen atom in HCOOH?

11.   Which hydrogen atom is the most acidic hydrogen atom in CH_3CH_2OH?

12.   Develop a consensus explanation describing why Model 4 is consistent with Model 3.

Model 5: Relative Acid Strength for Molecules with Similar Structures, X–Q–H, and the Q Atom is Held Constant.

Table 2.   Characteristics of some acids. Acids within each group have similar structures.

Similar Structures	Q atom	Acid	Partial Charge on Acidic Hydrogen (MOPAC; Water Solvent)	K_a
A	O	CH_3COOH	0.298	1.8×10^{-5}
A	O	$CH_2ClCOOH$	0.308	1.4×10^{-3}
A	O	$CHCl_2COOH$	0.317	5.1×10^{-2}
A	O	CCl_3COOH	0.325	0.22
B	O	HOCl	0.280	2.9×10^{-8}
B	O	HOBr	0.275	2.4×10^{-9}
B	O	HOI	0.270	2.3×10^{-11}

Critical Thinking Questions

13.   Provide a team consensus explanation for the increase in partial charge on the acidic hydrogen in this series:

   CH_3COOH, $CH_2ClCOOH$, $CHCl_2COOH$, CCl_3COOH

14. Provide a team consensus explanation for the decrease in the partial charge on the acidic hydrogen in the series: HOCl, HOBr, HOI .

15. a) Individually decide if the data in Table 2 are consistent with one or both of the following statements. Circle the consistent statement(s).

   • When the bond strengths between the acidic hydrogen and the atom to which it is attached are roughly comparable, the acid strength increases as the partial positive charge on the acidic hydrogen increases.

   • When the bond strengths between the acidic hydrogen and the atom to which it is attached are roughly comparable, the acid strength increases as the partial positive charge on the acidic hydrogen decreases.

   b) When all team members have completed part a, discuss your choices and come to consensus. Then write a team explanation for your answer.

16. As a team, predict the value of K_a for CF_3COOH. Explain the reasoning behind your team's prediction.

17. As a team:

   a) List the way (or ways) the acids in Table 1 are all structurally similar.

   b) List the way (or ways) the acids in Table 2 are all structurally similar.

   c) Provide a description for how the acids in Table 1 are structurally different than those in Table 2.

Model 6: Analyzing the Acids in Table 1.

Table 3.   Characteristics of the groups of acids from Table 1.

Structural Group	Non-H atoms present	Atom with highest EN	Species with H with highest partial charge	Strongest Acid
A	O, S	O or S	H_2O or H_2S	H_2S
B	N, P	N or P	NH_4^+ or PH_4^+	PH_4^+
C	F, Cl, Br, I	F or Cl or Br or I	HF or HCl or HBr or HI	HI

Critical Thinking Questions

Answer CTQs 18 and 19 as a team.

18.   For each Structural Group (A, B, C) in Table 3:

   a)   List the acids from Table 1 in that group.

      A:

      B:

      C:

   b)   Circle the atom with the highest electronegativity in the appropriate column in Table 3.

   c)   Circle the species that is expected to have the H atom with the highest partial positive charge in the appropriate column in Table 3.

19.   After their team completes CTQ 18, two students examine the information in Table 3 and comment on the results.

Student A says: "For a given structural type of acid where the acidic H is bonded to *different atoms*, the strongest acid is always the one that has the H atom with the highest partial positive charge."

Student B says: "For a given structural type of acid where the acidic H is bonded to *different atoms*, the strongest acid is always the one that has the weakest bond to the acidic H atom."

As a team, discuss these two comments and decide which (if either) of these two students is correct. Circle the correct statement(s) and then describe your team's reasoning for why each statement is either correct or incorrect using examples from the acids in Tables 1 and 3.

Exercises

1. For each of the following pairs of acids, predict which will have the larger value
    of K_a, and explain your reasoning.

    a) H_2S and H_2Se
    b)   HONO   and   HOPO
    c) NH_4^+ and Cl_3NH^+
    d) $(HO)_2SeO_2$ and $(HO)_2SO_2$
    e) H_2S and H_2Te
    f) $HONO_2$ and   HONO

2. Rank the following solutions in order of increasing pH *without referring to tables*
    of K_a or K_b values.. Explain your reasoning.

    x M HBr
    x M CH_3COOH
    x M CF_3COOH
    x M KBr
    x M NH_3

3. Consider the relative acid strengths of H_2O and HF. Which of the two factors
    dominates the determination of relative acidity for these acids? Why is this the
    case?

4. Indicate whether this statement is true or false and explain your reasoning

    CH_3COOH is expected to have a smaller value of K_a than CF_3COOH.

Problems

1. Salicylic acid (shown below) is a weak acid with $K_a = 3.0 \times 10^{-4}$.

    a)   Complete the following reaction of salicylic acid with water.

    b)   Calculate the pH of 50 mL of 0.15 M salicylic acid.

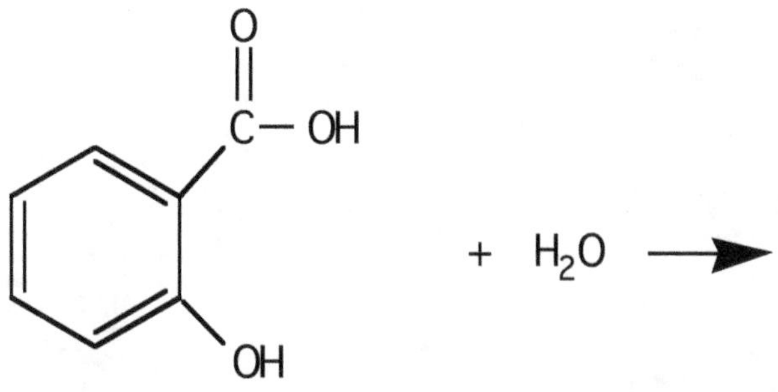

    $+ \ H_2O \longrightarrow$

2. Predict which will have the larger value for K_a and provide a clear explanation:
    $HOIO_3$ or $HSIO_3$.

ChemActivity 45

How Are K_a and K_b Related?

Model 1: The Mathematical Relationship between K_a and K_b of a Conjugate Pair.

Acid	K_a	Conjugate Base	K_b	$K_a \times K_b$
HF hydrofluoric acid	$\dfrac{[H_3O^+][F^-]}{[HF]}$	F^- fluoride ion	$\dfrac{[OH^-][HF]}{[F^-]}$	
HONO nitrous acid				
		NH_3 ammonia		

Critical Thinking Questions

1. Fill in the missing entries in Model 1.

2. For each acid and each conjugate base in Model 1, write the balanced chemical equation that has the K_a or K_b as its equilibrium constant. The conjugate base F^- is worked as an example. Including the example, there should be a total of *six* chemical equations and *six* corresponding K expressions.

$$F^-(aq) + H_2O(\ell) \rightleftharpoons HF(aq) + OH^-(aq) \qquad K_b = \frac{[OH^-][HF]}{[F^-]}$$

END OF WARM-UP

3. As a team, describe the common features of:

    a) all K_a expressions

    b) all K_b expressions

    c) all $K_a \times K_b$ products

4. Provide an expression relating K_w to K_a and K_b of a conjugate acid-base pair.

5. Show the mathematical relationship that allows you to determine the value of K_b for a base—given the value of K_a for its conjugate acid.

6. Consider two acids, HA and HX, with HA being a stronger acid than HX.

    Individually, answer parts a and b:

    a) Which acid has a larger value of K_a?

    b) Which conjugate base, A^- or X^-, has a larger value of K_b?

    Once all team members have completed a and b, compare answers and then answer part c as a team.

    c) Provide a qualitative description of the relationship between the relative strength of an acid and the relative strength of its conjugate base.

d)   Assume that K_a of HA is 1.0×10^{-5} and K_a of HX is 3.5×10^{-7}. Individually, calculate the K_b for A^- and for X^-. Once all team members are done, as a team confirm that your answers to parts b and c are correct.

Model 2: Ions are Potential Acids or Bases.

Statement A: All anions are *potential* bases:

$$Cl^-(aq) + H_2O(\ell) \rightleftharpoons HCl(aq) + OH^-(aq)$$

$$NO_2^-(aq) + H_2O(\ell) \rightleftharpoons HNO_2(aq) + OH^-(aq)$$

Statement B: All cations are *potential* acids:

$$NH_4^+(aq) + H_2O(\ell) \rightleftharpoons NH_3(aq) + H_3O^+(aq)$$

$$C_5H_5NH^+(aq) + H_2O(\ell) \rightleftharpoons C_5H_5N(aq) + H_3O^+(aq)$$

Statement C: Any molecule or ion that contains H is a *potential* acid.

Reminder: It is possible for a given chemical species to be a *potential* acid *and* a *potential* base.

Critical Thinking Questions

7.   As a team, discuss and decide which of the following are potential acids, potential bases, or both (potential acid and potential base). In addition, indicate which statement(s) above (A, B, C) supports your answer.

a) Al^{3+}

b) $CH_3NH_3^+$

c) HPO_4^{2-}

d) F^-

e) NH_4^+

f) H_2O

Model 3: Some Potential Acids and Some Potential Bases Are So Weak That They Do *Not* Alter the pH of the Solution.

- Any acid with a K_a less than 10^{-15} can be treated as if $K_a = 0$ (in water).
- Any acid with a K_b less than 10^{-15} can be treated as if $K_b = 0$ (in water).
- The cations of all alkali metals and alkaline earth metals act as neither acids nor bases in water.

Table 1.   The values of K_b for conjugate bases of some strong acids.

Acid	K_a	Conjugate Base	K_b
HBr	1×10^9		
HCl	1×10^6		
HNO_3	28		

Critical Thinking Questions

Answer CTQs 8 – 11 as a team.

8. Fill in the missing entries in Table 1.

9. The nitrate ion is the conjugate base of nitric acid, HNO_3. Explain why NO_3^- does not produce a basic solution when dissolved in water.

10. HNO_3 is considered to be the *weakest* of the strong acids. Explain why the conjugate bases of *all* strong acids do not produce basic solutions when dissolved in water.

11. To 2 significant figures, predict the pH of a 1.00 molar solution of NaBr. Explain your reasoning carefully.

Model 4: Three Solutions of Ionic Compounds.

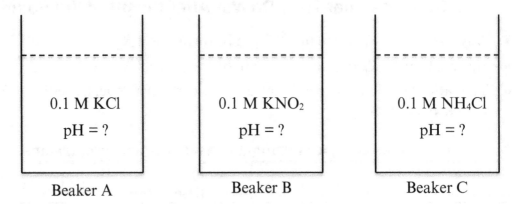

| Beaker A | Beaker B | Beaker C |

0.1 M KCl
pH = ?

0.1 M KNO₂
pH = ?

0.1 M NH₄Cl
pH = ?

Critical Thinking Questions

12. For each of the beakers in Model 4, individually identify the two ions that will be produced in solution when the ionic compound dissociates. Check your answers with your teammates when everyone on your team is finished.

   a)   Beaker A: _____   _____

   b)   Beaker B: _____   _____

   c)   Beaker C: _____   _____

13. A student measures the pH of the three solutions and gets these three values: 5.1, 7.0, 8.2 .

   Without performing any calculations, discuss as a team which beaker corresponds to each pH. After reaching consensus, explain your team's reasoning clearly by describing the effect on the pH of **each ion** in the solution.

14. The K_b for NH_3 is 1.8×10^{-5}. Use this information to verify that you have assigned the correct pH to Beaker C by performing the appropriate calculation.

Exercises

1. Give the conjugate base and the K_b of the conjugate base for each of the acids in the table below:

Acid	K_a	Base	K_b
CH_3COOH	1.8×10^{-5}		
H_2CO_3	4.5×10^{-7}		
H_2S	1.0×10^{-7}		
HNO_2	5.1×10^{-4}		
NH_4^+	5.6×10^{-10}		

2. Give the conjugate acid and the K_a of the conjugate acid for each of the bases in the table below:

Base	K_b	Acid	K_a
NH_3	1.8×10^{-5}		
CH_3COO^-	5.6×10^{-10}		
$C_6H_5NH_2$	4.0×10^{-10}		
NO_2^-	2.0×10^{-11}		
H_2NNH_2	1.2×10^{-6}		

3. Given that K_a for HCN is 6.2×10^{-10}, calculate the pH of a 0.15 M KCN solution.

4. For each of the following, indicate whether the resulting solution would be acidic, basic, or neutral, if 1.0 mole of each were dissolved in 1.0 liter of water.

    a) NaCl　　　　b)　KCl　　　　c)　KNO_3

    d) $NaCH_3CO_2$ (sodium acetate)　　　e)　NH_4Cl

    f) NH_4NO_3　　g)　$NaNO_2$　　h)　$CaCl_2$

    i) KCN　　　　j)　KF　　　　k)　NaBr

5. Consider the two acids, HBr and HOBr.

    a) Which acid has the larger K_a? Explain.

    b) Which conjugate base has the larger K_b? Explain.

    c) If you have 0.50 M solutions of each acid, which will have the higher pH? Explain.

6. Describe how the K_a and K_b for a conjugate acid-base pair are related.

7. For each of the following species, indicate whether the resulting solution would be acidic, basic, or neutral, if 1.0 mole of each were dissolved in 1.0 liter of water. Also provide the predominant acid-base reaction that would occur, and evaluate the equilibrium constant for that process. NaF is worked out as an example:

i)   NaF is an ionic compound. Na^+ and F^- ions exist in solution.

ii) Na^+ acts neither as an acid nor a base; it has no effect on the pH of the solution.

iii) The F^- ion is a weak base (the conjugate base of a weak acid). The solution will be basic.

iv)   The predominant reaction will be:

$$F^-(aq) + H_2O \rightleftharpoons HF(aq) + OH^-(aq) .$$

This is the chemical reaction that makes the solution basic.

v)   The equilibrium constant is $K_b = \dfrac{K_w}{K_a} = \dfrac{1.0 \times 10^{-14}}{1.0 \times 10^{-4}} = 1.4 \times 10^{-11}$

Recall that the strong acids are: HCl; HBr; HI; $HClO_4$; H_2SO_4; HNO_3

a) NH_4NO_3

b) CsI

c) CH_3COONa

d) $KClO_4$

e)   magnesium acetate

8. Determine the pH of each of the 1.0 M solutions in Exercise 4.

Problem

1. One mole of $CH_3CH_2NH_3{}^+Cl^-$ is added to one liter of water.

   a)   Will the solution be acidic, basic, or neutral? Explain briefly.

   b)   Provide the chemical reaction that occurs to justify your answer in part a. That is, give the chemical reaction that causes the solution to be acidic or basic or neutral in accordance with your answer to part a.

What is a Redox Reaction?

WARM-UP

Model 1: The Chemical Reaction of Zn(s) and Cu^{2+}(aq).

A student places a bar of zinc metal into a clear, dark blue solution of 1.0 M $Cu(NO_3)_2$ nitrate. After a while, the student observes that the blue solution has faded to a very light blue and that there is a solid deposit built up on the Zn bar that is a different color than the Zn itself. When the bar is examined, the new metal is determined to be solid copper, and the total mass of solid has decreased! When the faded solution is analyzed, Zn^{2+} ions are found along with the original Cu^{2+} in solution.

If the student repeats the experiment but waits long enough for equilibrium to be reached, the solution becomes completely colorless because essentially all of the copper ions are plated out as solid copper (assuming that Cu^{2+} is the limiting reagent). The reaction can be thought of as transferring electrons from one species to another according to the following chemical equation:

$$Zn(s) + Cu^{2+}(aq) \rightleftharpoons Zn^{2+}(aq) + Cu(s) \tag{1}$$

Critical Thinking Questions

1. Identify the reactant in equation 1 that:

   a) loses electrons.

   b) gains electrons.

2. How many electrons are transferred when:

   a) one Zn atom reacts with one Cu^{2+} ion?

   b) one mole of Zn reacts with one mole of Cu^{2+}?

3. Explain how one can conclude that, at equilibrium, $[Cu^{2+}]$ is essentially 0 M and $[Cu^{2+}]$ is essentially 1.0 M based on information given in Model 1.

END OF WARM-UP

Answer CTQ 4 as a team.

4. a)   Write the equilibrium constant expression, K, for reaction 1.

    b)   Indicate which of the following best describes K for this reaction:
          $K \ll 1$, $K < 1$, $K = 1$, $K > 1$, $K \gg 1$. Explain your reasoning.

Information

Reactions that involve the transfer of electrons between chemical species are known as **oxidation-reduction**, or **redox**, reactions. Equation 1 is an example of a redox reaction.

In redox reactions, the species that loses electrons is **oxidized**. This species is often referred to as the **reducing agent**. The species that gains electrons is **reduced**. This species is often referred to as the **oxidizing agent**.

Critical Thinking Questions

5. As a team, look at equation 1 and decide:
    a)   which species is oxidized?
    b)   which species is reduced ?
    c)   which species is the oxidizing agent?
    d)   which species is the reducing agent?

Model 2: Results of Placing Metal Bars in Solutions at 298 K.

Metal Bar	Ion Solution (1.0 M)	Concentration of Metal Ions at Equilibrium (M)		K
Zn	Cu^{2+}	$[Cu^{2+}] \approx 0$	$[Zn^{2+}] \approx 1.0$	
Zn	K^+	$[K^+] \approx 1.0$	$[Zn^{2+}] \approx 0$	
Co	Ni^{2+}	$[Ni^{2+}] \approx 0.1$	$[Co^{2+}] \approx 0.9$	
Co	Cu^{2+}	$[Cu^{2+}] \approx 0$	$[Co^{2+}] \approx 1.0$	
Co	Cr^{3+}	$[Cr^{3+}] \approx 1.0$	$[Co^{2+}] \approx 0$	

The results were obtained with metal bars large enough so that the limiting reagent in any redox reaction with the solution was the ion in solution.

Critical Thinking Questions

6. For each of the five experiments described in Model 2, write the balanced equation (no "e^-" appears in the balanced equation) for the redox reaction that *could* occur between the metal bar and the ion in solution. Note that the same number of electrons must be lost and gained in the transfer process. Do this individually and then check your answers with your teammates.

7. As a team, determine which species is the oxidizing agent and which is the reducing agent for each equation in CTQ 5. Put a circle around the oxidizing agent and a square around the reducing agent.

8. a) As a team, fill in the K column in Model 2 by indicating whether K is >1, K is <1, or it is impossible to deduce from the data given.

    b) Use the data in the first two rows of Model 2, to explain why $Cu^{2+}(aq)$ is considered to be a stronger oxidizing agent than K^+. Reach consensus on an explanation within your team and then provide your team's explanation below in a sentence.

9. Individually, use the data in the last three rows of Model 2 to rank the strength as oxidizing agents of the metal ions Ni^{2+}, Cu^{2+}, and Cr^{3+}. Then, reach consensus as a team.

10. As a team, rank the metal ions Ni^{2+}, Cu^{2+}, Cr^{3+}, and K^+ in terms of their strength as oxidizing agents – if this is possible. If this is not possible, rank as many as you can and propose an experiment (or series of experiments) that would enable you to complete the rankings.

Exercises

1. All of these reactions have $K > 1$. For each reaction, identify: the substance that is oxidized, the substance that is reduced, the oxidizing agent, the reducing agent, and the number of moles of electrons transferred when one mole of reaction takes place.

    a) $Br_2(aq) + Hg(s) \rightleftharpoons 2\,Br^-(aq) + Hg^{2+}(aq)$

    b) $2\,Co^{3+}(aq) + 2\,Br^-(aq) \rightleftharpoons Br_2(aq) + 2\,Co^{2+}(aq)$

    c) $Cl_2(aq) + 2\,Br^-(aq) \rightleftharpoons 2\,Cl^-(aq) + Br_2(aq)$

    d) $2\,H^+(aq) + Zn(s) \rightleftharpoons H_2(aq) + Zn^{2+}(aq)$

    e) $S_2O_8^{2-}(aq) + Zn(s) \rightleftharpoons Zn^{2+}(aq) + 2\,SO_4^{2-}(aq)$

    f) $Au^{3+}(aq) + Fe(s) \rightleftharpoons Au(s) + Fe^{3+}(aq)$

2. Indicate whether the following statement is true or false and explain your reasoning.

    > Based on the data in Model 2, $Cu^{2+}(aq)$ is a stronger oxidizing agent than $Cr^{3+}(aq)$.

3. What is a redox reaction?

Problem

1. Describe an experiment that would allow you to determine the relative strengths of zinc and nickel metals as reducing agents. Provide enough detail so that another student in your class could understand what to do, and also indicate what the observed results of the experiment would be. Make sure that you also indicate which of the two metals *is* the stronger reducing agent.

ChemActivity 47

What Are Oxidation Numbers?

WARM-UP

Model 1: Oxidation Numbers

Oxidation numbers are an accounting system that chemists use to keep track of electrons in chemical equations. **The main use of oxidation numbers is to identify the oxidized and reduced species in oxidation-reduction (redox) reactions.**

Figure 1.   Substances with oxidation numbers assigned to each atom.

$$\overset{+1\ +7\ -2}{HClO_4} \qquad \overset{0}{O_2} \qquad \overset{-4\ +1}{CH_4}$$

Note that equivalent atoms within a molecule are all assigned the same oxidation number. Thus, in CH_4 each H atom has an oxidation number of +1 even though there is only one "+1" above the H symbol in the molecule.

Critical Thinking Questions

1.   Where are the oxidation numbers located?

2.   Which of the following statements is correct? Provide evidence to support your answer.

   i)   Each molecule has an oxidation number.

   ii)   Each atom in a molecule has an oxidation number.

3.   Draw the Lewis structure for CH_4 and circle any atoms that have an oxidation number of +1.

END OF WARM-UP

Model 2: Redox Reactions and Oxidation Numbers.

$$5\,Cr^{3+}(aq) + 3\,MnO_4^-(aq) + 8\,H_2O \rightleftharpoons 5\,CrO_4^{2-}(aq) + 3\,Mn^{2+}(aq) + 16\,H^+(aq) \quad (1)$$

$$2\,CuI(s) \rightleftharpoons Cu(s) + Cu^{2+}(aq) + 2\,I^-(aq) \quad (2)$$

In these two redox reactions it is not obvious which species is being oxidized and which species is being reduced. Assigning oxidation numbers makes this determination very straightforward. In a redox reaction, the species that is oxidized undergoes an increase in oxidation number, and the species that is reduced undergoes a decrease in oxidation number. Several rules for assigning oxidation numbers are given below.

Read each of the rules and then answer the CTQs that follow each one.

Rule 1:   The oxidation number is zero for any atomic or elemental substance, regardless of the subscript.

$$\begin{array}{ccccc} 0 & 0 & 0 & 0 & 0 \\ H_2 & O_2 & O_3 & P_4 & Sn \end{array}$$

Example: H_2 O_2 O_3 P_4 Sn

Critical Thinking Questions

4. What is the oxidation number of:

   a)   P in P_4?

   b)   Cu in Cu(s)?

5. Look at redox reactions (1) and (2). Apply Rule 1 to the relevant species in both reactions and list your answers below so that they look like the Rule 1 examples shown. If the reaction does not have a substance that uses this rule, write "none".

   a)   Redox Reaction (1):

   b)   Redox Reaction (2):

Rule 2:   The oxidation number is the same as the charge on an ion if the ion consists of a single element.

$$\begin{array}{ccc} +1 & -1 & +4 \\ Na^+ & Cl^- & Sn^{4+} \end{array}$$

Example: Na^+ Cl^- Sn^{4+}

Critical Thinking Question

6. Look at redox reactions (1) and (2). Apply Rule 2 to the relevant species in both reactions and list your answers below. If the reaction does not have a substance that uses this rule, write "none".

   a)   Redox Reaction (1):

   b)   Redox Reaction (2):

Rule 3:   The oxidation number of H is +1 when the H is combined with a more electronegative element (typically a non-metal).

$$\overset{+1}{CH_4} \quad \overset{+1}{NH_3} \quad \overset{+1}{HCl}$$
Example:

Critical Thinking Question

7.   Apply Rule 3 to the relevant species in reactions (1) and (2) and list your answers below. Write "none" if the reaction has no relevant species.

   a)   Redox Reaction (1):

   b)   Redox Reaction (2):

Rule 4:   The oxidation number of H is is –1 when the H is combined with a less electronegative element (typically a metal).

$$\overset{-1}{LiH} \quad \overset{-1}{NaH} \quad \overset{-1}{CaH_2}$$
Example:

Critical Thinking Question

8.   Apply Rule 4 to the relevant species in reactions (1) and (2) and list your answers below. Write "none" if the reaction has no relevant species.

   a)   Redox Reaction (1):

   b)   Redox Reaction (2):

Rule 5:   The elements of Groups 1 and 2 form compounds in which the metal atoms have oxidation numbers +1 and +2, respectively.

$$\overset{+2}{CaCl_2} \quad \overset{+1}{LiOH} \quad \overset{+1}{Na_2S}$$
Example:

Critical Thinking Question

9.   Apply Rule 5 to the relevant species in reactions (1) and (2) and list your answers below. Write "none" if the reaction has no relevant species.

   a)   Redox Reaction (1):

   b)   Redox Reaction (2):

Rule 6:   Oxygen usually has an oxidation number of -2 when combined with other elements. Exceptions include molecules and polyatomic ions that contain an O-O single bond.

$$\overset{-1\,-1}{H\text{-}O\text{-}O\text{-}H}\ (H_2O_2) \qquad \overset{-2}{CaO}$$
Example:

Critical Thinking Question

10. Apply Rule 6 to the relevant species in reactions (1) and (2) and list your answers below. Write "none" if the reaction has no relevant species.

    a)   Redox Reaction (1):

    b)   Redox Reaction (2):

Rule 7:   F always has an oxidation number of -1 in any compound (other than F_2). All other Group 17 elements usually have an oxidation number of -1 when combined with other elements (except when as a central atom).

$$\overset{0}{F_2} \quad \overset{-1}{NaF} \quad \overset{0}{Cl_2} \quad \overset{-1}{CCl_4}$$

Example:

Critical Thinking Question

11. Apply Rule 7 to the relevant species in reactions (1) and (2) and list your answers below. Write "none" if the reaction has no relevant species.

    a)   Redox Reaction (1):

    b)   Redox Reaction (2):

Rule 8:   The sum of the oxidation numbers in a substance with no charge must be equal to zero.

Example:

$$\overset{+1 \ -2}{H_2O} \qquad \overset{+1 -1}{NaF}$$
$$2(+1) + (-2) = 0 \qquad +1 + (-1) = 0$$
$$\ \ \text{H} \qquad \text{O} \qquad\qquad \text{Na} \quad \text{F}$$

Critical Thinking Question

12. For each substance, show that the sum of the oxidation numbers equals zero:

    a)   NaCl

    b) K_2O

    c) H_2O_2

    d) CaF_2

Rule 9:   The sum of the oxidation numbers in in a polyatomic ion must be equal to the charge on the ion.

$$\overset{-2\ +1}{OH^-}$$

Example: OH^-

$$-2 + (+1) = -1$$
$$\underset{O\ \ \ H}{}$$

Information: Applying Rules 8 and 9

Rules 8 and 9, in combination with the other rules, provide a method to determine the oxidation numbers on all other substances.

Example 1:   Find the oxidation number for each element in $Na_2S_2O_4$.

$$\overset{+1}{Na}\ (\text{Rule 5}) \qquad \overset{-2}{O}\ (\text{Rule 6})$$

To find the oxidation number on S we can now use Rule 8:

$$0 = 2(+1) + 2(S) + 4(-2)$$
$$0 = -6 + 2(S)$$
$$+3 = S$$

$$\overset{+1\ +3\ -2}{Na_2S_2O_4}\ \text{ with oxidation numbers assigned}$$

Example 2:   Find the oxidation number for each element in ClO_4^-.

$$\overset{-2}{O}\ (\text{Rule 6})$$

To find the oxidation number on Cl we can now use Rule 9:

$$-1 = Cl + 4(-2)$$
$$+7 = Cl$$

$$\overset{+7\ -2}{ClO_4}\ \text{ with oxidation numbers assigned}$$

Critical Thinking Question

13.   Assign oxidation numbers to each element in each species.

   a) SO_4^{2-}

   b) Na_2CO_3

   c) $NiCl_2$

Information

Recall that in a redox reaction the electrons that are lost from one species must be gained by another species in the reaction.

- The species that is **oxidized** loses electrons and its oxidation number increases. The species that is oxidized is called the **reducing agent** because it provides the electrons for the reduction process to take place.
- The species that is **reduced** gains electrons and its oxidation number **decreases.** The species that is reduced is called the **oxidizing agent** because it accepts electrons and allows the oxidation process to take place.

Critical Thinking Questions

14. In every redox reaction, there is a species whose oxidation number increases when the reaction occurs. Is the species whose oxidation number increases:

    a)   being oxidized or reduced?

    b)   referred to as the oxidizing agent or the reducing agent?

15. Reactions 1 and 2 are rewritten below. Assign oxidation numbers to all atoms in both reactions.

$$5\,Cr^{3+}(aq) + 3\,MnO_4^-(aq) + 8\,H_2O \rightleftharpoons 5\,CrO_4^{2-}(aq) + 3\,Mn^{2+}(aq) + 16\,H^+(aq) \qquad (1)$$

$$2\,CuI(s) \rightleftharpoons Cu(s) + Cu^{2+}(aq) + 2\,I^-(aq) \qquad (2)$$

16. In reaction 1, which species is:

    a)   oxidized?

    b)   reduced?

17. In reaction 2, which species is:

    a)   oxidized?

    b)   reduced?

18. Describe, in one or two sentences, how one can determine whether or not a reaction is an oxidation-reduction reaction.

Exercises

1. Give the oxidation number for each atom in the following molecules.

   a) Br_2 b) $NaCl$ c) $CuCl_2$ d) CH_4 e) CO_2

   f) $SiCl_4$ g) CCl_4 h) SCl_2 i) Br_2O

2. Give the oxidation number for each atom in the following ions.

   a) Ni^{2+} b) NO_3^- c) CO_3^{2-} d) SO_4^{2-} e) NH_4^+

   f) ClO_4^- g) MnO_4^- h) CN^- i) IF_4^+ j) PO_4^{3-}

3. Give the oxidation number for each atom in the following molecules.

   a) $NiCl_2$ b) HNO_3 c) Na_2CO_3 d) $Al_2(SO_4)_3$

   e) NH_4Cl f) $KMnO_4$ g) KCN h) $HClO_4$

4. Give the oxidation number for each atom in the following ions.

   a) HCO_3^- b) HSO_4^- c) $H_2PO_4^-$ d) NH_2^- e) $Cr_2O_7^{2-}$

5. Give the oxidation number for each atom in the following molecules.

   a) CH_3OH b) H_2CCH_2 c) CH_3Cl d) CCl_4 e) CH_3CH_2OH

6. Give the oxidation number of N and H in NH_3. What is the oxidation number of Cu in $Cu(NH_3)_4^{2+}$?

7. Give the oxidation number of O and H in OH^-. What is the oxidation number of Al in $Al(OH)_4^-$?

8. An oxidation number need not be an integer. Give the oxidation number for each atom in the following molecules.

   a) P_4O_7 b) P_4O_6 c) P_4O_8 d) P_4O_9 .

9. Which of the following are redox reactions?

   a) $3 H_2(g) + N_2(g) \rightleftharpoons 2 NH_3(g)$

   b) $Ag^+(aq) + Cl^-(aq) \rightleftharpoons AgCl(s)$

   c) $C(s) + O_2(g) \rightleftharpoons CO_2(g)$

   d) $H_2CCH_2(g) + H_2(g) \rightleftharpoons H_3CCH_3(g)$

   e) $3 Cu(s) + 8 H^+(aq) + 2 NO_3^-(aq) \rightleftharpoons 3 Cu^{2+}(aq) + 2 NO(g) + 4 H_2O$

   f) $H_2(g) + Cl_2(g) \rightleftharpoons 2 HCl(g)$

   g) $Cu^{2+}(aq) + 4 NH_3(aq) \rightleftharpoons Cu(NH_3)_4^{2+}(aq)$

10. When natural gas (methane) burns, the chemical reaction is

$$CH_4(g) + 2\,O_2(g) \rightleftharpoons CO_2(g) + 2\,H_2O(g).$$

Is this an oxidation-reduction reaction?

11. When iron corrodes, the chemical reaction is

$$2\,Fe(s) + O_2(aq) + 2\,H_2O(\ell) \rightleftharpoons 2\,FeO{\cdot}H_2O(s).$$

Is this an oxidation-reduction reaction?

12. Plants convert carbon dioxide and water into carbohydrates and dioxygen by a series of reactions called photosynthesis. The overall chemical reaction is

$$6\,CO_2(g) + 6\,H_2O(\ell) \rightleftharpoons C_6H_{12}O_6(aq) + 6\,O_2(g)$$

Is this an oxidation-reduction reaction?

Problems

1. Give the oxidation number for the bromine atom in each of the species below. Then describe the relationship between the oxidation number on the bromine and the relative acidity of these compounds:

$$HOBrO_2 \quad HOBr \quad HOBrO.$$

2. Consider the three chlorine-containing acids: HCl   HOCl   HOClO

   a) Give the oxidation number for the Cl atom in each of the species.

   b) Identify the conjugate base of each of the three acids given, and then rank the conjugate bases in order of increasing values of K_b. Explain the reasoning for the ranking that you give.

How Does a Battery Work?

WARM-UP

Model 1: The Galvanic Cell.

It is possible to design a redox reaction such that the oxidation occurs at one location and the reduction occurs at another location. Such a device is called a **galvanic cell** or **voltaic cell**.

Figure 1.   Schematic Diagram of a Galvanic Cell (Voltaic Cell).

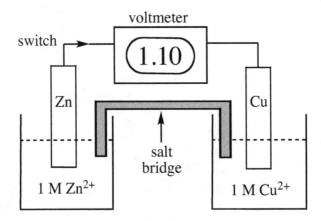

The beaker on the left contains a clear, colorless solution of 1 M $Zn(NO_3)_2$ and the beaker on the right contains a clear, dark blue solution of 1 M $Cu(NO_3)_2$.

If the switch is open (not shown), then nothing happens.

When the switch is closed (as shown in Figure 1), the following is observed:

- The mass of the Cu electrode increases.

- The dark blue color fades, indicating that the concentration of $Cu^{2+}(aq)$ decreases.

- The mass of the Zn electrode decreases.

- The concentration of $Zn^{2+}(aq)$ increases.

- Electrons (e^-) are observed to flow through the wire.

- The voltage measured with the voltmeter is 1.10 V.

- Nitrate ions flow through the salt bridge.

Critical Thinking Questions

1. There are two possible net chemical reactions that could occur in the galvanic cell of Model 1:

$$Cu(s) + Zn^{2+}(aq) \rightleftharpoons Zn(s) + Cu^{2+}(aq)$$

$$Cu^{2+}(aq) + Zn(s) \rightleftharpoons Zn^{2+}(aq) + Cu(s)$$

Based on the description given in Model 1, which of these chemical reactions describes the actual process that occurs. Explain your reasoning.

2. Based on your answer to CTQ 1:

    a) what species is oxidized in the overall process?

    b) what species is reduced in the overall process?

END OF WARM-UP

Information

The **cathode** is the electrode (usually a metal bar or carbon rod) where reduction takes place; the **anode** is the electrode where oxidation takes place. The **salt bridge** allows ions to slowly migrate from one beaker to the other to maintain electrical neutrality in each half-cell. The voltmeter measures the voltage (or potential), V, between the two electrodes. If the solutions are 1 M and the temperature is 298 K, then the beakers with the electrodes are each considered to be a **standard half-cell**.

Critical Thinking Questions

Answer CTQs 3 – 9 as a team.

3. Label the anode and the cathode in Figure 1.

4. In which direction (through the wire) are the electrons flowing when the switch is closed in Figure 1?

5. Electrons flow from the negative electrode to the positive electrode. Which electrode, Zn or Cu, is the negative electrode?

6. The overall charge in each beaker must remain neutral as the reaction proceeds. Based on this concept, in which direction do the nitrate ions flow through the salt bridge? Explain how your team reached that conclusion.

7. What happens when the switch in Model 1 is opened?

8. What use(s) could be made of the flow of electrons in the wire?

9. Give two advantages of a voltaic cell, as described in Model 1, compared to inserting a zinc bar into a Cu^{2+} solution (as in Model 1 of CA 46).

Model 2: Half-Reactions.

Oxidation-reduction reactions can be divided into **half-reactions** to separate and clarify the electron transfer process. Dividing redox reactions into half-reactions is particularly useful when considering voltaic cells where the oxidation and reduction processes take place in different physical locations. For example, the redox reaction

$$Co(s) + Ni^{2+}(aq) \rightleftharpoons Ni(s) + Co^{2+}(aq)$$

can be written as the sum of two half-reactions

$$Co(s) \rightleftharpoons Co^{2+}(aq) + 2e^-$$

$$Ni^{2+} + 2e^- \rightleftharpoons Ni(s)$$

Note that for any net oxidation-reduction reaction, one half-reaction must be an oxidation and the other half-reaction must be a reduction.

Critical Thinking Questions

Answer CTQs 10 and 11 individually. Check with your team before moving to CTQ 12.

10. For the reaction in Model 2:

    a)   which half-reaction represents an oxidation?

    b)   which half-reaction represents a reduction?

    c)   The two electrons that are lost by _____ are gained by _____ .

11. For the galvanic cell in Model 1:

    a)   what is the half-reaction occurring in the copper half-cell?

    b)   what is the half-reaction occurring in the zinc half-cell?

12. Given the overall process that occurs in the galvanic cell of Model 1, as summarized by your answers to CTQ 11, which has the greater attraction for electrons, $Cu^{2+}(aq)$ or $Zn^{2+}(aq)$? Discuss with your team and write a consensus explanation.

Model 3: Electron Pulling Strength.

The chemical processes taking place in a galvanic cell may be viewed as a "tug-of-war" for electrons between the two half-cells. The "winner" of the "tug-of-war" is the one containing the stronger oxidizing agent—it is the half-cell that gains the electrons and gets reduced. The voltage is a measure of the difference in electron-pulling strength.

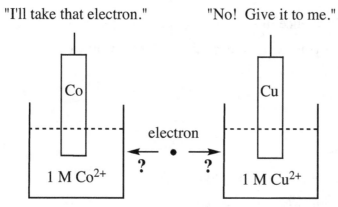

When a galvanic cell is constructed from the half-cells above, the electrons flow to the Cu(s) and the voltage is 0.62 V.

Critical Thinking Questions

Answer CTQs 13 and 14 individually.

13. Add a salt bridge, connecting wire, and a voltmeter (with the correct reading) to the figure in Model 3 to create a galvanic cell.

14. a) Draw an arrow on the connecting wire to indicate the flow of electrons.

   b) What is the half-reaction occurring in the cobalt half-cell?

   c) What is the half-reaction occurring in the copper half-cell?

   d) Label the anode and the cathode in the figure in Model 3.

   e) Circle the oxidizing agent and put a box around the reducing agent.

As a team, check your answers to CTQs 13 and 14 and then answer CTQs 15 and 16.

15. Given what occurs in this galvanic cell, as summarized by the answers to CTQ 14, decide which has the greater attraction for electrons: Cu^{2+}(aq) or Co^{2+}(aq)?

16. Note the voltage in the galvanic cell of Model 1 is 1.10 V. Compare this value to the voltage in the galvanic cell in Model 3. Which ion, Zn^{2+}(aq) or Co^{2+}(aq), has a stronger pull on electrons? Provide a consensus explanation.

Information

The **standard reduction potential**, $E°_{red}$, of a half-reaction is the relative strength of a half-cell for that reaction with all components in their standard states. The standard state for a solution is 1 M and for gases is 1 atm pressure, all at 298 K.

Critical Thinking Question

17. As a team, find the difference in standard reduction potential (in V) between Zn^{2+}(aq) and Co^{2+}(aq). Explain your team's reasoning and show all work.

Exercises

1. For the cell in Model 1:

    a) Which is the stronger oxidizing agent—Zn^{2+} or Cu^{2+}?

    b) How much stronger (in terms of volts) is the stronger oxidizing agent?

2. When a standard $Ni(s)/Ni^{2+}$ electrode is connected to a standard $Cu(s)/Cu^{2+}$ electrode, the mass of the nickel electrode is observed to decrease.

    a) Sketch this galvanic cell (as in Model 1) and indicate:

        i) the anode and the cathode;

        ii) the direction of flow of the electrons in the wire;

        iii) which electrode is positive and which electrode is negative.

    b) Write down the half-reactions that are occurring at each electrode, and then write down the overall chemical process occurring in the cell.

3. When a standard $Cr(s)/Cr^{3+}$ electrode is connected to a standard $Sn(s)/Sn^{2+}$ electrode, the tin electrode gains mass. The voltage is 0.60 V.

    a) Sketch this voltaic cell.

    b) Identify the anode and the cathode in this system.

    c) Identify the positive and negative electrode.

    d) Give the half-reaction occurring in each half-cell, and then give the net chemical reaction for the cell. Keep in mind that the number of electrons being given up and being received must be the same.

    e) Identify the oxidizing agent and the reducing agent in the overall process that is occurring.

    f) If the standard reduction potential for the chromium half-cell is –0.74, what is the standard reduction potential for the tin half-cell?

4. Describe the components of a battery (galvanic cell) and explain why electrons flow from one half-cell to the other in your own words.

What Determines the Cell Voltage?

WARM-UP

Model 1: The Standard Hydrogen Electrode.

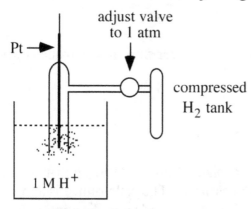

This half-cell consists of a platinum electrode submerged in a 1 M solution of ions at 298 K, and bathed by H_2 gas at 1 atm pressure. Pt is chemically inert, but it is an excellent conductor of electricity. The designation of H^+ is the same as H_3O^+, but is the representation used in half-reactions.

The Standard Hydrogen Electrode (SHE) is used as a reference point for all other standard reduction potentials. The standard reduction potential of the SHE is defined as zero volts.

$$2e^- + 2H^+(1\text{ M}) \;\rightleftharpoons\; H_2(g; 1\text{ atm}) \qquad E°_{red} \equiv 0.00 \text{ V}$$

When a SHE is connected to a standard Cu/Cu^{2+} half-cell, the Cu/Cu^{2+} half-cell exhibits a stronger pull on electrons than does the SHE half-cell. Thus, the following reaction takes place at the Cu electrode:

$$Cu^{2+}(1\text{ M}) + 2e^- \;\rightleftharpoons\; Cu(s)$$

Simultaneously, at the Pt electrode, the following reaction takes place:

$$H_2(g; 1\text{ atm}) \;\rightleftharpoons\; 2H^+(1\text{ M}) + 2e^-$$

The experimental voltage, $E°$, is 0.34 V.

Critical Thinking Questions

1. Which is the stronger oxidizing agent, $Cu^{2+}(aq)$ or $H^+(aq)$?

2. In terms of volts, how much stronger is the stronger of the two oxidizing agents in CTQ 1?

END OF WARM-UP

Answer CTQs 3 and 4 as a team.

3. What value (in volts) should be assigned as the standard reduction potential, $E°_{red}$, of the Cu/Cu^{2+} half-cell?

4. The standard reduction potentials for $Ag^+(aq)$ and $Au^+(aq)$ are

	$E°_{red}$ (V)
$Ag^+ + 1e^- \rightleftharpoons Ag(s)$	0.80
$Au^+ + 1e^- \rightleftharpoons Au(s)$	1.68

Which ion, $Ag^+(aq)$ or $Au^+(aq)$, exhibits a stronger pull on electrons? Explain your reasoning.

Model 2: The Cell Voltage.

Every redox reaction in a galvanic cell consists of an oxidation half-reaction at the anode and a reduction half-reaction at the cathode. The cell voltage is a measure of the difference in the electron pulling strength of the cathode and the anode. Because the standard reduction potential is a measure of the relative electron-pulling strength of the standard half-cell, the cell voltage under standard conditions, $E°_{cell}$, is given by the difference in standard reduction potentials of the cathode and anode:

$$E°_{cell} = E°_{red}(cathode) - E°_{red}(anode) \qquad (1)$$

Table 1.   Some standard reduction potentials.

Reaction	$E°_{red}$ (V)
$Zn^{2+}(aq) + 2e^- \rightleftharpoons Zn(s)$	–0.76
$2 H^+(aq) + 2e^- \rightleftharpoons H_2(g)$	0.00
$Cu^{2+}(aq) + 2e^- \rightleftharpoons Cu(s)$	0.34

Critical Thinking Questions

5. Consider a galvanic cell composed of a Cu/Cu^{2+}(1 M) half-cell and a Zn/Zn^{2+} (1 M) half-cell.

   a) Which half-cell has a stronger pull on electrons, Cu/Cu^{2+}(1 M) or Zn/Zn^{2+}(1 M)?

   b) Write the cathode half-reaction.

   c) Write the anode half-reaction.

   d) Using the data in Table 1, provide a calculation to confirm that the cell voltage, $E°_{cell}$, is 1.10 V.

Model 3: Measured Voltages for Some Galvanic Cells Using Standard Electrodes (all ions at 1 M and all gases at 1 atm).

Cathode	Anode	E°_{cell} (V)
Cu/Cu^{2+}	Zn/Zn^{2+}	1.10
Cu/Cu^{2+}	SHE	0.34
Br_2/Br^-	Zn/Zn^{2+}	1.85
Zn/Zn^{2+}	K/K^+	2.16
Cl_2/Cl^-	Ag/Ag^+	0.56
Ag/Ag^+	K/K^+	3.72

Critical Thinking Questions

6. As a team, determine the missing standard reduction potentials, E°_{red}, for all of the following half-reactions using only the data in Model 3. In each case, give a brief explanation of how your team determined the answer.

	E°_{red} (V)	Brief Explanation
$Cl_2 + 2e^- \rightleftharpoons 2Cl^-$		
$Br_2 + 2e^- \rightleftharpoons 2Br^-$		
$Ag^+ + e^- \rightleftharpoons Ag$		
$Cu^{2+} + 2e^- \rightleftharpoons Cu$	0.34	
$2H^+ + 2e^- \rightleftharpoons H_2$	0.00	
$Zn^{2+} + 2e^- \rightleftharpoons Zn$		
$K^+ + e^- \rightleftharpoons K$		

7. Use the results from CTQ 6 to confirm that E°_{cell} = 0.29 V for a galvanic cell composed of a Br_2/Br^- half-cell and a Ag/Ag^+ half-cell. Show all work.

8. As a team, examine the results from CTQ 6.

    a)   What is the strongest oxidizing agent?

    b)   What is the weakest oxidizing agent?

9. The stronger the oxidizing agent, the weaker the resulting reducing agent that is produced by the acquisition of electrons. In this case:

    a)   What is the strongest reducing agent on the right-hand side of the list in CTQ 2?

    b)   What is the weakest reducing agent?

Exercises

1. Draw a galvanic cell consisting of a SHE and a standard copper electrode. Indicate:

    a)   the anode and the cathode.
    b)   the direction of flow of the electrons in the wire.
    c)   which electrode is positive and which electrode is negative.
    d)   Write down the half-reactions that are occurring at each electrode, and then write down the overall chemical process occurring in the cell.

2. When a standard $Al(s)/Al^{3+}$ cell is connected to a SHE, the electrons are observed to flow in the direction of the SHE. The voltage is 1.66 V.

    a)   Sketch this galvanic cell.
    b)   Identify the anode and the cathode in this system.
    c)   Identify the positive and negative electrode.
    d)   Give the half-reaction occurring in each half-cell, and then give the net chemical reaction for the cell. Keep in mind that the number of electrons being given up and being received must be the same.
    e)   What is the standard reduction potential for the $Al(s)/Al^{3+}$ half-cell? Explain your reasoning.

3. When a standard $Cr(s)/Cr^{3+}(1\ M)$ cell is connected to a standard hydrogen electrode (SHE), the electrons are observed to flow in the direction of the SHE. The measured voltage is 0.74 V.

    a)   Is the SHE the cathode or the anode? Explain your reasoning.

    b)   Give the half-reaction occurring in each half-cell, and then give the net chemical reaction for the cell.

4. Describe how to determine the cell voltage for an electrochemical cell given the balanced redox reaction that occurs and a table of standard reduction potentials.

Use a table of standard reduction potentials for the following exercises.

5. You decide to construct a zinc/aluminum galvanic cell in which the electrodes are connected by a wire and the solutions are connected with a salt bridge. One electrode consists of an aluminum bar in a 1.0 M solution of aluminum(III) nitrate. The other electrode consists of a zinc bar in a 1.0 M solution of zinc(II) nitrate. Zn(II) has a more positive standard reduction potential than Al(III).

    a) Which electrode is the cathode and which is the anode?

    b) What is the direction of electron flow?

    c) Which electrode is negative? Positive?

    d) What chemical reactions are occurring at each electrode?

    e) What is the overall chemical reaction?

    f) After a period of time, will the bar of zinc become heavier, lighter, or stay the same weight? Will the bar of aluminum become heavier, lighter, or stay the same weight?

6. Indicate whether each of the following statements is true or false and explain your reasoning:

    a) The half-cell with the larger standard reduction potential is always the anode in a galvanic cell.

    b) Whenever an oxidation half-reaction takes place, a reduction half-reaction must also take place.

7. For each of the chemical equations below assume that at the start of the reaction the concentration of each ion (on the left-hand side and on the right-hand side) is 1.0 M, each gas (on the both sides) has a pressure of 1.0 atm, and each solid (on both sides) is present. Determine the cell voltage for each reaction, as written. Which of these reactions will proceed to the right? Which of these reactions will proceed to the left?

    a) $Cr(s) + Pb^{2+}(aq) \rightleftharpoons Pb(s) + Cr^{2+}(aq)$

    b) $H_2(g) + 2\,Ag^+(aq) \rightleftharpoons 2\,Ag + 2\,H^+(aq)$

    c) $2\,Cr^{2+}(aq) + Mg^{2+} \rightleftharpoons 2\,Cr^{3+}(aq) + Mg(s)$

    d) $NO_2^-(aq) + ClO^-(aq) \rightleftharpoons NO_3^-(aq) + Cl^-(aq)$

    e) $4\,AgBr(s) + 4\,OH^-(aq) \rightleftharpoons O_2(g) + 2\,H_2O + 4\,Ag(s) + 4\,Br^-(aq)$

8. For each of the chemical reactions in Exercise 7 assume that only the reactants (the species on the left-hand side) are present. Which of these chemical reactions will occur? Which will not occur?

Use a table of standard reduction potentials as needed for the following Problems.

Problems

1. Assuming standard conditions, indicate whether each of the following statements is true or false:

    a) $H_2(g)$ can reduce $Ag^+(aq)$

    b) $H_2(g)$ can reduce $Ni^{2+}(aq)$

    c) $Fe^{2+}(aq)$ can reduce $Cu^{2+}(aq)$

    d) $H^+(aq)$ can oxidize $Mg(s)$

    e) $Pb^{2+}(aq)$ can oxidize $Ni(s)$

2. A student places some $Zn(s)$ powder in a beaker of 1 M nitric acid, and some $Cu(s)$ powder in another beaker also containing 1 M nitric acid. In which, if either, of the beakers would you expect the solid to react and evolve hydrogen gas? Explain your reasoning.

3. Find a reagent that can oxidize Br^- to Br_2 but cannot oxidize Cl^- to Cl_2.

4. Use a table of standard reduction potentials to determine whether or not a reaction occurs when a tin (Sn) rod is placed into 500 mL of 1.0 M Ni^{2+}. Explain your reasoning.

5. A 20.00 mL sample of oxalic acid solution, $H_2C_2O_4$, was titrated with 0.256 M $KMnO_4$ solution. What is the molarity of the oxalic acid solution if it took 14.6 mL of the $KMnO_4$ solution to completely react with the oxalic acid? The oxidation-reduction reaction is:

    $5 H_2C_2O_4(aq) + 2 MnO_4^-(aq) + 6 H^+(aq) \rightleftharpoons$

    $$10 CO_2(g) + 2 Mn^{2+}(aq) + 8 H_2O(\ell)$$

What is Entropy?

WARM-UP

Information

Water flows downhill, not uphill. Ice melts on a warm day; water does not freeze on a warm day. If we throw a handful of confetti out of a window, we do not expect all of the confetti to accumulate in the refuse container at the end of the street. Similarly, when a piece of zinc metal dissolves in a strong acid solution, bubbles of hydrogen gas evolve.

$$Zn(s) + 2 H_3O^+(aq) \rightleftharpoons Zn^{2+}(aq) + H_2(g) + 2 H_2O(\ell) \qquad (1)$$

Although perhaps not as familiar as the melting of ice, this process is also not surprising. However, if we saw a video in which H_2 bubbles formed at the surface of a solution and sank through the solution until they disappeared, while a strip of zinc metal formed in the middle of the solution, we would likely think that the video was being run backward.[1]

Most important of all, my desk gets messy.

Clearly, many physical and chemical processes proceed **naturally** in one direction, but not in the other. (They are sometimes referred to as being **spontaneous** in the direction in which they proceed naturally.) This raises the question: What factor (or factors) determines the direction in which reactions proceed naturally?

Model 1: A Ball Tends to Roll Downhill.

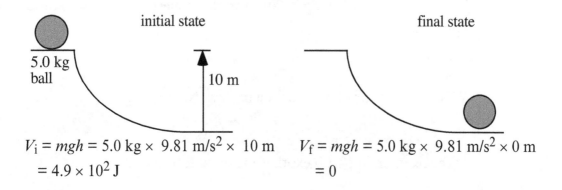

initial state   final state

5.0 kg ball   10 m

$V_i = mgh = 5.0 \text{ kg} \times 9.81 \text{ m/s}^2 \times 10 \text{ m}$ $V_f = mgh = 5.0 \text{ kg} \times 9.81 \text{ m/s}^2 \times 0 \text{ m}$
$= 4.9 \times 10^2 \text{ J}$ $= 0$

---

[1] J. N. Spencer, G. M. Bodner, and L. H. Rickard, *Chemistry: Structure & Dynamics*, Fifth Edition, John Wiley & Sons, 2011, Section 13.1.

Critical Thinking Question

1. A ball tends to roll down a hill.

    a)   Which is the lower energy state: the ball at the top of the hill or the ball at the bottom of the hill?

    b)   Is the change in the potential energy for this process, $V_f - V_i$, positive, negative, or zero?

    c)   Why doesn't the ball roll up the hill on its own?

END OF WARM-UP

Model 2:   The Formation of Solid Sodium Chloride from Gaseous Ions.

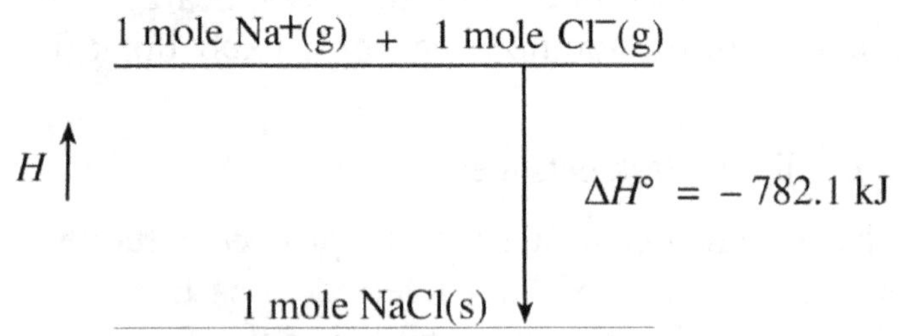

$$\underline{1 \text{ mole } Na^+(g) \ + \ 1 \text{ mole } Cl^-(g)}$$

$H \uparrow$

$\Delta H° = -782.1 \text{ kJ}$

$$\underline{1 \text{ mole } NaCl(s) \downarrow}$$

Critical Thinking Questions

Answer CTQ 2 as a team.

2. Gaseous sodium ions and gaseous chloride ions will combine to form solid sodium chloride.

    a)   Which is the lower energy state: 1 mole of $NaCl(s)$ or 1 mole of $Na^+(g)$ and 1 mole of $Cl^-(g)$?

    b)   What is the value of $\Delta H°$ for the process $Na^+(g) + Cl^-(g) \rightleftharpoons NaCl(s)$?

    c)   Is the reaction in part b exothermic or endothermic?

    d)   Why doesn't a salt crystal suddenly become gaseous sodium ions and gaseous chloride ions?

3. a) Individually, write a chemical equation that describes the melting of ice.

    b) Individually, indicate whether ΔH for the melting process is positive, negative, or zero.

    Once all team members have completed parts a and b compare your answers and then answer part c as a team.

    c) Under what temperature conditions will this process naturally occur?

4. a) Individually, write a chemical equation that describes the freezing of water.

    b) Individually, indicate whether ΔH for the freezing process is positive, negative, or zero.

    Once all team members have completed parts a and b compare your answers and then answer part c as a team.

    c) Under what temperature conditions will this process naturally occur?

5. A student says "The only processes that occur naturally are exothermic processes." As a team, use the answers to CTQs 3 and 4 to explain why this student is not correct.

6. As a team, use the answers to CTQs 3 and 4, to discuss what factor (or factors) other than the sign of ΔH must be considered to determine whether or not a process will occur naturally under a given set of conditions. Write your consensus answer(s) in the space below.

Information

Many naturally occurring processes *tend* to be exothermic, but this is not a requirement. The temperature at which a process occurs also plays a role in determining in which direction a process will proceed naturally. Thus, there appear to be two important factors in this determination—the ΔH of the reaction and another factor whose impact is influenced by the temperature. This second factor, known as **entropy**, S, is a measure of disorder or randomness. The more disorder, the higher (more positive) the entropy. The entropy can never be less than zero; that is, entropy values are always positive.

Model 3: Gaseous Molecules in a Box.

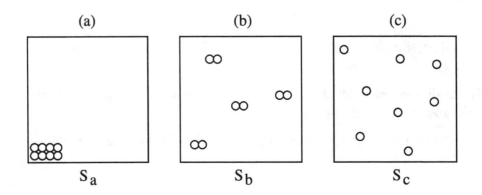

Critical Thinking Questions

Answer CTQs 7 – 11 as a team.

7. In which case in Model 3 are the molecules most disordered: (a), (b), or (c)?

8. Which case in Model 3 has the greatest entropy: (a), (b), or (c)?

9. Suppose that at some temperature the naturally occurring process starts with case (a) and ends with case (c).

    a)   Is $S_a > S_c$ or is $S_c > S_a$?

    b)   Is ΔS for this naturally occurring process positive or negative?

10. Suppose that at some temperature (different than the temperature in CTQ 9) the naturally occurring process starts with case (c) and ends with case (a). Is ΔS for this naturally occurring process positive or negative?

11. a) Which process is more like the freezing of ice: the process described in CTQ 9 or the process described in CTQ 10?

     b) A student says "The only processes that occur naturally are those that have $\Delta S > 0$." Use the examples of the melting of ice and freezing of water to demonstrate that this statement is not correct.

Model 4: Dissolving Sodium Chloride in Water.

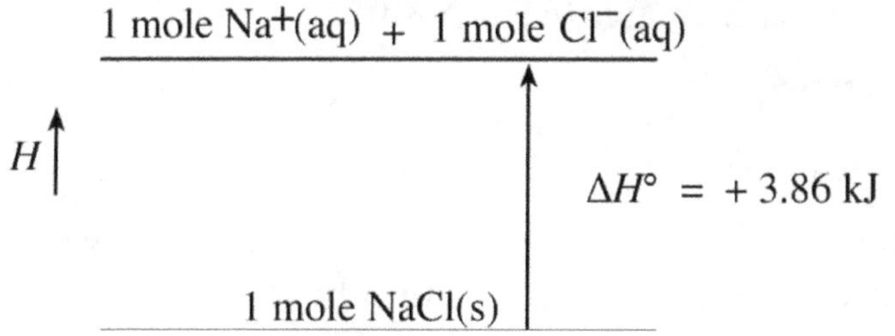

1 mole Na^+(aq) + 1 mole Cl^-(aq)

H↑

$\Delta H° = +3.86$ kJ

1 mole NaCl(s)

Critical Thinking Question

12. As a team, use Model 4 to address these questions about NaCl dissolving in water:

     a) Is the process exothermic or endothermic?

     b) Is $\Delta H > 0$ or $\Delta H < 0$?

     c) Is $\Delta S > 0$ or $\Delta S < 0$?

     d) Provide an explanation for your answer to part c) including the evidence used to arrive at the team answer.

Information

Dissolving NaCl in water is another example of an endothermic reaction that occurs naturally. However, ΔS for the process is positive. Thus, in addition to the tendency for processes to be exothermic, another factor that determines the direction in which reactions proceed naturally is entropy: chemical (and physical) processes tend to proceed toward the state of highest entropy.

The following are some generalizations that can often be used in considering the entropy associated with a chemical species, or the change in entropy (ΔS) associated with a chemical reaction:

  i.   As the number of particles in the system increases, the amount of disorder increases (ΔS is positive).

  ii.   As the volume in which particles can move increases, the amount of disorder increases (ΔS is positive).

  iii. As the temperature of a system increases, the motion of the particles and the amount of disorder increases (ΔS is positive).

Critical Thinking Questions

Answer CTQs 13 and 14 as a team.

13. For each process below, indicate whether ΔS is positive or negative. Then indicate which of the three generalizations from the above Information supports your conclusion.

    a) $C_4H_8(g) \rightleftharpoons 2\,C_2H_4(g)$

    b) $C_4H_8(g; 298\ K; 1\ atm) \rightleftharpoons C_4H_8(g; 298\ K; 0.5\ atm)$

    c) $C_4H_8(g; 298\ K; 1\ atm) \rightleftharpoons C_4H_8(g; 398\ K; 1\ atm)$

14. Describe how, in general, the entropy of the solid, liquid, and gaseous phases of a particular compound are related. Explain your reasoning.

Exercises

1. In your own words, describe what "entropy" means.

2. For each of the following processes, predict whether $\Delta S°$ (for the chemical reaction) is expected to be positive or negative. Explain your reasoning.

    a) $N_2(g) + 3\,H_2(g) \rightleftharpoons 2\,NH_3(g)$

    b) $CO_2(g) \rightleftharpoons CO_2(s)$

    c) $CaCO_3(s) \rightleftharpoons CaO(s) + CO_2(g)$

    d)   The air in a balloon escapes out a hole and the balloon flies wildly around the room. (Consider ΔS for the air molecules originally in the balloon.)

    e)   A precipitate of $Pb(OH)_2$ forms when solutions of lead(II) nitrate and sodium hydroxide are mixed.

3. Consider these two reactions:

    $$N_2(g) + O_2(g) \rightleftharpoons 2\,NO(g) \qquad\qquad N_2(g) + 2\,O_2(g) \rightleftharpoons N_2O_4(g)$$

    How would you expect the values of ΔS for these reactions to compare? Would they be equal, and if not, which one would be larger? Explain your reasoning.

4. Indicate whether each of the following statements is true or false and explain your reasoning.

    a)   For the reaction $2\,SO_3(g) \rightleftharpoons 2\,SO_2(g) + O_2(g)$, $\Delta S°$ is expected to be negative.

    b)   At a given temperature, the value of $\Delta S°$ for the reaction

    $$3\,F_2(g) + Cl_2(g) \rightleftharpoons 2\,ClF_3(g)$$

    is expected to be negative.

What Determines if Reactions Occur?

WARM-UP

Recall that exothermic reactions *tend to* occur naturally (spontaneously). The temperature can also have an impact on whether or not a particular process occurs naturally. This temperature effect is related to the concept of entropy. In fact, it is the entropy change, ΔS, which must be considered in helping to determine whether or not a process occurs naturally.

Model 1: The Melting of Ice.

$$H_2O(s) \rightleftharpoons H_2O(\ell) \quad (T = 273 \text{ K})$$

Critical Thinking Questions

1. Explain why ΔH is positive ($\Delta H > 0$) for the melting of ice.

2. Do you expect ΔS to be positive ($\Delta S > 0$) or negative ($\Delta S < 0$) for the melting of ice? Explain your reasoning.

3. Consider the freezing of water: $H_2O(\ell) \rightleftharpoons H_2O(s)$.

   a) Will ΔH be positive (+) or negative (–)?

   b) Will ΔS be positive (+) or negative (–)?

   c) Explain your reasoning for both of your answers.

END OF WARM-UP

Model 2: Relationships Between ΔH, ΔS, and T for a Chemical Process to Be Naturally Occurring.

Row Number	ΔH	ΔS	Occurs at Higher T?	Occurs at Lower T?
1	−	−	no	yes
2	−	+	yes	yes
3	+	−	no	no
4	+	+	yes	no

Critical Thinking Questions

Answer CTQs 4 - 12 as a team.

4. a) Based on your answers to CTQs 1 – 3, which row in Model 2 corresponds to the melting of ice?

　　b) Based on your answers to CTQs 1 – 3, which row in Model 2 corresponds to the freezing of water?

　　c) Think about the temperature conditions under which melting and freezing occur. Explain how the information in Model 2 confirms that your answers to parts a and b are correct.

5. a) Circle the row numbers that correspond to exothermic reactions.

　　b) Put a box around the row numbers that correspond to endothermic reactions.

6. Consider the rows that correspond to exothermic reactions.

　　a) When $\Delta S < 0$, can the process occur naturally? If so, under what temperature conditions?

　　b) When $\Delta S > 0$, can the process occur naturally? If so, under what temperature conditions?

7. Consider the rows that correspond to endothermic reactions.

　　a) When $\Delta S < 0$, can the process occur naturally? If so, under what temperature conditions?

　　b) When $\Delta S > 0$, can the process occur naturally? If so, under what temperature conditions?

8. Consider the answers to CTQs 6 and 7, paying particular attention to the range of conditions under which each type of reaction (exothermic and endothermic) allow the process to occur naturally.

    Discuss with your team and then generate a consensus explanation for how the information presented in Model 2 is consistent with the statement that exothermic reactions tend to occur naturally, but endothermic reactions do not tend to occur naturally.

9. a)   Put a star next to the row numbers for which $\Delta S > 0$.

    b)   Put an asterisk next to the row numbers for which $\Delta S < 0$.

10. Consider the rows that correspond to $\Delta S > 0$.

    a)   When $\Delta H < 0$, can the process occur naturally? If so, under what temperature conditions?

    b)   When $\Delta H > 0$, can the process occur naturally? If so, under what temperature conditions?

11. Consider the rows that correspond to $\Delta S < 0$.

    a)   When $\Delta H < 0$, can the process occur naturally? If so, under what temperature conditions?

    b)   When $\Delta H > 0$, can the process occur naturally? If so, under what temperature conditions?

12. Consider the answers to CTQs 10 and 11, paying particular attention to the range of conditions under which each change in entropy ($\Delta S > 0$ and $\Delta S < 0$) allows the process to occur naturally.

    Discuss with your team and then generate a consensus explanation for how the information presented in Model 2 is consistent with the previous statement that "chemical (and physical) processes tend to be driven toward the state of highest entropy."

Information

Because processes for which the enthalpy decreases ($\Delta H < 0$) tend to occur naturally, we often say that these processes are **enthalpically favorable**.

Similarly, because processes for which the entropy increases ($\Delta S > 0$) tend to occur naturally, we often say that these processes are **entropically favorable**.

Critical Thinking Questions

13. For each process below, circle the term(s) that apply.

    a)   melting of ice

        enthalpically favorable   entropically favorable   neither

    b)   freezing of water

        enthalpically favorable   entropically favorable   neither

Answer CTQs 14 and 15 as a team.

14. Under what conditions can an endothermic reaction occur naturally? Explain your reasoning, using information from Model 2 to support your answer.

15. Based on the information in Model 2, explain why the following reaction must be exothermic if it is to occur naturally:

$$A_2(g) + B_2(g) \rightleftharpoons A_2B_2 (g)$$

Exercises

1. What factors determine if a reaction occurs naturally?

2. When $NH_4NO_3(s)$ dissolves in water, the temperature of the solution is observed to decrease. Which phrase below describes what makes this dissolution a naturally occurring process? Explain.

    i)   enthalpically favored

    ii)   entropically favored

    iii)   both enthalpically favored and entropically favored

    iv)   neither enthalpically favored nor entropically favored

3. When concentrated sulfuric acid (18 M) is added to water, the resulting solution has a lower concentration of sulfuric acid and the temperature of the solution increases. (As a matter of fact, it is important not to add water to concentrated sulfuric acid because the water may boil and bring some of the acid along with the steam.) Which phrase below describes what makes this a naturally occurring process? Explain.

    i)   enthalpically favored

    ii) entropically favored

    iii) both enthalpically favored and entropically favored

    iv) neither enthalpically favored nor entropically favored

Problems

1. Assume that five hydrogen fluoride molecules are arranged as shown in Figure A. For the transformation of these molecules to the arrangement in Figure B:

    a) Is ΔS positive or negative? Explain.

    b) Is ΔH positive or negative? Explain.

    c) Will this transformation tend to be naturally occurring at high temperatures, low temperatures, or both high and low temperatures? Explain.

Figure A	Figure B
H—F	H—F
H—F	F—H
H—F	H—F
H—F	F—H
H—F	H—F

2. For the reaction: $O_3(g) \rightarrow O_2(g) + O(g)$

    a) Draw the best Lewis structures for $O_3(g)$ and $O_2(g)$

    b) Which represents the lowest enthalpy, the reactant or the products? Explain.

    c) Is $\Delta H < 0$ or $\Delta H > 0$ for this process? Explain.

    d) Is $\Delta S < 0$ or $\Delta S > 0$ for this process? Explain.

    e) Will this transformation tend to be naturally occurring at high temperatures, low temperatures, or both high and low temperatures? Explain.

How is a Change in Entropy Calculated?

WARM-UP

Information

When a chemical reaction takes place, the entropy associated with the chemical system can increase, decrease, or remain constant. This change in entropy can be determined in a manner analogous to the approach that we have taken in calculation of changes in enthalpy, ΔH.

Because factors such as temperature, pressure, and concentration can have an effect on thermodynamic values, we need to define a set of reference conditions, called **standard state conditions**, at which measurements are made. By convention, the standard state conditions for thermodynamic measurements are:

- $T = 298$ K

- All gases have partial pressure of 1 atm.

- All solutes have concentrations of 1 M.

The entropy of atom combination, ΔS_{ac}°, is the change in entropy when a mole of a substance is produced from its constituent atoms in the gas phase at 1 atmosphere pressure and 25 °C.

Model 1: The Entropy of Atom Combination, ΔS_{ac}°, of $NO_2(g)$ at 25 °C.

1 mole N(g) + 2 mole O(g) ← entropy of one mole of N(g) and two moles of O(g)

$S\uparrow$ increasing entropy

$\Delta S^{\circ} = -235.35$ J /K

1 mole NO_2 (g) ← entropy of one mole of NO_2 (g)

ΔS_{ac}° of $NO_2(g) = -235.35$ J/mol•K

Table 1. Standard state entropies of atom combination, ΔS_{ac}°.

Substance	ΔS_{ac}° (J/mol•K)	Substance	ΔS_{ac}° (J/mol•K)
N(g)	0	$H_2O(g)$	–202.23
O(g)	0	$H_2O(\ell)$	–320.57
$N_2(g)$	–114.99	$CCl_4(g)$	–509.04
$O_2(g)$	–116.972	$CCl_4(\ell)$	–602.49
$NO_2(g)$	–235.35	$C_6H_6(g)$	–1367.7
$N_2O_4(g)$	–646.53	$C_6H_6(\ell)$	–1464.1

Critical Thinking Questions

1. Do you expect ΔS for the following reaction to be positive or negative? Explain your reasoning.

$$N(g) + 2\ O(g) \rightleftharpoons NO_2(g)$$

2. Why is ΔS_{ac}° of N(g) $= 0$?

3. Why are the entropies of atom combination of $NO_2(g)$ and $N_2O_4(g)$ negative?

END OF WARM-UP

4. As a team, discuss and write a consensus explanation about why all of the values for entropies of atom combination are negative.

5. Discuss and explain why the entropies of atom combination generally become more negative as the number of atoms in the molecule increases.

6. As a team, describe why the entropies of atom combination are more negative for liquids than the corresponding entropies of atom combination for gases.

7. Individually, use the data in Table 1 to determine the entropy change associated with breaking one mole of $N_2O_4(g)$ into its constituent atoms (under standard conditions)? Consider both the magnitude and the sign associated with this transformation. When all teammates are done, compare answers.

8. As a team, use the data in Table 1 to answer these questions:

    a) What is the entropy change associated with forming one mole of $NO_2(g)$ (under standard conditions) from its constituent atoms?

    b) What is the entropy change associated with forming 2 moles of $NO_2(g)$ from its constituent atoms?

9. a) Individually, decide if ΔS for the following reaction is expected to be positive or negative? (circle the answer)

    $$N_2O_4(g) \rightleftharpoons 2\,NO_2(g)$$

    b) As a team, discuss your answers and then write a consensus explanation for your answer.

Information

When the change in entropy for a chemical reaction is measured under standard conditions, the result is the **standard state entropy of reaction**, $\Delta S°$.

Model 2: The Entropy Diagram for a Chemical Reaction.

$$N_2O_4(g) \rightleftharpoons 2\,NO_2(g)$$

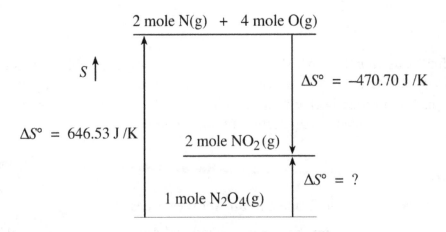

Critical Thinking Questions

Answer CTQs 10 – 13 as a team.

10. a)   Why is ΔS° associated with the upward arrow (left-side of Model 2) a positive number?

     b)   How was the magnitude of ΔS° associated with the upward arrow determined?

11. a)   Why is ΔS° associated with the downward arrow (right-side of Model 2) a negative number?

     b)   How was the magnitude of ΔS° associated with the downward arrow determined?

12. Use the data in Model 2 to calculate the ΔS° for the following reaction:

$$N_2O_4(g) \rightleftharpoons 2\,NO_2(g)$$

13. Complete the diagram below, similar to that in Model 2, to depict $\Delta S°$ for the reaction:

$$A_2X_2(g) \; + \; B_2(g) \; \rightleftharpoons \; 2\,XB(g) \; + \; A_2(g)$$

using $\Delta S_{ac}°(A_2X_2)$, $\Delta S_{ac}°(B_2)$, $\Delta S_{ac}°(XB)$, $\Delta S_{ac}°(A_2)$ — not numerical values.

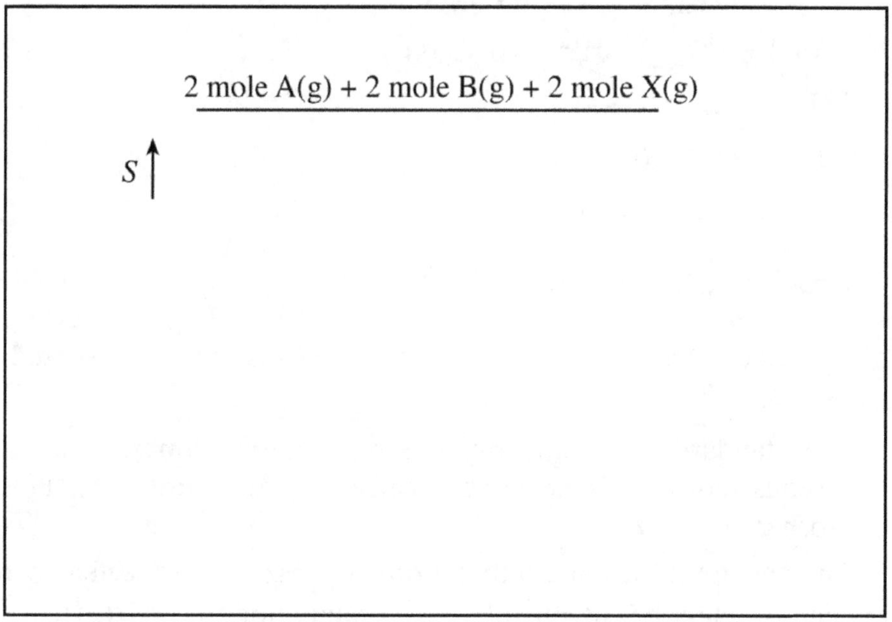

$$
\begin{array}{|l|}
\hline
\\
\underline{2 \text{ mole A(g)} + 2 \text{ mole B(g)} + 2 \text{ mole X(g)}} \\
\\
S \uparrow \\
\\
\\
\\
\\
\\
\\
\hline
\end{array}
$$

14. Individually, describe how to calculate the $\Delta S°$ for the reaction in CTQ 13 using the values of $\Delta S_{ac}°$ of the four species. When all team members are done, compare answers and write one consensus description using a few sentences below your individual answer.

Exercises

1. For each of the following reactions, predict whether $\Delta S°$ will be positive, negative, or zero. Then, use an appropriate table to calculate $\Delta S°$ for each and compare the value to your predictions.

   a) $N_2(g) + 3 H_2(g) \rightleftharpoons 2 NH_3(g)$

   b) $4 Al(s) + 3 O_2(g) \rightleftharpoons 2 Al_2O_3(s)$

   c) $2 HCl(g) \rightleftharpoons H_2(g) + Cl_2(g)$

   d) $P_4(g) \rightleftharpoons 2 P_2(g)$

   e) $3 O_2(g) \rightleftharpoons 2 O_3(g)$

   f) $2 Fe(s) + \dfrac{3}{2} O_2(g) \rightleftharpoons Fe_2O_3(s)$

2. Indicate whether each of the following statements is true or false and explain your reasoning:

   a)   The standard state entropy of atom combination for any diatomic gaseous molecule is negative because the formation of a bond is an exothermic process.

   b)   The entropy of atom combination for $CH_4(g)$ is expected to be more negative than the entropy of atom combination for $NH_3(g)$.

3. Which $\Delta S°_{ac}$ given below is obviously incorrect?

   i) $Hg(\ell)$ $\Delta S°_{ac} = +34.71$ J/mol•K

   ii) $P(g)$ $\Delta S°_{ac} = 0$

   iii) $N_2(g)$ $\Delta S°_{ac} = -122.10$ J/mol•K

4. Given a balanced chemical equation, describe how to determine the entropy change associated with the reaction.

5. One of the key steps toward transforming coal into a liquid fuel involves the reaction of carbon monoxide with hydrogen to form liquid methanol:

   $$CO(g) + 2 H_2(g) \rightleftharpoons CH_3OH(\ell)$$

   a)   Calculate $\Delta S°$ for this reaction.

   b)   Provide the oxidation numbers for each of the atoms in these species, and explain whether or not this reaction is an oxidation-reduction process.

6. For the following reaction at 25 °C:

$$Fe_2O_3(s) + 2\ Al(s) \rightleftharpoons Al_2O_3(s) + 2\ Fe(s)$$

a)   Determine the values of $\Delta S°$ and $\Delta H°$.

b)   Is the reaction favorable or unfavorable with respect to the entropy factor?

c)   Is the reaction favorable or unfavorable with respect to the enthalpy factor?

d)   Is this reaction an oxidation-reduction process? Explain your reasoning.

Problem

1. Which of the following processes should have the most positive $\Delta S°$? Explain.

i) $N_2(g) + O_2(g) \rightleftharpoons 2\ NO(g)$

ii) $H_2O(g) \rightleftharpoons H_2O(\ell)$

iii) $3\ C_2H_2(g) \rightleftharpoons C_6H_6(\ell)$

iv) $4\ Al(s) + 3\ O_2(g) \rightleftharpoons 2\ Al_2O_3(s)$

v) $2\ H_2(g) + O_2(g) \rightleftharpoons H_2O(g)$

What Determines the Magnitude of the Equilibrium Constant?

WARM-UP

Model 1: Lower Enthalpy and Higher Entropy are Driving Forces for Chemical Reactions.

Two important ideas we have developed about reactions are that:

- When the products are at a lower enthalpy than the reactants ($\Delta H° < 0$), a chemical reaction is *enthalpically (or energetically) favored*.
- When the products are more disordered than the reactants ($\Delta S > 0$), a chemical reaction is *entropically favored*.

Table 1. Standard state enthalpy changes and entropy changes (at 25 °C) for several chemical reactions.

Reaction	$\Delta H°$ (kJ/mol$_{rxn}$)	Enthalpy Favorable ?	$\Delta S°$ (J/mol$_{rxn}$·K)	Entropy Favorable ?
1) NaCl(s) $\rightleftharpoons$ Na$^+$(aq) + Cl$^-$(aq)	3.86		43.3	
2) NH$_4$NO$_3$(s) $\rightleftharpoons$ NH$_4^+$(aq) + NO$_3^-$(aq)	28.07		108.6	
3) Zn(s) + Cu^{2+}(aq) $\rightleftharpoons$ Cu(s) + Zn^{2+}(aq)	–218.67		–21.0	
4) 2Cl$^-$(1M) + Br$_2$(ℓ) $\rightleftharpoons$ 2Br$^-$(aq) + Cl$_2$(g)	91.23		106.6	
5) CH$_3$COOH(aq) $\rightleftharpoons$ CH$_3$COO$^-$(aq) + H$^+$(aq)	–0.25		–92.0	

Critical Thinking Questions

1. a) What values of $\Delta H°$ indicate that a reaction is enthalpically favorable?

   b) What values of $\Delta S°$ indicate that a reaction is entropically favorable?

2. For each of the reactions in Table 1:

   a) According to the sign of $\Delta H°$, is the reaction favorable or unfavorable with respect to the enthalpy factor? Enter Y or N in the table.

   b) According to the sign of $\Delta S°$, is the reaction favorable or unfavorable with respect to the entropy factor? Enter Y or N in the table.

3. a) Circle all of the reactions in Table 1 for which both the enthalpy and the entropy factors are favorable.

    b) Put a box around all of the reactions in the Table 1 for which both the enthalpy and the entropy factors are unfavorable.

    c) What combinations of $\Delta H°$ and $\Delta S°$ characterize the reactions in Table 1 that are neither circled nor boxed?

END OF WARM-UP

Model 2: Equilibrium Constants and Various Thermodynamic Quantities at 25 °C for Several Chemical Reactions.

Reaction	$\Delta H°$ (kJ/mol$_{rxn}$)	$T\Delta S°$ (kJ/mol$_{rxn}$)	$\Delta H° - T\Delta S°$ (kJ/mol$_{rxn}$)	K
1) $NaCl(s) \rightleftharpoons Na^+(aq) + Cl^-(aq)$	3.86	12.9	−9.00	38
2) $NH_4NO_3(s) \rightleftharpoons NH_4^+(aq) + NO_3^-(aq)$	28.07	32.38	−4.31	5.7
3) $Zn(s) + Cu^{2+}(aq) \rightleftharpoons Cu(s) + Zn^{2+}(aq)$	−218.67	−6.3	−212.4	1.6×10^{37}
4) $2Cl^-(aq) + Br_2(\ell) \rightleftharpoons 2Br^-(aq) + Cl_2(g)$	91.23	31.78	59.45	3.9×10^{-11}
5) $CH_3COOH(aq) \rightleftharpoons CH_3COO^-(aq) + H^+(aq)$	−0.25	−27.43	27.18	1.7×10^{-5}

A reaction is called *favorable* if $K > 1$. A reaction is called *unfavorable* if $K < 1$.

Critical Thinking Questions

Answer CTQs 4 – 8 as a team.

4. a) Circle all of the reactions in Model 2 that are favorable.

    b) Put a box around all of the reactions in Model 2 that are unfavorable.

5. Circle below the factor in Model 2 that indicates whether $K > 1$ or $K < 1$:

$$\Delta H° \qquad T\Delta S° \qquad \Delta H° - T\Delta S°$$

Provide specific evidence from Model 2 that enables you to eliminate the other two factors as indicative of a favorable reaction.

6. When $K > 1$, is the factor identified in CTQ 5 positive or negative?

7. When $K < 1$, is the factor identified in CTQ 5 positive or negative?

8. Provide a qualitative description of the relationship between the value of the factor identified in CTQ 5 and the magnitude of K.

Model 3: The Gibbs Free Energy.

An equation that describes the quantitative relationship between the enthalpy, the entropy and the equilibrium constant was developed by J. Willard Gibbs, a professor of mathematical physics at Yale in the late nineteenth century. He defined a new quantity, **Gibbs free energy** (G), which describes the balance between the enthalpy and entropy factors for a chemical reaction.

$$G = H - TS.$$

For a chemical reaction which takes place at a constant temperature:

$$\Delta G = G(\text{products}) - G(\text{reactants}) = \Delta H - T\Delta S$$

If the reactants and products are in standard states at 25 °C:

$$\Delta G° = G°(\text{products}) - G°(\text{reactants}) = \Delta H° - T\Delta S°$$

Critical Thinking Questions

Answer CTQs 9 – 12 as a team.

9.   For a chemical reaction with $K > 1$, is $\Delta G°$ positive or negative?

10.   For a chemical reaction with $K < 1$, is $\Delta G°$ positive or negative?

11.   For what combination of values of $\Delta H°$ and $\Delta S°$:

   a)   will a chemical reaction always have $K < 1$?

   b)   will a chemical reaction always have $K > 1$?

12.   If $\Delta H° = T\Delta S°$, what is the value of $\Delta G°$? Predict the value of K in this case.

Exercises

1. For each of the following reactions, use the appropriate tables to determine ΔH° and ΔS° (at 25 °C). Then, indicate whether the equilibrium constant is expected to be greater than, less than, or equal to 1, or that it cannot be deduced.

    a) $H_2O(\ell) \rightleftharpoons H_2O(g)$

    b) $2\ C(graphite) + 2\ H_2(g) \rightleftharpoons C_2H_4(g)$

    c) $CuO(s) + H_2(g) \rightleftharpoons Cu(s) + H_2O(\ell)$

    d) $N_2(g) + 3\ H_2(g) \rightleftharpoons 2\ NH_3(g)$

    e) $\frac{1}{8}\ S_8(s) + O_2(g) \rightleftharpoons SO_2(g)$

2. a)   Use enthalpies of atom combination and entropies of atom combination to determine if any of the reactions below (i – iii) have an equilibrium constant greater than 1.

    b)   Find the reaction with the greatest equilibrium constant.

    c)   Find the reaction with the smallest equilibrium constant.

    i) $HF(aq) \rightleftharpoons H^+(aq) + F^-(aq)$

    ii) $N_2(g) + 3\ H_2(g) \rightleftharpoons 2\ NH_3(g)$

    iii) $PbCl_2(s) \rightleftharpoons Pb^{2+}(aq) + 2\ Cl^-(aq)$

3. Consider the following exothermic reaction at room temperature:

    $$C_3H_8(g) + 5\ O_2(g) \rightleftharpoons 3\ CO_2(g) + 4\ H_2O(g)$$

    Without referring to tables to calculate ΔH° and ΔS°, predict whether the equilibrium constant at room temperature for the following exothermic reaction will be greater than, less than, or equal to 1. Explain your reasoning.

4. Describe what determines the magnitude of the equilibrium constant for a given chemical reaction.

5. Calculate ΔH° and ΔS° for the reaction:

    $$3\ Fe(s) + 4\ H_2O(\ell) \rightleftharpoons Fe_3O_4(s) + 4\ H_2(g)$$

    Recalling that hydrogen gas is quite flammable, explain why it is a mistake to use water to put out a fire that contains white-hot iron metal.[1]

---

[1]J. N. Spencer, G. M. Bodner, and L. H. Rickard, *Chemistry: Structure & Dynamics*, Fifth Edition, John Wiley & Sons, 2011, Chapter 13, Problem 39.

ChemActivity 54

How Are ΔG° and K Related?

Model 1: The Mathematical Relationship Between ΔG° and K.

Table 1. Standard state free energy changes and equilibrium constants for several chemical reactions (25 °C).

Reaction	ΔG° (kJ/mol$_{rxn}$)	K
$NaCl(s) \rightleftharpoons Na^+(aq) + Cl^-(aq)$	−9.00	38
$NH_4NO_3(s) \rightleftharpoons NH_4^+(aq) + NO_3^-(aq)$	−4.31	5.7
$Zn(s) + Cu^{2+}(aq) \rightleftharpoons Cu(s) + Zn^{2+}(aq)$	−212.4	1.6×10^{37}
$2Cl^-(aq) + Br_2(\ell) \rightleftharpoons 2Br^-(aq) + Cl_2(g)$	59.45	3.9×10^{-11}
$CH_3COOH(aq) \rightleftharpoons CH_3COO^-(aq) + H^+(aq)$	27.18	1.8×10^{-5}

Critical Thinking Questions

1. Circle all of the reactions in Table 1 that are redox reactions.

2. When one of the redox reactions in Table 1 reaches equilibrium, the amount of products is much, much larger than the amount of reactants. So much larger, that in most cases the amount of reactants remaining is essentially zero.

   Indicate which reaction shows this behavior and describe how you reached your conclusion.

END OF WARM-UP

Information

The symbol ∝ means "proportional to."

Recall that when two quantities (for example, m and V) are proportional, that means that $m = c \times V$ where "c" is some proportionality constant.

In this case, we could also write: $m \propto V$. We also note that in this case $\dfrac{m}{V} = c$.

Critical Thinking Questions

3. a) As a team, decide which relationship below describes the mathematical relationship between $\Delta G°$ and K.

    i) Is $\Delta G° \propto K$?

        (If so, then $\dfrac{\Delta G°}{K}$ = same number, or proportionality constant, for all entries in Table 1.)

    ii) Is $\Delta G° \propto -K$?

    iii) Is $\Delta G° \propto -\sqrt{K}$?

    iv) Is $\Delta G° \propto -\ln K$?

    b) What is the value (with units) of the proportionality constant for the correct relationship in part a?

Information

The equation $\Delta G° = -RT\ln K$ is one of the most important equations in chemistry. It relates the change in standard state free energies for a chemical reaction to the equilibrium constant. Thus, if $\Delta G°$ is known, it is possible to calculate the value of an equilibrium constant for a reaction *without performing an experiment!*

Critical Thinking Questions

Answer CTQs 4 - 7 as a team.

4. Show that the value of the proportionality constant found in CTQ 3b is equal to RT, where the ideal gas constant $R = 8.3145 \dfrac{J}{K \, \text{mole}}$ and T = 25 °C.

5. Recall that $\Delta G°$ can be written as a function of $\Delta H°$ and $\Delta S°$. Assume that $\Delta H°$ and $\Delta S°$ are not temperature dependent. Starting with the two equations

$$\Delta G° = -RT\ln K \qquad \text{and} \qquad \Delta G° = \Delta H° - T\Delta S°$$

show how the relationship $\ln K = \dfrac{\Delta S°}{R} - \dfrac{1}{T}\dfrac{\Delta H°}{R}$ can be obtained.

6. We now use the relationship derived in CTQ 5 to analyze how a change in temperature affects the equilibrium constant for reactions for which $\Delta H° > 0$.

   a) If $\Delta H° > 0$, is $\ln K > \dfrac{\Delta S°}{R}$ or is $\ln K < \dfrac{\Delta S°}{R}$?

   b) If $\Delta H° > 0$ and T increases, what happens to the magnitude of the term that contains $\Delta H°$ - that is, does the magnitude increase or decrease?

   c) Given your answers to parts b and c, provide an explanation for why the equilibrium constant K (or $\ln K$) increases when the temperature increases for reactions with $\Delta H° > 0$.

7. Repeat the analysis from CTQ 6 for reactions that have $\Delta H° < 0$. Provide an explanation for why the equilibrium constant K (or $\ln K$) decreases when the temperature increases for reactions with $\Delta H° < 0$.

8. Individually, determine whether the equilibrium constant for the reaction $H_2O(\ell) \rightleftharpoons H_2O(g)$ will increase or decrease when the temperature is increased. Explain your analysis in terms of $\Delta H°$. When everyone is finished, compare answers and revise your explanation as needed.

Model 2: The Mathematical Relationship Between $E°$ and K.

Table 2.   Measured voltages and equilibrium constants for some galvanic cells using standard electrodes at 25 °C (all ions and soluble species at 1 M and all gases at 1 atm).

Cathode	Anode	$E°$ (V)	K
Cu/Cu^{2+}	Zn/Zn^{2+}	1.10	1.6×10^{37}
Cu/Cu^{2+}	SHE	0.34	3.1×10^{11}
Br_2/Br^-	Zn/Zn^{2+}	1.85	3.5×10^{62}
Zn/Zn^{2+}	K/K^+	2.16	1.1×10^{73}
Cl_2/Cl^-	Ag/Ag^+	0.56	8.6×10^{18}

Critical Thinking Questions

Answer CTQs 9 and 10 as a team.

9. Write balanced chemical equations for each of the galvanic cells in Table 2.

10. a) Which relationship below describes the mathematical relationship between $E°$ and K?

   i) Is $E° \propto K$?   ii) Is $E° \propto -K$?

   iii) Is $E° \propto \sqrt{K}$?   iv) Is $E° \propto \ln K$?

   b) What is the value (with units) of the proportionality constant for the correct relationship in part a?

Information

The equation $E° = \dfrac{RT}{nF} \ln K$ relates the standard state cell potential for a chemical reaction to the equilibrium constant. Thus, it is possible to determine the value of an equilibrium constant for a reaction by measurement of the cell potential.

Critical Thinking Questions

11. As a team, show that the proportionality constant found in CTQ 10b is equal to $\dfrac{RT}{nF}$, where the universal gas constant $R = 8.314\ \dfrac{J}{K\ mole}$, F is Faraday's constant, 96485 coulombs per mole (of electrons), and "n" is the number of moles of electrons transferred in the balanced chemical reaction. (Make sure to keep units with all of your numerical values.)

12. Individually, use the equations in the two Information sections above to derive an equation that relates $ΔG°$ and $E°$. When all teammates are done, compare your answers.

Exercises

1. Describe how $\Delta G°$ and K are related using a mathematical expression and also using your own words.

2. Calculate $\Delta G°$ for the reaction

    $$HF(aq) = H^+(aq) + F^-(aq)$$

    Use this datum to calculate K_a for hydrofluoric acid.

3. Consider the reaction $CO_2(g) + H_2(g) \rightleftharpoons CO(g) + H_2O(g)$. Calculate $\Delta H°$, $\Delta S°$, $\Delta G°$, and K for this reaction at 25 °C. Predict the effect on the equilibrium constant when the temperature of the system is increased.

4. Without referring to the tables of thermodynamic data, predict the signs of $\Delta H°$ and $\Delta S°$ for the reaction $NH_3(aq) \rightleftharpoons NH_3(g)$. Explain why the odor of $NH_3(g)$ that collects above an aqueous solution of ammonia becomes more intense as the temperature is increased.[1]

5. Explain why the equilibrium constant for the reaction:

    $$N_2(g) + 3\,H_2(g) \longrightarrow 2\,NH_3(g)$$

    decreases as the temperature increases.

6. Assume that a liquid boils at the temperature at which $\Delta G° = 0$ for the reaction liquid $\longrightarrow$ gas.

    a) Adding salt to water does not change $\Delta H°$ for the process

        $$H_2O(\ell) \longrightarrow H_2O(g)$$

        However, $\Delta S°$ for the process is decreased because the entropy of the liquid is increased without changing the entropy of the gas. Show how this can be used to explain the fact that adding salt to water raises its boiling point.

    b) Using the appropriate values of $\Delta H°$ and $\Delta S°$, estimate the boiling point of methanol (CH_3OH).

7. Consider the reaction:

    $$PbCl_2(s) \rightleftharpoons Pb^{2+}(aq) + 2\,Cl^-(aq) \qquad K = 1.6 \times 10^{-5}$$

    a) Calculate $\Delta G°$ for this reaction at 298 K.

    b) Predict the signs (positive or negative) of $\Delta S°$ and $\Delta H°$ for this reaction. Explain your reasoning.

---

[1] J. N. Spencer, G. M. Bodner, and L. H. Rickard, *Chemistry: Structure & Dynamics*, Fifth Edition, John Wiley & Sons, 2011, Chapter 13, Problem 31.

8. Calculate the equilibrium constant at 25 °C for each of the following reactions (from the standard cell potential).

   a) $Zn(s) + 2 H^+(aq) \rightleftharpoons H_2(g) + Zn^{2+}(aq)$

   b) $2 Na(s) + 2 H_2O(\ell) \rightleftharpoons H_2(g) + 2 Na^+(aq) + 2 OH^-(aq)$

   c) $Cu(s) + 2 H^+(aq) \rightleftharpoons H_2(g) + Cu^{2+}(aq)$

Problems

1. A voltaic cell has the following overall reaction:

$$I_3^-(aq) + 2 S_2O_3^{2-}(aq) \rightleftharpoons 3 I^-(aq) + S_4O_6^{2-}(aq)$$

   a) Determine the cell voltage, $E°$, when run under standard conditions.

   b) Which chemical species is the oxidizing agent?

   c) Determine the value of the equilibrium constant for this reaction at   25 °C.

2. Le Châtelier's Principle states that when a system at equilibrium is subjected to a change in concentration, temperature, volume, or pressure, the system responds in a way that partly counteracts that change.

   a) Explain how the change in equilibrium constant observed in Exercise 2 is consistent with Le Châtelier's Principle.

   b) Explain how the change in equilibrium constant observed in Exercise 4 is consistent with Le Châtelier's Principle.

How Do Reactant Concentrations Affect the Rate?

WARM-UP

Model 1: The Rate of a Reaction Varies with Time.

We have previously defined the **rate of reaction** as

$$\text{rate} = -\frac{\Delta(\text{reactant})}{\Delta\text{time}} \tag{1}$$

for any chemical reactant with a stoichiometric coefficient of 1 in the balanced chemical equation.

A better measure of the rate of a reaction is the *instantaneous rate of reaction,* generally written as

$$\text{rate} = -\frac{d(\text{reactant})}{dt} \tag{2}$$

The value of the instantaneous rate of reaction (for reactants with a stoichiometric coefficient of 1 in the balanced chemical equation) can be obtained by plotting the concentration of the reactant versus time, drawing a tangent to the curve, and determining the slope of the tangent line, as shown in Figure 1 on the next page.

Information

In equation (1), the use of the Δ symbol represents some measurable change – for example, Δtime represents some time interval. In equation (2), the Δ symbol is replaced with a "d"; this is a convention from calculus that indicates that the "change" has become infinitesimally small. That is, dt represents an infinitesimally small time interval. That is why equation (2) is described as the *instantaneous* rate of reaction – because the time interval is just an "instant" in duration.

It is not necessary to be familiar with calculus to complete this activity. But it is important to understand that the slope of a graph of concentration vs. time represents the rate of reaction – and that the rate is equal to the slope of the tangent line to the curve at each point.

Figure 1.   Nitrite concentration versus time for the reaction of ammonium ion with nitrite ion.

$$NH_4^+(aq) + NO_2^-(aq) \rightleftharpoons N_2(g) + 2\,H_2O(\ell)$$

$$(NO_2^-)_o = 0.00500\ M \qquad (NH_4^+)_o = 0.100\ M$$

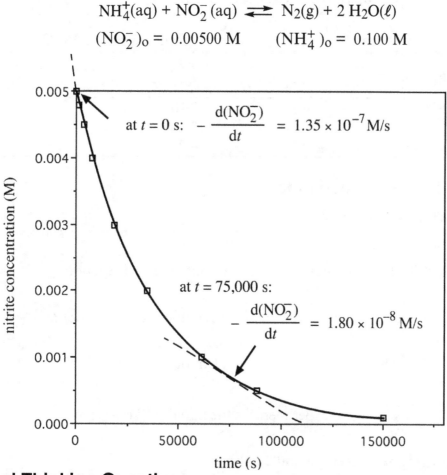

at $t = 0$ s: $-\dfrac{d(NO_2^-)}{dt} = 1.35 \times 10^{-7}\,M/s$

at $t = 75{,}000$ s:

$-\dfrac{d(NO_2^-)}{dt} = 1.80 \times 10^{-8}\,M/s$

nitrite concentration (M)

time (s)

Critical Thinking Questions

1. What is the rate of reaction at:

    a) $t = 0$ s?

    b) $t = 75{,}000$ s?

2. What is the rate of production of $H_2O(\ell)$ at $t = 75{,}000$ s?

3. As (NO_2^-) decreases, does the rate of reaction increase, decrease, or remain constant?

4. Estimate the value of the rate of reaction at $t = 175{,}000$ s. Explain your reasoning.

END OF WARM-UP

Model 2a: The Effect of Concentration on Reaction Rate.

$$Br_2(g) + 2\,NO(g) \rightleftarrows 2\,NOBr(g)$$

Table 1a.   Initial reaction rates for several experiments at 25 °C.

Experiment	$(Br_2)_o$ (M)	$(NO)_o$ (M)	Initial Rate of Reaction (M/min)
1	0.10	0.10	slow
2	0.10	0.20	faster
3	0.30	0.20	fastest

Critical Thinking Questions

Answer CTQs 5 – 7 as a team.

5. For the three experiments in Table 1a:

   a)   Which experiment has the fastest initial rate of reaction?

   b)   Which experiment has the slowest initial rate of reaction?

   c)   For which two experiments is the initial (Br_2) the same?

   d)   For which two experiments is the initial (NO) the same?

6. Comparing experiments **1** and **2** only:

   a)   What is the ratio of the initial concentrations of Br_2 expressed as a fraction, $(Br_2)_2/(Br_2)_1$?

   b)   What is the ratio of the initial concentrations of NO expressed as a fraction, $(NO)_2/(NO)_1$?

   c)   Based on the answers to parts a and b above, explain why it *is not* possible to determine whether or not the initial rate of reaction depends on the initial (Br_2) using only the data from experiments 1 and 2.

   d)   Based on the answers to parts a and b above, explain why it *is* possible to determine whether or not the initial rate of reaction depends on the initial (NO) using only the data from experiments 1 and 2.

7. Comparing experiments **2** and **3** only:

   a) What is the ratio of the initial concentrations of Br_2 expressed as a fraction, $(Br_2)_3/(Br_2)_2$?

   b) What is the ratio of the initial concentrations of NO expressed as a fraction, $(NO)_3/(NO)_2$?

   c) Based on the answers to parts a and b above, explain why it *is* possible to determine whether or not the initial rate of reaction depends on the initial (Br_2) using only the data from experiments 2 and 3.

   d) Based on the answers to parts a and b above, explain why it *is not* possible to determine whether or not the initial rate of reaction depends on the initial (NO) using only the data from experiments 2 and 3.

Model 2b: The Effect of Concentration on Reaction Rate.

Table 1b.   Initial reaction rates for several experiments at 25 °C.

Experiment	$(Br_2)_0$ (M)	$(NO)_0$ (M)	Initial Rate of Reaction (M/min)
1	0.10	0.10	1.30×10^{-3}
2	0.10	0.20	5.20×10^{-3}
3	0.30	0.20	1.56×10^{-2}

Critical Thinking Questions

Answer CTQs 8 and 9 as a team.

8. Consider the data for Experiments 1 and 2 in Table 1b.

   a) What is the ratio of the initial rates of reaction expressed as a fraction, initial $rate_2$/initial $rate_1$?

   b) Describe how your answer to part a (the ratio of initial rates) compares to your answer to CTQ 6b (the ratio of initial concentrations of NO).

c)   The results of comparing experiments 1 and 2 indicate that the initial rate of reaction is proportional to the initial (NO) raised to some power. Show that this is true, and determine the power.

9.   Consider the data for Experiments 2 and 3 in Table 1b.

a)   What is the ratio of the initial rates of reaction expressed as a fraction, initial rate$_3$/initial rate$_2$?

b)   Describe how your answer to part a (the ratio of initial rates) compares to your answer to CTQ 7b (the ratio of initial concentrations of Br_2).

c)   The results of comparing experiments 2 and 3 indicate that the initial rate of reaction is proportional to the initial (Br_2) raised to some power. Show that this is true, and determine the power.

Model 3: The Rate Law.

In general, the rate of reaction is proportional to the concentration of a reactant raised to some power (usually an integer such as 0, 1, 2, ...). For example, if

$$\text{rate} = k\,(R)^x .$$

Frequently, it is convenient to measure the rate of a reaction when it first begins and when the initial concentrations of the reactants are known. Then, the ratio of the initial rates is related to the ratios of the initial concentrations of reactants by

$$\frac{\text{initial rate}_2}{\text{initial rate}_1} = \frac{k(R)_2^x}{k(R)_1^x} = \left(\frac{(R)_2}{(R)_1}\right)^x$$

where   initial rate$_i$ = the initial rate of experiment i ; and
         $(R)_i$ = the initial concentration of the reactant R for experiment i .

The relationship between the rate of a reaction and the concentrations of reactants is known as the **rate law.** An example of a typical rate law is

$$\text{rate} = k\,(Br_2)^x\,(NO)^y \tag{1}$$

where k is the proportionality constant, known as the **rate constant**, and x and y are the numerical values of the exponents described previously. The exponents are often referred to as the **order** of the reaction with respect to the respective reactants. For example, if $y = 3$, we say that the reaction is third order with respect to NO. The rate constant and the orders can be determined by experiment only.

The rate constant, k, is characteristic of a particular reaction at a given temperature. That is, if the temperature changes, the rate constant also changes. Typically, the orders of the reaction are not affected by changes in temperature.

Critical Thinking Questions

Answer CTQs 10 - 12 as a team.

10. Based on your previous answers (see CTQs 8 and 9), determine the order of the reaction in the Model 2 with respect to:

   a) Br_2

   b)   NO

11. Based on your answers to CTQ 10, calculate the value of the rate constant k (with units) in the rate law for the reaction using

   a)   data from Experiment 1.

   b)   data from Experiment 2.

   c)   data from Experiment 3.

12. Compare the three answers from CTQ 11. Explain why the three relative values are reasonable.

Model 4: More Experimental Rate Laws

Table 2.   Experimental rate laws for several chemical reactions.

Reaction	Experimental Rate Law
i) $CH_3Br(aq) + OH^-(aq) \rightleftharpoons CH_3OH(aq) + Br^-(aq)$	rate = $k_i(CH_3Br)$
ii) $2NO(g) + O_2(g) \rightleftharpoons 2NO_2(g)$	rate = $k_{ii}(NO)^2(O_2)$
iii) $2HI(g) \rightleftharpoons H_2(g) + I_2(g)$	rate = $k_{iii}(HI)^2$
iv) $NH_4^+(aq) + NO_2^- \rightleftharpoons N_2(g) + 2H_2O(\ell)$	rate = $k_{iv}(NH_4^+)(NO_2^-)$
v) $BrO_3^-(aq) + 5Br^-(aq) + 6H^+(aq) \rightleftharpoons 3Br_2(aq) + H_2O$	rate = $k_v(BrO_3^-)(Br^-)(H^+)^2$
vi) $CH_3CHO(g) \rightleftharpoons CH_4(g) + CO(g)$	rate = $k_{vi}(CH_3CHO)^{3/2}$

Critical Thinking Questions

13.   Individually, indicate whether each statement is true or false based on the data presented in Table 2. If false, provide at least one example to support your conclusion. When all team members are done, compare your answers.

a)   The order of a reaction with respect to a reactant cannot be 0.

True   False

Example:

b)   The order of a reaction with respect to a reactant must be an integer.

True   False

Example:

c)   The order of a reaction with respect to a reactant is always equal to its stoichiometric coefficient in the balanced chemical reaction.

True   False

Example:

d)   The order of a reaction with respect to a reactant is never equal to its stoichiometric coefficient in the balanced chemical reaction.

True   False

Example:

14. As a team, discuss each statement and comment on the appropriateness of the following methods to determine the order of a reaction.

   i)   Examine the stoichiometric coefficients in the chemical equation. In this method, the order of a reaction with respect to a component is equal to the stoichiometric coefficient of that component in the chemical equation.

   ii) Perform experiments. In this method, the order of a reaction with respect to a component is determined by how the reaction rate changes when the concentration(s) is changed.

15. Discuss and answer as a team:

   a)   In reaction iii in Table 2, what will happen to the initial rate of reaction if the initial concentration of HI is doubled without a change in temperature?

   b)   In reaction i in Table 2, what will happen what will happen to the initial rate of reaction if the initial concentration of OH⁻ is doubled and the initial concentration of CH_3Br remains the same without a change in temperature?

Exercises

1. A student considers this balanced reaction: $A(g) + 2 B(g) \rightleftarrows 2 C(g) + D(g)$

   The student says: "I know that the rate law for this reaction is first order in A and second order in B by examining the given balanced chemical reaction." Is the student correct? Explain why or why not.

2. What is the initial rate of production of N_2 in experiment 3 of Table 1?

3. If the initial concentration of a reactant is doubled, and all other experimental conditions are kept the same, how does this change in initial concentration affect the initial rate of reaction if the reaction is:

   a)   first order in the reactant?

   b)   second order in the reactant?

   c)   zeroth order in the reactant?

4. These initial reaction rates were observed for the oxidation of Fe^{2+} by Ce^{4+}:

Experiment	Initial Concentration of Ce^{4+} (M)	Initial Concentration of Fe^{2+} (M)	Initial Rate of Reaction (M /sec)
1	1.5×10^{-5}	2.5×10^{-5}	3.79×10^{-7}
2	1.5×10^{-5}	5.0×10^{-5}	7.58×10^{-7}
3	3.0×10^{-5}	5.0×10^{-5}	1.52×10^{-6}

a) Determine the order of the reaction with respect to Ce^{4+} and with respect to Fe^{2+}.

b) Write the rate law for this reaction.

c) Calculate the rate constant, k, and give its units.

d) Predict the initial reaction rate for a solution in which:

   (Ce^{4+}) is 1.0×10^{-5} M and (Fe^{2+}) is 1.8×10^{-5} M.

5. Determine the rate law and evaluate the rate constant for the following reaction:

   $$NH_4^+(aq) + NO_2^-(aq) \rightleftharpoons N_2(g) + 2\,H_2O(\ell)$$

Experiment	Initial Concentration of NH_4^+ ((M)	Initial Concentration of NO_2^- (M)	Initial Rate of Reaction (M /sec)
1	0.100	0.0050	1.35×10^{-7}
2	0.100	0.010	2.70×10^{-7}
3	0.200	0.010	5.40×10^{-7}

6. The following reaction was studied experimentally at 25 °C.

   $$S_2O_8^{2-}(aq) + 2\,I^-(aq) \rightleftharpoons I_2(aq) + 2\,SO_4^{2-}(aq)$$

   The reaction was found to be first order in I^- and first order in $S_2O_8^{2-}$. A reaction was run with $(I^-)_o = 0.080$ M and $(S_2O_8^{2-})_o = 0.040$ M. The initial rate of formation of I_2 was found to be $1.25 \times 10^{-6} \frac{mole}{liter\ s}$. Provide an expression for the rate law for this reaction, and determine the initial rate of formation of I_2 when $(I^-)_o = 0.080$ M and $(S_2O_8^{2-})_o = 0.060$ M.

7. Indicate whether the following statement is true or false and explain your reasoning.

   The rate law for a reaction can be obtained by examining the chemical equation for the reaction.

Problems

1. One of the major irritants found in smog is formaldehyde, $CH_2O(g)$, formed by the reaction of ethene and ozone in the atmosphere:

$$C_2H_4(g) + 2 O_3(g) \rightleftharpoons 4 CH_2O(g) + O_2(g)$$

From the following initial rate data, deduce the rate law for this reaction. Clearly indicate how you arrived at your answer.

Experiment	Initial Concentration of O_3 (M)	Initial Concentration of C_2H_4 (M)	Initial Rate of Reaction (M /sec)
1	0.5×10^{-7}	1.0×10^{-8}	1.0×10^{-12}
2	1.5×10^{-7}	1.0×10^{-8}	3.0×10^{-12}
3	1.0×10^{-7}	2.0×10^{-8}	4.0×10^{-12}

2. For the following reaction:

$$2 HgCl_2(aq) + C_2O_4^{2-}(aq) \rightleftharpoons Hg_2Cl_2(s) + 2 Cl^-(aq) + 2 CO_2(g)$$

Experiment	Initial Concentration of $HgCl_2$ (M)	Initial Concentration of $C_2O_4^{2-}$ (M)	Initial Rate of Reaction (M /sec)
1	0.096	0.13	2.1×10^{-7}
2	0.096	0.21	5.5×10^{-7}
3	0.171	0.21	9.8×10^{-7}

a) Determine the order of the reaction with respect to $HgCl_2$ and with respect to $C_2O_4^{2-}$.

b) Write the rate law for this reaction.

c) Calculate the rate constant and give its units.

3. Consider the reaction

$$2 UO_2^+(aq) + 4 H^+(aq) \rightleftharpoons U^{4+}(aq) + UO_2^{2+}(aq) + 2 H_2O(\ell)$$

a) From the following initial rate data, deduce the rate law for this reaction. Clearly indicate how you arrived at your answer.

b) Find the rate constant k, including units, for the reaction above.

Experiment	Initial Concentration of UO_2^+ (M)	Initial Concentration of H^+ (M)	Initial Rate of Reaction (M /sec)
1	0.0012	0.22	4.12×10^{-5}
2	0.0012	0.35	6.55×10^{-5}
3	0.0030	0.35	4.10×10^{-4}

4. In a laboratory, a team of students collected the following data for the reaction at a constant temperature:

$$2 NO(g) + O_2(g) \rightleftarrows 2 NO_2(g)$$

Initial NO Concentration (mol/L)	Initial O_2 Concentration (mol/L)	Initial Rate of reaction (mol/Ls)
5.38×10^{-3}	5.38×10^{-3}	2.0×10^{-5}
8.07×10^{-3}	5.38×10^{-3}	4.6×10^{-5}
13.45×10^{-3}	5.38×10^{-3}	11.8×10^{-5}
8.07×10^{-3}	6.99×10^{-3}	5.7×10^{-5}
8.07×10^{-3}	9.59×10^{-3}	7.5×10^{-5}

Assuming that the reaction is either first, second, or zeroth order with respect to each reactant, determine the rate law for this reaction, including the best estimate of the rate constant at the experimental temperature.

How Does Reactant Concentration Change as a Reaction Proceeds?

WARM-UP

Model 1: Integrated First- and Second-Order Rate Laws.

The concentration of a reactant decreases as a reaction proceeds. In some cases, the decrease in concentration of a reactant is a (relatively) simple function of time. We will examine two such cases.

For a reaction that is *first order* in a single reactant, R, the rate law is

$$\text{rate} = -\frac{d(R)}{dt} = k\,(R)^1 \tag{1}$$

This equation can be rearranged and integrated to provide the explicit relationship between (R) and time. The resulting equation is

$$\ln(R) = \ln(R)_0 - kt \tag{2}$$

where $(R)_0$ is the (R) at time 0 (the initial concentration) and t is the time. Equation 2 is called the **integrated form** of a first order rate law.

For a reaction that is *second order* in a single reactant, the rate law is

$$\text{rate} = -\frac{d(R)}{dt} = k\,(R)^2 \tag{3}$$

and the corresponding relationship between concentration and time is

$$\frac{1}{(R)} = \frac{1}{(R)_0} + kt \tag{4}$$

Equation 4 is the integrated form of a second-order rate law. Note that equations 2 and 4 each contain four potential variables: (R), $(R)_0$, k, and t. Knowledge of any three of these variables permits the calculation of the fourth variable.

Critical Thinking Questions

1. Show that (R) decreases as t increases for each integrated rate law, equations 2 and 4.

END OF WARM-UP

2. A student obtains data for *a first-order reaction* at a given temperature, and then makes a graph of ln(R) (along the vertical axis) versus t (along the horizontal axis). They note that the resulting plot appears to correspond to a straight-line relationship with a negative slope. The student then determines the values for the slope and the intercept of the best-fit straight line.

    As a team, describe how the student could use the slope and/or the intercept of the best-fit straight line to determine:

    a)   the rate constant for the reaction at the given temperature.

    b)   the value of $(R)_0$.

    (Hint: Compare the first-order integrated rate law to the equation for a straight line: $y = mx + b$.)

3. A student obtains data for a *second-order reaction* at a given temperature, and then makes a graph of 1/(R) (along the vertical axis) versus t (along the horizontal axis). They note that the resulting plot appears to correspond to a straight-line relationship with a positive slope. The student then determines the values for the slope and the intercept of the best-fit straight line.

    As a team, describe how the student could use the slope and/or the intercept of the best-fit straight line to determine:

    a)   the rate constant for the reaction at the given temperature.

    b)   the value of $(R)_0$.

Model 2: A Simple Decomposition Reaction.

Chloroethane decomposes at 800 K:

$$CH_3CH_2Cl(g) \rightleftharpoons C_2H_4(g) + HCl(g)$$

The reaction is first-order with respect to chloroethane.

Figure 1.   The concentration of chloroethane versus time at 800 K.

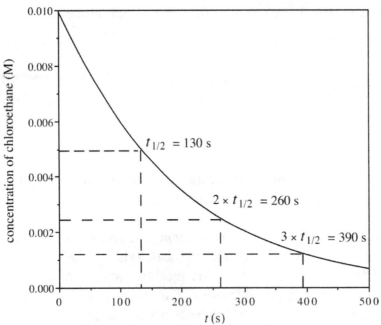

Critical Thinking Questions

Answer CTQs 4 and 5 as a team.

4.   a)   Complete this table showing (CH_3CH_2Cl) at various times:

	$t = 0$ s	$t = 130$ s	$t = 260$ s	$t= 390$ s
(CH_3CH_2Cl)				

   b)   What is the ratio of the concentration of chloroethane at t = 130 s to the concentration of chloroethane at $t = 0$ s?

   c)   What is the ratio of the concentration of chloroethane at $t = 260$ s to the concentration of chloroethane at $t = 130$ s?

   d)   What is the ratio of the concentration of chloroethane at $t = 390$ s to the concentration of chloroethane at $t = 260$ s?

   e)   Based on your answers to parts b – d above, what conclusion can be reached about what happens to (CH_3CH_2Cl) after 130 seconds elapses?

5. a) Use Figure 1 to estimate the concentration of chloroethane at $t = 50$ s.

    b) Estimate the concentration of chloroethane at $t = 180$ s.

    c) Are your answers to parts a and b consistent with your answers to CTQ 4? Explain your reasoning.

Model 3: The Half-Life of a Reaction.

The half-life of a reaction, $t_{1/2}$, is the time that it takes for the concentration of a single reactant to reach one-half of its original value.

Critical Thinking Questions

6. Based on your team's answers to CTQs 4 and 5, does $t_{1/2}$ for the first-order reaction in Model 2 depend on the concentration of chloroethane? Discuss as a team and provide a consensus explanation.

7. When $t = t_{1/2}$, what is the value of (R) in terms of $(R)_o$?

8. Recall that for a first-order reaction:

$$\ln (R) = \ln (R)_o - kt$$

Use your answer to CTQ 7 to show that $t_{1/2} = \dfrac{\ln 2}{k} = \dfrac{0.693}{k}$ for a first-order reaction.

9. Recall that for a second-order reaction:

$$\frac{1}{(R)} = \frac{1}{(R)_o} + kt$$

Use your answer to CTQ 7 to show that $t_{1/2} = \dfrac{1}{k(R)_o}$ for a second-order reaction.

Exercises

1. Consider the decomposition of N_2O_5 in the gas phase:

$$N_2O_5(g) \longrightarrow 2\ NO_2(g) + \frac{1}{2}\ O_2(g)$$

At room temperature, the following data were collected:

Time (s)	(N_2O_5) (M)
0	0.1000
50	0.0707
100	0.0500
200	0.0250
400	0.00625

a) Copy these data into an appropriate computer file or use your calculator to construct two plots to determine whether the data is consistent with a first-order rate law or a second-order rate law. Once you have determined which rate law applies, determine the value of the rate constant.

b) What is the concentration of $N_2O_5(g)$ at $t = 10$ s?

c) Based on the rate law obtained in part a, describe in words how the concentration of $N_2O_5(g)$ changes as the reaction proceeds.

2. The chemical equation for the decomposition of hypobromite ion, BrO^-, is:

$$3\ BrO^-\ (aq) \rightleftharpoons BrO_3^-(aq) + 2\ Br^-(aq)$$

The concentration of hypobromite was monitored as a function of time:

time (s)	BrO^- conc. (M)
0	0.750
20	0.408
40	0.280
60	0.213
80	0.172
100	0.144

Explain, in detail, how to determine if the reaction is first- or second-order.

3. The isomerization reaction

$$CH_3NC(g) \rightleftharpoons CH_3CN(g)$$

obeys the first-order rate law. At 500 K, the concentration of CH_3NC is 85% of its original value after 247 s.

a) What is the rate constant for this decomposition at 500 K?

b) At what time will the concentration of CH_3NC be 25% of its original value?

4. A student is studying the reaction A $\rightleftharpoons$ B. They notice that the amount of time it takes for the concentration of A to reach 50% of its original value is less than the amount of time it takes for the concentration of A to go from 50% to 25% of its original value. The student concludes that this implies that the reaction is NOT first order in A. Is he correct in this conclusion? Explain your reasoning.

5. The isomerization reaction

$$CH_3NC(g) \rightleftharpoons CH_3CN(g)$$

obeys a first-order rate law at 500 K. (See Exercise 3a for the rate constant at 500 K.)

a) What is the half-life of this decomposition?

b) How long will it take for the concentration of CH_3NC to reach 25% of its original value?

c) How well does this answer agree with your answer in Exercise 3?

6. Indicate whether the following statement is true or false and explain your reasoning:

    For the first-order reaction A ⟶ products, the rate of reaction remains constant as the reaction proceeds.

7. Which graph (I, II, III, IV, V) best describes the following reaction if the reaction is first order in N_2O_4?[1]

$$N_2O_4(g) \longrightarrow 2\,NO_2(g)$$

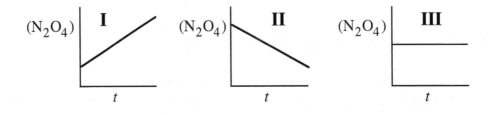

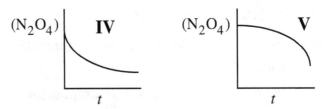

8. What fraction of reactant remains after 3 half-lives of a first-order reaction?

    i)   1/2
    ii)   1/3
    iii) 1/6
    iv)   1/8
    v)   1/12

9. One way to determine the age of a rock is to measure the extent to which the ^{87}Rb in the rock has decayed to ^{87}Sr (a first-order process).

$$^{87}Rb \rightleftharpoons\ ^{87}Sr + e^- \qquad k = 1.42 \times 10^{-11}\ \text{year}^{-1}$$

    What fraction of the original ^{87}Rb would still remain in the rock after 1.0×10^{10} years (10 billion years)?

10. The radioactive decay of ^{14}C is a first-order process with a half-life of 5730 years. If living wood gives 15.3 disintegrations per minute per gram, and a wooden bowl found in an archeological dig gives 6.29 disintegrations per minute per gram, how old is the bowl?

---

[1]J. N. Spencer, G. M. Bodner, and L. H. Rickard, *Chemistry: Structure & Dynamics*, Fifth Edition, John Wiley & Sons, 2011, Chapter 14, Problem 56.

Problems

1. The exothermic reaction $2 A_2B_2(g) \rightleftharpoons 2 A_2(g) + 2 B_2(g)$ has the experimental rate law: rate $= k (A_2B_2)^2$. Explain how the rate constant for this reaction can be determined from experimental measurements of (A_2B_2) at 10-minute intervals. (That is, from experimental determinations of (A_2B_2) when $t = 0$ min, $t = 10$ min, $t = 20$ min, etc.)

2. The rate law for a reaction is known to involve only the reactant A, and is suspected to be either a first-order reaction or a second-order reaction. Describe, using one or more sentences, how the order of the reaction can be determined by measuring how long it takes for the concentration of A to reach 50% and 25% of its original value.

3. The reaction $A \rightleftharpoons B + C$ is known to follow a first-order rate law. What feature of the plot of the concentration of A vs. time (shown below) clearly indicates that the reaction is indeed first-order, not second-order.

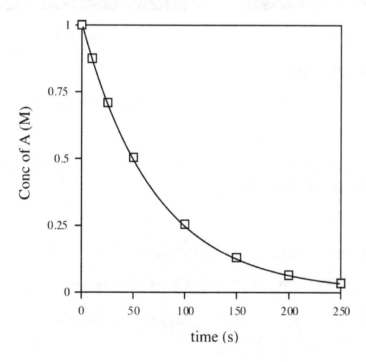

How Fast Will a Reaction Be?

WARM-UP

Model 1: Eight Balls in a Lopsided Double-box.

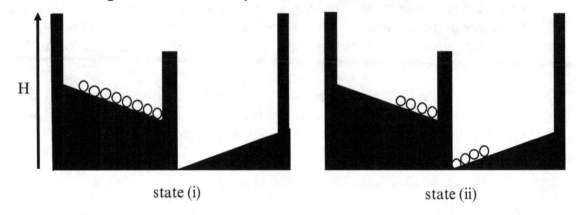

state (i)   state (ii)

Critical Thinking Questions

1. Explain why state (ii) is at a lower energy (enthalpy) than state (i).

2. Use the sign of ΔH for the process to explain why the transformation from state (i) to state (ii) is enthalpically favorable.

3. Explain why state (ii) is a higher entropy state than state (i).

4. Use the sign of ΔS for the process to explain why the transformation from state (i) to state (ii) is entropically favorable.

5. a) Use your answers to CTQs 2 and 4 to determine if ΔG is positive or negative for the process: state (i) $\longrightarrow$ state (ii). Explain your analysis.

   b) Use your answer to part a to explain why the transformation from state (i) to state (ii) is thermodynamically favorable.

6. Based on the analysis thus far, the transformation state (i) ⟶ state (ii) is expected to be a naturally occurring process. However, if we place eight balls in the left-side box, as in state (i), and we wait several hours, the transformation to state (ii) does not take place. Why? What needs to be done in order for the transformation state (i) ⟶ state (ii) to take place?

Information: A Theory of Reaction Rates.

The $\Delta G°$ for the reaction of hydrogen and oxygen at 25 °C is very negative:

$$H_2(g) + \frac{1}{2} O_2(g) = H_2O(\ell) \qquad \Delta G° = -237 \text{ kJ/mol}_{rxn} \qquad (1)$$

Thermodynamically, this reaction is expected to be a naturally occurring process, just like the process in Model 1. However, hydrogen gas and oxygen gas can be mixed at room temperature and no water is detected after years. However, if additional energy is provided (e.g., a spark) the reaction does occur (explosively).

Many other chemical reactions are similar to reaction 1 in the sense that they are thermodynamically favorable, but the rate of reaction is exceptionally slow. A simple theory has been proposed to explain why there is a large variation in the observed rates of chemical reactions. This theory of reaction rates provides a basis for understanding why some chemical reactions are fast and others are slow:

1) Molecules must collide in order for a reaction to occur.

2) Not all collisions between molecules are effective in producing a reaction.

    a)   There is a minimum energy of collision required for a reaction to occur.

    b)   Colliding molecules must be oriented properly for the reaction to proceed.

Point 2 above implies that the rate at which molecules collide (the **collision frequency**) is generally greater than the rate of reaction involving those molecules. An explanation for 2a and 2b is that is that in order for the reaction to proceed, particular bonds must be broken – and frequently other bonds must be formed.

Critical Thinking Questions

7. For each item below, indicate whether it would be expected to *increase* or *decrease* the rate of a reaction occurring in the gas phase.

    a)   The volume is increased resulting in fewer collisions between molecules occur.

    b)   The temperature is increased resulting in the collisions between molecules becoming more energetic on average.

END OF WARM-UP

Model 2: Reaction Coordinate Diagrams.

The energetics of a reaction are often depicted by a **reaction coordinate diagram**, a graph showing how the energy (enthalpy) of the molecules changes as the reaction proceeds. A reaction coordinate diagram is shown below for the reaction:

$$ONBr(g) + ONBr(g) \rightleftharpoons 2\,NO(g) + Br_2(g). \tag{2}$$

Figure 1.   A Reaction Coordinate Diagram.

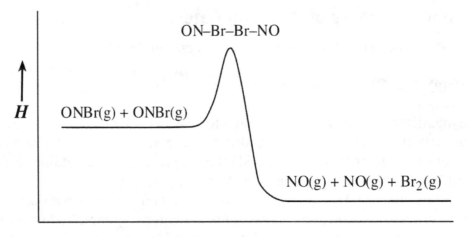

The reaction coordinate is a measure of the progress of a reaction. It represents all the changes that must occur in the course of the reaction, including the bending, breaking, and making of bonds.

Critical Thinking Questions

Answer CTQs 8 – 12 as a team.

8. Assume that reaction 2 occurs by having two ONBr molecules collide.

    a) What bond in each ONBr molecule must break in order for the reaction to proceed to form the indicated products?

    b) What bond(s) must be formed to create the indicated products?

9. The bond between the N atom and Br atom must be weakened or broken for reaction 2 to proceed upon collision of two ONBr molecules. Note that a violent collision between two ONBr molecules is more likely to weaken or break the bonds than a gentle collision. Based on this idea, explain why there will be more collisions that will be effective in weakening or breaking the N-Br bond at high temperature compared to low temperature.

10. If two ONBr molecules collide as diagrammed below, is the collision likely to lead to two NO molecules and one Br_2 molecule? Explain your reasoning.

$$BrNO \longrightarrow \longleftarrow ONBr$$

11. Propose a more effective collision (one that is more likely to lead to two NO molecules and one Br_2 molecule) between two ONBr molecules.

12. Provide two major reasons that all collisions between molecules might not be effective in causing a reaction.

Complete all parts of this question individually. When all team members are done, compare your answers and make any changes needed.

13. a) Circle the reactants on Figure 1 and put a box around the products.

   b) Draw a vertical line on Figure 1 that indicates the magnitude of ΔH for the reaction.

   c) Is the reaction in Figure 1 an exothermic or endothermic reaction? Explain your reasoning by including an indication of whether ΔH is positive or negative.

Information

The state of the reacting system in which the molecules are colliding, and in which bonds are being broken (and new bonds are being formed), is known as the **transition state**, or the **activated complex**. The minimum energy needed to create this transition state is the **activation energy**, E_a.

Critical Thinking Questions

Answer CTQs 14 – 16 individually. When all team members are finished, compare answers and reach consensus before moving to CTQ 17.

14. Circle the activated complex (or transition state) in Figure 1.

15. Indicate on Figure 1 the magnitude of E_a for the forward reaction

$$ONBr(g) + ONBr(g) \longrightarrow 2\,NO(g) + Br_2(g) \,.$$

16. Indicate on Figure 1 the magnitude of E_a for the reverse reaction

$$2\,NO(g) + Br_2(g) \longrightarrow 2\,ONBr(g) \,.$$

17. After discussing as a team, write the mathematical relationship between E_a(forward), E_a(reverse), and ΔH.

Exercises

1. Describe the factors that determine how fast a reaction will be.

2. Construct a reaction coordinate diagram (as in Figure 1) for a typical endothermic reaction. Which has the larger activation energy, the forward reaction or the reverse reaction?

3. The reaction $O_3(g) + NO(g) \longrightarrow O_2(g) + NO_2(g)$ has $E_a = 10.7$ kJ/mole and $\Delta H = -199.8$ kJ/mole. What is the activation energy for the following reaction?

$$O_2(g) + NO_2(g) \longrightarrow O_3(g) + NO(g)$$

4. The reaction $2\,N_2O(g) \rightleftharpoons 2\,N_2(g) + O_2(g)$ is exothermic.

   a) Construct a reaction coordinate diagram (with enthalpy, H, on the y-axis and the reaction coordinate on the x-axis) for this reaction.

   b) Clearly indicate the magnitude of the activation energy for both the forward reaction and the reverse reaction with lines on the diagram.

   c) Give two reasons why not all collisions between N_2O molecules will necessarily be effective in causing this reaction to occur.

Problems

1. The reaction $H_2O + H^+ \rightleftharpoons H_3O^+$ has a very small activation energy (forward). Draw the Lewis structure for H_2O and give two reasons why the activation energy is small.

2. Why is the forward activation energy for the following reaction so large?

$$N_2(g) + 3\,H_2(g) \rightleftharpoons 2\,NH_3(g)$$

What is a Reaction Mechanism?

WARM-UP

Model 1: Mechanistic Steps

Chemical reactions occur on the molecular level by a sequence of one or more **steps** known as a **mechanism**. Typically, a single-headed arrow ($\longrightarrow$) is used to indicate the transformation that occurs in a step. Each step describes a process happening on a molecular level – for example, two molecules colliding and being transformed into two different species, one molecule falling apart into two pieces, or two species coming together and combining to form one large species.

Table 1 contains individual steps from several different mechanisms describing different chemical reactions.

Table 1.   Individual steps from several different mechanisms.

Label	Step	Rate of Step
A	$Br_2(g) \longrightarrow Br(g) + Br(g)$	rate = k_A (Br_2)
B	$CH_3Cl(aq) + I^-(aq) \longrightarrow CH_3I(aq) + Cl^-(aq)$	rate = k_B (CH_3Cl) (I^-)
C	$(CH_3)_3CBr(aq) \longrightarrow (CH_3)_3C^+(aq) + Br^-(aq)$	rate = k_C (($CH_3)_3CBr$)
D	$CH_3I(aq) + Cl^-(aq) \longrightarrow CH_3Cl(aq) + I^-(aq)$	rate = k_D (CH_3I) (Cl^-)
E	$NO(g) + NO(g) \longrightarrow N_2O_2(g)$	rate = k_E $(NO)^2$

Critical Thinking Questions

1. Which steps in Table 1 involve:

    a)   two species colliding to produce two new species?

    b)   one species falling apart into two pieces?

    c)   two species coming together to form one larger species?

2. Two of the steps in Table 1 come from the same mechanism. They represent a forward process and the reverse of that process. Which two steps are these?

3. Based on the data in Table 1, write a sentence describing how to determine the rate of a step from the reactants in that step.

Information

Every step in a mechanism is either a **unimolecular step** or a **bimolecular step.**

A **unimolecular step** involves one species (molecule or ion) undergoing a decomposition: a bond breaks and the species becomes two new fragments. The rate of a unimolecular step depends on the concentration of the species that decomposes.

A **bimolecular step** involves two colliding species. As the two species collide, one or more bonds are broken and new bonds may or may not form. The rate of a bimolecular step depends on the rate of collisions between the two species (remember that not all collisions lead to a reaction). The rate of collisions between the two molecules depends on the product of the concentrations of the two species.

The "k" for a bimolecular or unimolecular step is called a **specific rate constant**; the value of a specific rate constant depends on the given step and the temperature.

Critical Thinking Questions

4.   Which steps in Table 1 are:

   a)   unimolecular steps?

   b)   bimolecular steps?

5.   Consider this mechanistic step from a reaction describing the decomposition of ozone: $O_3(g) \longrightarrow O_2(g) + O(g)$

   a)   Is this a unimolecular step or a bimolecular step?

   b)   Using k_1 as the specific rate constant, provide the expression for the rate of this step.

   rate =

END OF WARM-UP

Information

In general, it is not possible to directly observe the sequence of steps that occur as a reaction proceeds. For this reason, there could be several possible sequences of steps (or mechanisms) that would result in the overall transformation described by a chemical reaction.

Model 2: Three proposed mechanisms for a chemical reaction.

Three scientists have each proposed a mechanism (labeled A, B, C) for the gas phase chemical reaction of NO_2 and CO.

Chemical Equation: $NO_2(g) + CO(g) \longrightarrow NO(g) + CO_2(g)$

Proposed Mechanism A:

Step Number	Step
A1	$NO_2(g) + CO(g) \longrightarrow NO(g) + CO_2(g)$
Overall Reaction:	$NO_2(g) + CO(g) \longrightarrow NO(g) + CO_2(g)$

Proposed Mechanism B:

Step Number	Step
B1	$NO_2(g) + NO_2(g) \longrightarrow NO(g) + NO_3(g)$
B2	$NO_3(g) + CO(g) \longrightarrow NO_2(g) + CO_2(g)$
Overall Reaction:	

Proposed Mechanism C:

Step Number	Step
C1	$NO_2(g) + NO_2(g) \longrightarrow NO(g) + NO_3(g)$
C2	$NO_2(g) + CO(g) \longrightarrow NO(g) + CO_2(g)$
Overall Reaction:	

Critical Thinking Questions

Complete CTQs 6 – 8 as a team.

6. A student describes Mechanism A as "One NO_2 molecule collides with one CO molecule. As a result, one NO molecule and one CO_2 molecule are produced." Construct a similar consensus description in words for Mechanism B.

7. It is straightforward to determine the overall reaction described by Mechanism A because there is only one step. The transformation described in that step is equal to the overall reaction produced by the mechanism, as shown below Mechanism A. We now determine the overall reactions described by Mechanisms B and C.

    a)   For Mechanism B, we can add up the reactants in the two steps and the products in the two steps to obtain:

    $$NO_2(g) + NO_2(g) + NO_3(g) + CO(g) \longrightarrow NO(g) + NO_3(g) + NO_2(g) + CO_2(g)$$

    i)   Identify the individual molecules that appear as both reactants and products and cross them off in the equation above to generate the overall reaction predicted by this mechanism.

    ii)   Copy the overall reaction in the space below Mechanism B.

b)   Repeat the process used in part a to generate the overall reaction predicted by Mechanism C. Copy that overall reaction into the appropriate place below Mechanism C.

8. Examine the overall reactions predicted by Mechanisms B and C. Only one of them is consistent with the chemical equation provided in Model 2.

a)   Which mechanism describes an overall reaction that is *not* the same as the chemical equation?

b)   Explain why the mechanism indicated in part a cannot be a valid mechanism for the reaction described in Model 2.

Information

As is often true in science, in general it is not possible to *prove* that a particular mechanism is the correct one. However, it is possible to determine whether a proposed mechanism is (or is not) *possibly correct* for a particular reaction. The potential validity of a proposed mechanism is determined from two important features:

i)   the sum of the elementary steps must give the overall chemical transformation described in the chemical equation.

ii)   the rate law predicted by the proposed mechanism must agree with the experimentally determined rate law.

In Model 2, the sum of elementary steps in Mechanism C does not give the overall chemical transformation for the chemical equation, so Mechanism C is *not* a valid mechanism for that reaction.

Model 3: The experimentally determined rate law for a chemical reaction.

Chemical Equation: $NO_2(g) + CO(g) \longrightarrow NO(g) + CO_2(g)$

Experimentally determined rate law: rate $= k(NO_2)^2$

Critical Thinking Questions

Answer CTQs 9 and 10 as a team.

9. Based on the experimentally determined rate law, determine the order of the reaction with respect to:

    a) NO_2

    b)   CO

10. a)   What is the rate of Step A1?

     b)   Mechanism A in Model 2 consists of a single step – Step A1. Therefore, the rate of the overall transformation (the rate of reaction) predicted by Mechanism A is equal to the rate of this step.

         What is the rate law predicted by Mechanism A?

     c)   Explain why Mechanism A is not a possible valid mechanism for the chemical reaction described in Model 2.

Model 4: The rate-limiting step of a mechanism.

Thus far we have shown that proposed Mechanisms A and C are not valid as possible mechanisms for the chemical reaction described in Model 2. But what about Mechanism B? We know that Mechanism B satisfies requirement i) for a possibly valid mechanism, but what about requirement ii) – that the proposed mechanism predicts the experimentally determined rate law. It is not obvious what rate law is predicted by Mechanism B as it was for Mechanism A, as there is more than one step in the mechanism.

The rate law for a proposed mechanism is based on a mathematical analysis of the sequence of steps in the mechanism. This analysis can become very complicated for multi-step mechanisms. However, in many cases the analysis can be substantially simplified because one of the steps in the mechanism is assumed to be very much slower than all of the other steps. This slowest step in a proposed mechanism is called the **rate-limiting step** (also called the **rate-determining step**).

The overall rate at which reactants can be transformed into products can be no faster than the slowest step in the reaction – the **rate-limiting step**. We assume that the overall rate of a reaction predicted by a proposed mechanism with more than one step is equal to the rate of the rate-limiting step.

Critical Thinking Questions

11. Provide the rate for each step in Mechanism B.

    a) Step B1:

    b) Step B2:

12. What is the predicted rate law from Mechanism B if we assume that:

    a) Step B1 is the rate-limiting step?

    b) Step B2 is the rate-limiting step?

13. A student says: "I think that Mechanism B is a possible mechanism for the overall reaction in Model 2 if Step B1 is the rate determining step." As a team, explain why this student is correct by referring to both of the requirements for a possible mechanism to be valid.

Information: Intermediate Species

Mechanism B includes a chemical species, NO_3, that does not appear in the overall reaction in Model 2. It is neither a reactant nor a product; rather, NO_3 is a chemical species that is both produced and consumed as the reaction takes place according to this mechanism. This type of species is called an **intermediate species**.

Normally, it is quite difficult to measure the concentration of an intermediate species. For this reason, intermediate species are not normally included in experimentally determined rate laws. When they appear in predicted rate laws from mechanisms, some additional analysis is needed to compare the predicted rate law to the experimentally determined rate law.

Model 5: A Proposed Mechanism for a Chemical Reaction.

Chemical Equation: $2\,NO(g) + O_2(g) \longrightarrow 2\,NO_2(g)$

Proposed Mechanism

Step Number	Step	Rate of Step
1	$NO\,(g) + NO(g) \longrightarrow N_2O_2$	rate =
2	$N_2O_2(g) + O_2(g) \longrightarrow NO_2(g) + NO_2(g)$	rate =

Overall Reaction:

Critical Thinking Questions

14. Fill in the proposed mechanism in Model 5 by indicating the rate for each step and the overall reaction.

15. What is the intermediate species in the proposed mechanism in Model 5?

16. If the experimental rate law for the reaction is rate $= k(NO)^2(O_2)$, is the proposed mechanism a valid one if Step 1 is rate-limiting? Explain your reasoning clearly.

Model 5A: Reactions Steps are Reversible

Recall that in Model 1, Steps B and D represent a forward process and the reverse of that process. In general, *every* step in a mechanism is reversible. Often, however, the reverse reaction is so slow as to be negligible and so it is not explicitly included in the mechanism.

The mechanisms that we have been considering so far have not included the reverse of each forward step. However, the reversibility of a step is frequently considered as an important part of a mechanism. Below is a proposed mechanism for the reaction in Model 3 that includes the reversibility of each step.

Chemical Equation: $2\,NO(g) + O_2(g) \rightleftharpoons 2\,NO_2(g)$

Experimental rate law: rate $= k_{exp}\,(NO)^2\,(O_2)$

Proposed Mechanism:

Step Number	Step	Rate of Forward Step	Relative Rate
1	$NO(g) + NO(g) \rightleftharpoons N_2O_2(g)$	$k_1\,(NO)^2$	fast equilibrium
2	$N_2O_2(g) + O_2(g) \rightleftharpoons 2\,NO_2(g)$	$k_2\,(N_2O_2)\,(O_2)$	slow forward

Overall Reaction: $NO(g) + NO(g) + O_2(g) \rightleftharpoons 2\,NO_2(g)$

In this mechanism, note that Step 1 is described as reaching equilibrium fast and involves both the intermediate (N_2O_2) and a reactant (NO). In this case, we assume that Step 1 remains in an equilibrium state as Step 2 slowly consumes O_2 as the reaction proceeds forward.

Given that Step 1 is considered to be at equilibrium, we can write an equilibrium expression for that step in the mechanism:

$$K_{step1} = \frac{(N_2O_2)}{(NO)_2} \tag{1}$$

Critical Thinking Questions

Complete CTQs 17 and 18 as a team.

17. For the mechanism in Model 5A:

     a)   what is the rate-limiting step?

     b)   what is the predicted rate law, given your answer to part a?

18. a)   Rearrange the expression for the Step 1 equilibrium constant to solve for the concentration of the intermediate species, N_2O_2.

     b)   Substitute the result from part a into the predicted rate law from CTQ 17b to produce a new rate law expression that does not include N_2O_2.

     c)   A student compares the answer to part b to the experimental rate law for the reaction and says: "The proposed mechanism is a valid mechanism for the reaction and it must be the case that $k_{exp} = k_2K$."

          Produce a consensus explanation for why the student is correct that addresses both criteria for a valid mechanism and clearly shows that the stated relationship is required.

19. Consider this proposed mechanism for the reaction in Model 2 in which both steps are considered to be reversible.

     Proposed Mechanism BB:

Step Number	Step	Relative Rate
BB1	$NO_2(g) + NO_2(g) \rightleftharpoons NO(g) + NO_3(g)$	fast equilibrium
BB2	$NO_3(g) + CO(g) \rightleftharpoons NO_2(g) + CO_2(g)$	slow forward

     Individually, determine whether this proposed mechanism is possibly a valid mechanism for the reaction in Model 2 and clearly explain your reasoning. When all team members are done, compare answers and reach a consensus decision.

Model 6: A Proposed Mechanism for the Chemical Reaction
$(CH_3)_3CBr(aq) + OH^-(aq) \rightleftharpoons (CH_3)_3COH(aq) + Br^-(aq)$

It is found experimentally that when the initial concentration of $(CH_3)_3CBr$ is doubled (keeping the initial hydroxide concentration constant) the rate of the reaction doubles. Furthermore, it is found that when the initial concentration of hydroxide is doubled (keeping the initial concentration of $(CH_3)_3CBr$ constant) the rate of the reaction remains the same.

Experimental rate law: rate $= k_{exp} ((CH_3)_3CBr) (OH^-)^0 = k_{exp} ((CH_3)_3CBr)$

Proposed Mechanism:

Step Number	Step	Relative Rate
C1	$(CH_3)_3CBr(aq) \rightleftharpoons (CH_3)_3C^+(aq) + Br^-(aq))$	slow forward
C2	$(CH_3)_3C^+(aq) + H_2O \rightleftharpoons (CH_3)_3COH_2^+(aq)$	fast equilibrium
C3	$(CH_3)_3COH_2^+(aq) + OH^-(aq) \rightleftharpoons (CH_3)_3COH(aq) + H_2O$	fast equilibrium

Critical Thinking Questions

Answer CTQs 20 – 22 individually. When all team members have completed, reach consensus on the answers and make any necessary changes.

20. Based on the information in Model 1, how do we know that the rate law for the overall reaction does not depend on (OH^-)?

21. A student says: "In the overall reaction given in Model 6, two species react. Therefore, the rate law for the reaction should be:

$$\text{rate} = k_{experimental} ((CH_3)_3CBr) (OH^-) \text{ "}$$

Explain why this student is *not correct*.

22. Is the proposed mechanism a possibly valid mechanism for the reaction described in Model 6? Explain your reasoning by referring to both criteria for a possibly valid mechanism.

Model 7: Thermodynamic and Kinetic Control.

There are two major reasons that a chemical reaction might produce very little product even after a very long time.

Thermodynamic control. Many chemical reactions are thermodynamically unfavorable ($K < 1$). To reach equilibrium, these reactions occur only to a very limited extent (as determined from $\Delta G°$ and the equilibrium constant).

These reactions are said to be under **thermodynamic control**.

$$CH_3COOH(aq) \rightleftharpoons CH_3COO^-(aq) + H^+(aq) \qquad K_a = 1.8 \times 10^{-5}$$

$$2\ Cl^-(1M) + Br_2(\ell) \rightleftharpoons 2\ Br^-(1M) + Cl_2(g) \qquad K = 3.9 \times 10^{-11}$$

Kinetic control. Some chemical reactions are thermodynamically favorable but no reaction is apparent over long time periods.

$$H_2(g) + \frac{1}{2}\ O_2(g) \rightleftharpoons H_2O(\ell) \qquad\qquad K = 10^{41}$$

$$C(diamond) \rightleftharpoons C(graphite) \qquad\qquad K = 3.2$$

$$C(diamond) + O_2(g) \rightleftharpoons CO_2(g) \qquad\qquad K = 10^{69}$$

These reactions are said to be under **kinetic control**.

Critical Thinking Questions

Answer CTQs 23 – 25 as a team.

23. For a certain chemical reaction $\Delta G° = 200$ kJ/mol. When the reactants are mixed, no chemical reaction is apparent. Is this reaction under thermodynamic or kinetic control?

24. For a certain chemical reaction $\Delta G° = -200$ kJ/mol. When the reactants are mixed, no chemical reaction is apparent. Is this reaction under thermodynamic or kinetic control?

25. What *one* feature of a reaction coordinate diagram is indicative of kinetic control of a reaction? Explain your reasoning.

    i) $\Delta H° < 0$

    ii) $\Delta H° > 0$

    iii) Activation energy is large

    iv) Activation energy is small

Exercises

1. Indicate whether each of the following steps is unimolecular or bimolecular and then give the rate expression for the step. An example is shown involving the decomposition of ozone.

   Example: $O_3(g) \longrightarrow O_2(g) + O(g)$ unimolecular   rate = k' (O_3)

   a) $ONBr(g) + ONBr(g) \longrightarrow NO(g) + NO(g) + Br_2(g)$

   b) $N_2O_2(g) \longrightarrow NO(g) + NO(g)$

   c) $NO(g) + NO(g) \longrightarrow N_2(g) + O_2(g)$

   d) $I(g) + H_2(g) \longrightarrow HI(g) + H(g)$

2. The following reaction is first order with respect to both NO and F_2:[1]

   $$2\,NO_2(g) + F_2(g) \rightleftharpoons 2\,NO_2F(g)$$

   experimental rate law: rate = k_{exp} (NO_2) (F_2)

   a)   Which of the mechanisms below is consistent with the experimental rate law?

   i) $NO_2 + F_2 \rightleftharpoons NO_2F + F$ fast

        $NO_2 + F \rightleftharpoons NO_2F$ slow

   ii) $NO_2 + F_2 \rightleftharpoons NO_2F + F$ slow

        $NO_2 + F \rightleftharpoons NO_2F$ fast

   iii) $F_2 \rightleftharpoons F + F$ slow

        $2\,NO_2 + 2\,F \rightleftharpoons 2\,NO_2F$ fast

   b)   Add the molecular species for the two steps in each of the mechanisms. How is this sum related to the stoichiometry of the overall reaction?

3. The equilibrium constant for the following reaction is quite large. Is it possible to predict the extent of reaction in a reasonable time period (a few minutes or hours)?

   $$Zn(s) + 2\,H^+(aq) \rightleftharpoons Zn^{2+}(aq) + H_2(g)$$

4. The equilibrium constant for the following reaction is quite small. Is it possible to predict the extent of reaction in a reasonable time period (a few minutes or hours)?

   $$Cu(s) + 2\,H^+(aq) \rightleftharpoons Cu^{2+}(aq) + H_2(g)$$

---

[1]J. N. Spencer, G. M. Bodner, and L. H. Rickard, *Chemistry: Structure & Dynamics*, Fifth Edition, John Wiley & Sons, 2011, Chapter 14, Problem 32.

5. The diamond to graphite reaction is thermodynamically favorable but does not appear to happen during the lifetime of an engagement ring. Use the appropriate tables to determine if this reaction is endothermic or exothermic. Construct a reaction coordinate diagram that shows the endothermic or exothermic nature of the reaction and illustrates why this reaction is under kinetic control.

6. Each diagram below (I, II, III, IV) describes a possible reaction:

$$A_2(g) + B_2(g) \rightleftharpoons 2\ AB(g)$$

Assuming that you begin with equal amounts of $A_2(g)$ and $B_2(g)$, but no AB, and assuming that $\Delta S°$ is the same for all of the possible reactions, for which of these diagrams would:

    a)   the reaction proceed fastest in the forward direction?
    b)   the amount of AB(g) at equilibrium be the greatest?
    c)   the equilibrium constant be the smallest?
    d)   equilibrium be reached in the shortest amount of time?

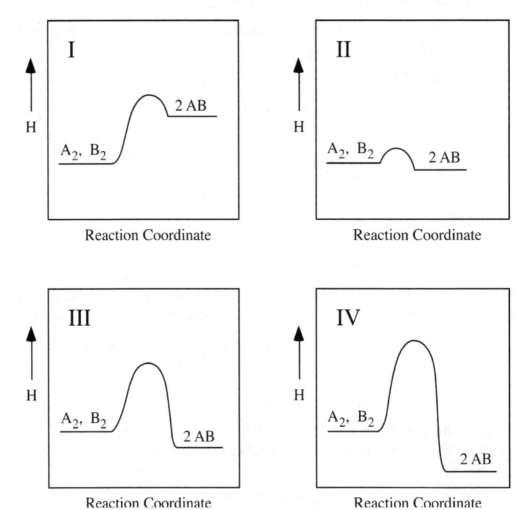

7. Consider the following reaction:

$$2 NO_2(g) + O_3(g) \rightleftharpoons N_2O_5(g) + O_2(g)$$

Several experiments were performed at 298 K beginning with only NO_2 and O_3. The results are shown in the table below:

$(NO_2)_o$ (mol/L)	$(O_3)_o$ (mol/L)	Initial rate of reaction, (mol/L sec)
0.50	1.00	2.5×10^4
2.00	1.00	1.0×10^5
2.00	2.00	2.0×10^5

a) Determine the rate law for this reaction, and the value of the rate constant at 298 K.

b) Determine $\Delta G°$ at 298 K for this reaction.

c) Construct the best reaction coordinate diagram that you can for this reaction. (Remember that a reaction coordinate diagram plots enthalpy, H, along the y-axis, and the reaction coordinate along the x-axis.) Use one or two sentences to explain how your diagram accounts for both

   i) the fast rate of reaction as shown in the table, and

   ii) the exothermic or endothermic nature of this reaction.

d) Determine whether or not the proposed mechanism below is consistent with the rate law obtained in part a.

   Proposed Mechanism:

   $NO_2 + O_3 \longrightarrow NO_3 + O_2$ slow

   $NO_3 + O_2 \longrightarrow NO_2 + O_3$ fast

   $NO_3 + NO_2 \longrightarrow N_2O_5$ fast

8. What is a reaction mechanism? Provide a description or definition in your own words.

Problems

1. Consider the following reaction:

$$NO_2(g) + CO(g) \rightleftharpoons NO(g) + CO_2(g)$$

Several experiments were performed at 400 K beginning with only NO_2 and CO. The results are shown in the table below:

$(NO_2)_o$, M	$(CO)_o$, M	Initial rate of reaction, M/hr
0.38×10^{-4}	5.1×10^{-4}	3.5×10^{-8}
0.76×10^{-4}	5.1×10^{-4}	1.4×10^{-7}
0.38×10^{-4}	8.6×10^{-4}	3.5×10^{-8}

a) Determine the rate law for this reaction, and the value of the rate constant at 400 K.

b) Determine whether or not the proposed mechanism below is consistent with the rate law obtained in part a.

         PROPOSED MECHANISM:

         $NO_2 + NO_2 \longrightarrow NO_3 + NO$ slow

         $NO_3 + CO \longrightarrow NO_2 + CO_2$ fast

2. The conversion of ozone to molecular oxygen in the upper atmosphere,

$$2\, O_3(g) \rightleftharpoons 3\, O_2(g)$$

is thought to occur via the following mechanism:

         $O_3 \rightleftharpoons O_2 + O$ (fast equilibrium)

         $O + O_3 \rightleftharpoons 2\, O_2$ (slow forward)

a) What is the rate law for this mechanism (remember that only the concentrations of the reactants and the products can appear in the rate law)?

b) The rate law from the mechanism above is consistent with the experimental rate law. Explain the experimental fact that the rate decreases as the concentration of O_2 increases.

3. A possible mechanism for a chemical reaction is:

$Fe^{2+}(aq) + I_2(aq) \rightleftharpoons Fe^{3+}(aq) + I_2^-(aq)$ (fast equilibrium)

$Fe^{2+}(aq) + I_2^-(aq) \longrightarrow Fe^{3+}(aq) + 2\, I^-(aq)$ (slow forward)

What is the overall chemical reaction for this mechanism?

ChemActivity 59

What is a Catalyst?

Model 1: Hydrolysis of Glycylglycine.

In the following reaction, glycylglycine is split into two glycine molecules by a water molecule.

$$H_2NCH_2CONHCH_2COOH(aq) + H_2O(\ell) \rightleftharpoons 2\ H_2NCH_2COOH(aq) \qquad (1)$$

The mechanism is one-step bimolecular process wherein the partial negatively charged oxygen atom of the water molecule collides with the partial positively charged carbon atom, as shown in Figure 1 below.

Figure 1. Reaction of Glycylglycine with Water.

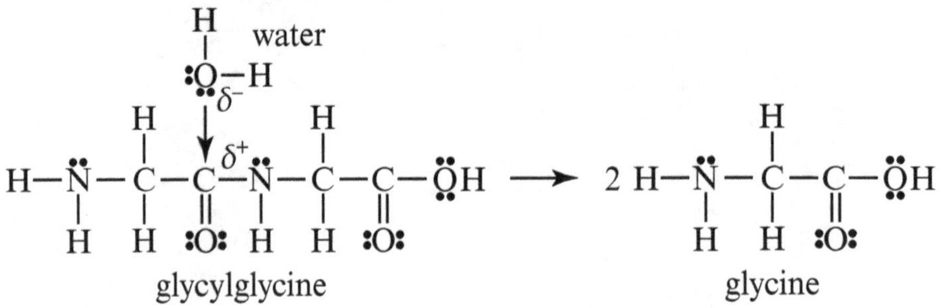

glycylglycine   glycine

The reaction is exothermic and thermodynamically favorable, but the activation energy is very high and the reaction is extremely slow.

Critical Thinking Questions

1. Confirm that reaction 1 is a balanced chemical reaction by completing this table:

Element	Number of Reactant Atoms	Number of Product Atoms
H		
C		
N		
O		

2. In reaction 1, where do the two hydrogen atoms and the oxygen atom from the water molecule end up?

3.   a)   Is reaction 1 a redox reaction? How can you tell?

     b)   Is reaction 1 an acid/base reaction? How can you tell?

END OF WARM-UP

4. A student suggests that the reason that the reaction described in Model 1 is so slow is that it is under thermodynamic control. As a team, indicate whether or not the student is correct and provide a consensus explanation.

5. Individually, sketch a reaction coordinate diagram for the hydrolysis of glycylglycine as described in Model 1. When all team members have finished the drawing, compare your answers and make any necessary changes.

Information

The hydrolysis of glycylglycine is extremely rapid in the presence of a specific large protein. This large protein interacts with the glycylglycine molecule to increase the rate of hydrolysis by several orders of magnitude. As the reaction proceeds in the presence of this protein, the overall balanced reaction is unchanged, the protein is neither consumed nor altered, but the reaction proceeds much more rapidly than without this protein.

Critical Thinking Questions

6. Write the overall reaction for the hydrolysis of glycylglycine in the presence of the large protein as described in the above Information section.

7. As a team, use the description of the hydrolysis of glycylglycine in the presence of the large protein to discuss how the presence of the protein changes the energetics of the reaction. Once consensus is reached, add a new line to the reaction coordinate diagram in CTQ 5 to include this process. Clearly label the diagram in a way that indicates what aspects of the diagram relate to the reaction in the presence of the protein and what aspects relate to the reaction without the protein.

Model 2: Catalysts.

A **catalyst** is a substance that is neither produced nor consumed in a chemical reaction, yet causes the rate of the reaction to be increased without changing the temperature. For example, the reaction $H_2(g) + I_2(g) \rightleftharpoons 2\,HI(g)$ proceeds about 10^8 times faster in the presence of Pt dust than without it. In this case, Pt acts as a catalyst. The large protein that increases the rate of hydrolysis of glycylglycine is a biological catalyst known as an **enzyme**. The presence of a catalyst enables a reaction to take place using a *different mechanism* than would otherwise be possible.

Critical Thinking Questions

Answer CTQs 8 – 11 as a team.

8. What effect does a catalyst have on the stoichiometry of the balanced chemical equation describing a reaction? Explain your reasoning.

9. What effect does a catalyst have on the $\Delta H°$ of a chemical reaction? Explain your reasoning.

10. How does the rate of the rate-limiting step in a mechanism involving a catalyst compare to the rate of the rate-limiting step of the mechanism without the catalyst present? Explain your reasoning.

11. What effect does a catalyst have on the activation energy of an overall reaction?

Exercise

1. What is a catalyst? Provide a definition or description in your own words.

2. Modify the following reaction coordinate diagram (drawn in the absence of a catalyst) for the presence of a catalyst.

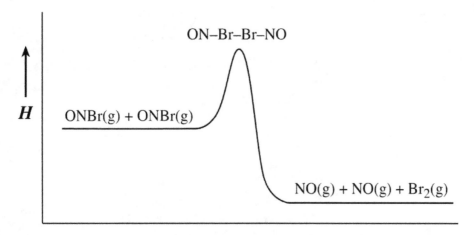

ON–Br–Br–NO

H | ONBr(g) + ONBr(g)

NO(g) + NO(g) + Br$_2$(g)

Reaction Coordinate ⟶

Problem

1. At 1000 °C, the reaction 2 HI(g) ⇌ I$_2$(g) + H$_2$(g) has E_a (forward) = 183 kJ/mol and $\Delta H°$ = 9.5 kJ/mole.

    a) Draw a reaction coordinate diagram (H vs. reaction coordinate) for this reaction. Graph paper is not necessary, but make some attempt to scale properly. Clearly indicate E_a (forward), E_a (reverse), and $\Delta H°$ on the diagram.

    b) Determine the value of E_a (reverse).

    c) A platinum catalyst is added and E_a (forward) is reduced to 58 kJ/mole. What is the value of $\Delta H°$ when the catalyst is present?

How Does Temperature Influence Rate of Reaction?

WARM-UP

Model 1: A Chemical Reaction at Different Temperatures

$$NO(g) + O_3(g) \rightleftharpoons NO_2(g) + O_2(g)$$

Experimental rate law: rate $= k(NO)(O_3)$

Three students separately perform experiments to determine the value of the rate constant for this reaction. Each student uses a different temperature.

Table 1.   Rate constants obtained by three students.

Student	Temperature, T (K)	Rate constant, k (L/mol s)
1	238	3.7×10^9
2	268	7.2×10^9
3	298	12.3×10^9

Critical Thinking Questions

1. What is the order of the reaction in Model 1 with respect to:

    a)   NO ?

    b) O_3 ?

2. Based on the data in Table 1, which word or phrase best describes how the rate constant, k, changes as temperature is increased:

    remains roughly constant   increases   decreases

3. The three students wonder whether the relationship between rate constant and temperature is a *linear relationship* – that is, whether the relationship between k and T is described by $k = m\,T + b$ where m and b are constants.

    How could the students plot this data in order to test this hypothesis? That is, what variable goes on the x-axis and what variable goes on the y-axis to see whether or not this relationship holds?

END OF WARM-UP

Model 2: The Arrhenius Equation.

The rate of a reaction depends on the temperature because the magnitude of the rate constant, k, is typically a function of the temperature – as seen in Model 1. In general, the relationship between k and T is found to be

$$k = A\, e^{-E_a/RT}$$

By taking the natural logarithm of both sides of this relationship, equation (10 can be obtained. Either form of the relationship is known as the **Arrhenius Equation.**

$$\ln k = \ln A - \frac{E_a}{RT} \tag{1}$$

Here, A is the **frequency factor** and E_a is the **activation energy** in units of joules per mole, T is the absolute temperature in Kelvin, and R is the gas constant (8.314 J/mol K). Both A and E_a are characteristic of the particular reaction being studied, and they are both *always* positive numbers. If the rate constant for a given reaction is examined at two temperatures, T_1 and T_2, and if the observed rate constants at those temperatures are k_1 and k_2, respectively, then equation 1 can be used to derive the following relationship:

$$\ln \frac{k_1}{k_2} = \frac{E_a}{R}\left[\frac{1}{T_2} - \frac{1}{T_1}\right] \tag{2}$$

Critical Thinking Questions

4. At how many different temperatures must the rate constant be determined in order to evaluate the activation energy for a reaction?

5. According to equation 1, if the temperature increases, does the rate constant increase or decrease? As a team, construct an explanation that does not involve doing any calculations involving specific numbers.

6. A student is studying a reaction in detail and uses experimental data to calculate that at a given temperature, T, $k > A$ for the reaction.

   As a team, explain why it must be that the student has made an error.

7. Individually, use appropriate data from Table 1 and equation 2 to determine the activation energy (*with units*) for the reaction in Model 1. Once all team members are done, compare your answers and reach consensus. Note that there is more than one correct choice of "appropriate data" to use – but any choice should generate the same value for the activation energy.

8. The three students from Model 1 decide to plot their data to obtain values for the activation energy and frequency factor for the reaction they were studying.

    Student A suggests making a plot of k vs. T.

    Student B suggests making a plot of $\ln k$ vs. $1/T$.

    Student C suggests making a plot of $\ln k$ vs. T.

    As a team, discuss these suggestions and decide which one will provide a linear fit to the data. Provide a consensus explanation describing how A and E_a can be obtained from the slope and/or intercept of the linear fit to the data.

9. Consider a situation in which the activation energy for some reaction, Q, is greater than the activation energy for a different reaction, W. Assume that the value of A, the frequency factor, is identical in both reactions.

    As a team, consider equation 1 and discuss which has the greater rate constant— reaction Q or reaction W. Write a consensus explanation.

Exercises

1. A chemist's "rule of thumb" is that the rate of a chemical reaction doubles for every 10 °C increase in temperature. Use equation 2 to demonstrate this rule of thumb. Assume that a typical chemical reaction has an activation energy of 50 kJ/mol and that the measurements are taking place around 300 K.

   Recall that $R = 8.314 \dfrac{J}{K\,mol}$.

2. A great Martian chemist enunciated the following chemical principle:

   The rate of a chemical reaction doubles for every 7 K increase in temperature.

   Assume that the average temperature on Mars is –40 °C, and determine if the Martian chemist was correct or not.

3. Indicate whether the following statement is true or false and explain your reasoning.

   In general, the higher the activation energy, the faster a reaction occurs at a given temperature.

4. A chemist determines the rate constant, k, for a particular reaction at a number of different temperatures. Explain how the activation energy for the reaction can be determined in kJ/mole from a graph of ln k vs. $1/T$.

5. The following experimental data were obtained for the initial rate of production of ABX at 298 K, according to the equation:

$$A_2\,(aq) + 2\,BX(aq) \rightleftharpoons 2\,ABX(aq)$$

$(A_2)_o$ (mol/L)	$(BX)_o$ (mol/L)	Initial rate of reaction (mol/L sec)
0.37	0.60	0.18
0.37	1.20	0.71
0.74	1.20	1.43

   a)   Determine the rate law for the reaction and calculate the rate constant at 298 K.

   b)   The rate constant for this reaction at 314 K is 3.0 times larger than the rate constant at 298 K. What is the activation energy for this reaction?

6. Describe in a few sentences how temperature influences the rate of reaction. Be as specific and complete as you can be.

Problems

1. $H_2(g) + I_2(g) \longrightarrow 2\,HI(g)$

    The rate constant for the above reaction at two temperatures was determined:

Temperature (K)	Rate Constant $(M^{-1}\,sec^{-1})$
400	0.0234
500	0.750

    Determine the rate constant at 400 K for the reverse reaction

    $$2\,HI(g) \longrightarrow H_2(g) + I_2(g)$$

    as precisely as you can, assuming that $A = 5 \times 10^5\,M^{-1}\,s^{-1}$ for the reverse reaction.

2. Consider a generic reaction:

    $$AB\,(g) + CD\,(g) \rightleftharpoons AC\,(g) + BD\,(g)$$

    a) Construct a reaction coordinate diagram for this reaction assuming that it has a large equilibrium constant, but that it reaches equilibrium very slowly. Explain your reasoning clearly.

    b) Indicate how the addition of a catalyst would change the reaction coordinate diagram from part a, and describe what effect this would have on the equilibrium constant and the rate at which equilibrium is reached.

Appendix

TABLE A.1   Values of Selected Fundamental Constants

Speed of light in a vacuum (c)	$c = 2.99792458 \times 10^8$ m/s
Charge on an electron (q_e)	$q_e = 1.6021892 \times 10^{-19}$ C
Rest mass of an electron (m_e)	$m_e = 9.109534 \times 10^{-28}$ g
	$m_e = 5.4858026 \times 10^{-4}$ amu
Rest mass of a proton (m_p)	$m_p = 1.6726485 \times 10^{-24}$ g
	$m_p = 1.00727647$ amu
Rest mass of a neutron (m_n)	$m_n = 1.6749543 \times 10^{-24}$ g
	$m_n = 1.008665012$ amu
Faraday's constant (F)	$F = 96{,}484.56$ C/mol
Planck's constant (h)	$h = 6.626176 \times 10^{-34}$ J $\cdot$ s
Ideal gas constant (R)	$R = 0.0820568$ L-atm/mol-K
	$R = 8.31441$ J/mol-K
Atomic mass unit (amu)	1 amu $= 1.6605655 \times 10^{-24}$ g
Boltzmann's constant (k)	$k = 1.380662 \times 10^{-23}$ J/K
Avogadro's constant (N)	$N = 6.022045 \times 10^{23}$ mol^{-1}
Rydberg constant (R_H)	$R_H = 1.09737318 \times 10^7$ m^{-1}
	$= 1.09737318 \times 10^{-2}$ nm^{-1}
Heat capacity of water	$C = 75.376$ J/mol-K

TABLE A.2   Selected Conversion Factors

Energy	1 J $= 0.2390$ cal $= 10^7$ erg $= 1$ volt$\bullet$coulomb
	1 cal $= 4.184$ J (by definition)
	1 ev/atom $= 1.6021892 \times 10^{-19}$ J/atom $= 96.484$ kJ/mol
Temperature	K $= {}^\circ$C $+ 273.15$
	$^\circ$C $= (5/9)(^\circ$F $- 32)$
	$^\circ$F $= (9/5)(^\circ$C$) + 32$
Pressure	1 atm $= 760$ mm Hg $= 760$ torr $= 101.325$ kPa
Mass	1 kg $= 2.2046$ lb
	1 lb $= 453.59$ g $= 0.45359$ kg
	1 oz $= 0.06250$ lb $= 28.350$ g
	1 ton $= 2000$ lb $= 907.185$ kg
	1 tonne (metric) $= 1000$ kg $= 2204.62$ lb
Volume	1 mL $= 0.001$ L $= 1$ cm^3 (by definition)
	1 oz (fluid) $= 0.031250$ qt $= 0.029573$ L
	1 qt $= 0.946326$ L
	1 L $= 1.05672$ qt
Length	1 m $= 39.370$ in
	1 mi $= 1.60934$ km
	1 in $= 2.54$ cm (by definition)

TABLE A.3   Standard-State Enthalpies, Free Energies, and Entropies of Atom Combination

Substance	ΔH°_{ac} (kJ/mol)	ΔG°_{ac} (kJ/mol)	ΔS°_{ac} (J/mol-K)
Aluminum			
Al(s)	−326.4	−285.7	−136.21
Al(g)	0	0	0
Al^{+3}(aq)	−857	−77.1	−486.2
Al$_2$O$_3$(s)	−3076.0	−2848.9	−761.33
AlCl$_3$(s)	−1395.6	−1231.5	−549.46
AlF$_3$(s)	−2067.5	−1896.4	−574.36
Al$_2$(SO$_4$)$_3$(s)	−7920.1	−7166.9	−2525.9
Barium			
Ba(s)	−180	−146	−107.4
Ba(g)	0	0	0
Ba^{+2}(aq)	−718	−707	−160.6
BaO(s)	−983	−903	−260.88
Ba(OH)$_2$·8H$_2$O(s)	−9931.6	−8915	−3419
BaCl$_2$(s)	−1282	−1168	−376.96
BaCl$_2$(aq)	−1295	−1181	−378.04
BaSO$_4$(s)	−2929	−2673	−850.1
Ba(NO$_3$)$_2$(s)	−3612	−3217	−1229.4
Ba(NO$_3$)$_2$(aq)	−3573	−3231	−1140.7
Beryllium			
Be(s)	−324.3	−286.6	−126.77
Be(g)	0	0	0
Be^{+2}(aq)	−707.1	−666.3	−266.0
BeO(s)	−1183.1	−1026.6	−283.18
BeCl$_2$(s)	−1058.1	−943.6	−383.99
Bismuth			
Bi(s)	−207.1	−168.2	−130.31
Bi(g)	0	0	0
Bi$_2$O$_3$(s)	−1735.6	−1525.3	−705.8
BiCl$_3$(s)	−951.2	−800.2	−505.6
BiCl$_3$(g)	−837.8	−741.2	−323.79
Bi$_2$S$_3$(s)	−1393.7	−1191.8	−677.2
Boron			
B(s)	−562.7	−518.8	−147.59
B(g)	0	0	0
B$_2$O$_3$(s)	−3145.7	−2926.4	−736.10
B$_2$H$_6$(g)	−2395.7	−2170.4	−763.07
B$_5$H$_9$(ℓ)	−4729.7	−4251.4	−1615.45
B$_{10}$H$_{14}$(s)	−8719.3	−7841.2	−2963.92

(continued)

TABLE A.3   Standard-State Enthalpies, Free Energies, and Entropies of Atom Combination (continued)

Substance	ΔH_{ac}° (kJ/mol)	ΔG_{ac}° (kJ/mol)	ΔS_{ac}° (J/mol-K)
$H_3BO_3(s)$	−3057.5	−2792.7	−891.92
$BF_3(g)$	−1936.7	−1824.9	−375.59
$BCl_3(\ell)$	−1354.9	−1223.2	−442.7
$B_3N_3H_6(\ell)$	−4953.1	−4535.4	−1408.9
$B_3N_3H_6(g)$	−4923.9	−4532.8	−1319.84
Bromine			
$Br_2(\ell)$	−223.768	−164.792	−197.813
$Br_2(g)$	−192.86	−161.68	−104.58
$Br(g)$	0	0	0
$HBr(g)$	−365.93	−339.09	−91.040
$HBr(aq)$	−451.08	−389.60	−207.3
$BrF(g)$	−284.72	−253.49	−104.81
$BrF_3(g)$	−604.45	−497.56	−358.75
$BrF_5(g)$	−935.73	−742.6	−648.60
Calcium			
$Ca(s)$	−178.2	−144.3	−113.46
$Ca(g)$	0	0	0
$Ca^{+2}(aq)$	−721.0	−697.9	−208.0
$CaO(s)$	−1062.5	−980.1	−276.19
$Ca(OH)_2(s)$	−2097.9	−1912.7	−623.03
$CaCl_2(s)$	−1217.4	−1103.8	−380.7
$CaSO_4(s)$	−2887.8	−2631.3	−860.3
$CaSO_4 \cdot 2H_2O(s)$	−4256.7	−4383.2	−1553.8
$Ca(NO_3)_2(s)$	−3557.0	−3189.0	−1234.5
$CaCO_3(s)$	−2849.3	−2639.5	−703.2
$Ca_3(PO_4)_2(s)$	−7278.0	−6727.9	−1843.5
Carbon			
$C(graphite)$	−716.682	−671.257	−152.36
$C(diamond)$	−714.787	−668.357	−155.719
$C(g)$	0	0	0
$CO(g)$	−1076.377	−1040.156	−121.477
$CO_2(g)$	−1608.531	−1529.078	−266.47
$COCl_2(g)$	−1428.0	−1318.9	−366.02
$CH_4(g)$	−1662.09	−1535.00	−430.68
$HCHO(g)$	−1509.72	−1412.01	−329.81
$H_2CO_3(aq)$	−2599.14	−2396.02	−683.3
$HCO_3^{-}(aq)$	−2373.83	−2156.47	−664.8
$CO_3^{-2}(aq)$	−2141.33	−1894.26	−698.16
$CH_3OH(\ell)$	−2075.11	−1882.25	−651.2
$CH_3OH(g)$	−2037.11	−1877.94	−538.19
$CCl_4(\ell)$	−1338.84	−1159.19	−602.49
$CCl_4(g)$	−1306.3	−1154.57	−509.04
$CHCl_3(\ell)$	−1433.84	−1265.20	−567.3

TABLE A.3   Standard-State Enthalpies, Free Energies, and Entropies of Atom Combination (continued)

Substance	ΔH_{ac}° (kJ/mol)	ΔG_{ac}° (kJ/mol)	ΔS_{ac}° (J/mol-K)
$CHCl_3(g)$	–1402.51	–1261.88	–472.69
$CH_2Cl_2(\ell)$	–1516.80	–1356.37	–540.1
$CH_2Cl_2(g)$	–1487.81	–1354.98	–447.69
$CH_3Cl(g)$	–1572.15	–1444.08	–432.9
$CS_2(\ell)$	–1184.59	–1082.49	–342.40
$CS_2(g)$	–1156.93	–1080.64	–255.90
$HCN(g)$	–1271.9	–1205.43	–224.33
$CH_3NO_2(\ell)$	–2453.77	–2214.51	–805.89
$C_2H_2(g)$	–1641.93	–1539.81	–344.68
$C_2H_4(g)$	–2251.70	–2087.35	–555.48
$C_2H_6(g)$	–2823.94	–2594.82	–774.87
$CH_3CHO(\ell)$	–2745.43	–2515.35	–775.9
$CH_3CO_2H(\ell)$	–3286.8	–3008.86	–937.4
$CH_3CO_2H(g)$	–3234.55	–2992.96	–814.7
$CH_3CO_2H(aq)$	–3288.06	–3015.42	–918.5
$CH_3CO_2^-(aq)$	–3070.66	–2785.03	–895.8
$CH_3CH_2OH(\ell)$	–3266.12	–2968.51	–1004.8
$CH_3CH_2OH(g)$	–3223.53	–2962.22	–882.82
$CH_3CH_2OH(aq)$	–3276.7	–2975.37	–1017.0
$C_6H_6(\ell)$	–5556.96	–5122.52	–1464.1
$C_6H_6(g)$	–5523.07	–5117.36	–1367.7

Chlorine

Substance	ΔH_{ac}° (kJ/mol)	ΔG_{ac}° (kJ/mol)	ΔS_{ac}° (J/mol-K)
$Cl_2(g)$	–243.358	–211.360	–107.330
$Cl(g)$	0	0	0
$Cl^-(aq)$	–288.838	–236.908	–108.7
$ClO_2(g)$	–517.5	–448.6	–230.47
$Cl_2O(g)$	–412.2	–345.2	–225.24
$Cl_2O_7(\ell)$	–1750	-	-
$HCl(g)$	–431.64	–404.226	–93.003
$HCl(aq)$	–506.49	–440.155	–223.4
$ClF(g)$	–255.15	–223.53	–106.06

Chromium

Substance	ΔH_{ac}° (kJ/mol)	ΔG_{ac}° (kJ/mol)	ΔS_{ac}° (J/mol-K)
$Cr(s)$	–396.6	–351.8	–150.73
$Cr(g)$	0	0	0
$CrO_3(s)$	–1733.6	-	-
$CrO_4^{-2}(aq)$	–2274.4	–2006.47	–768.51
$Cr_2O_3(s)$	–2680.4	–2456.89	–751.0
$Cr_2O_7^{-2}(aq)$	–4027.7	–3626.8	–1214.5
$(NH_4)_2Cr_2O_7(s)$	–7030.7	-	-
$PbCrO_4(s)$	–2519.2	-	-

Cobalt

Substance	ΔH_{ac}° (kJ/mol)	ΔG_{ac}° (kJ/mol)	ΔS_{ac}° (J/mol-K)
$Co(s)$	–424.7	–380.3	–149.475
$Co(g)$	0	0	0

(continued)

TABLE A.3   Standard-State Enthalpies, Free Energies, and Entropies of Atom Combination (continued)

Substance	ΔH_{ac}° (kJ/mol)	ΔG_{ac}° (kJ/mol)	ΔS_{ac}° (J/mol-K)
$Co^{+2}(aq)$	−482.9	−434.7	−293
$Co^{+3}(aq)$	−333	−246.3	−485
$CoO(s)$	−911.8	−826.2	−287.60
$Co_3O_4(s)$	−3162	−2842	−1080.3
$Co(NH_3)_6^{+3}(aq)$	−7763.5	−6929.5	−3018.
	Copper		
$Cu(s)$	−338.32	−298.58	−133.23
$Cu(g)$	0	0	0
$Cu^+(aq)$	−266.65	−248.60	−125.8
$Cu^{+2}(aq)$	−273.55	−233.09	−266.0
$CuO(s)$	−744.8	−660.0	−284.81
$Cu_2O(s)$	−1094.4	−974.9	−400.68
$CuCl_2(s)$	−807.8	−685.6	−388.71
$CuS(s)$	−670.2	−590.4	−267.7
$Cu_2S(s)$	−1304.9	−921.6	−379.7
$CuSO_4(s)$	−2385.17	−1530.44	−869
$Cu(NH_3)_4^{+2}(aq)$	−5189.4	−4671.13	−1882.5
	Fluorine		
$F_2(g)$	−157.98	−123.82	−114.73
$F(g)$	0	0	0
$F^-(aq)$	−411.62	−340.70	−172.6
$HF(g)$	−567.7	−538.4	−99.688
$HF(aq)$	−616.72	−561.98	−184.8
	Hydrogen		
$H_2(g)$	−435.30	−406.494	−98.742
$H(g)$	0	0	0
$H^+(aq)$	−217.65	−203.247	−114.713
$OH^-(aq)$	−696.81	−592.222	−286.52
$H_2O(\ell)$	−970.30	−875.354	−320.57
$H_2O(g)$	−926.29	−866.797	−202.23
$H_2O_2(\ell)$	−1121.42	−990.31	−441.9
$H_2O_2(aq)$	−1124.81	−1003.99	−407.6
	Iodine		
$I_2(s)$	−213.676	−141.00	−245.447
$I_2(g)$	−151.238	−121.67	−100.89
$I(g)$	0	0	0
$HI(g)$	−298.01	−272.05	−88.910
$IF(g)$	−281.48	−250.92	−103.38
$IF_5(g)$	−1324.28	−1131.78	−646.9
$IF_7(g)$	−1603.7	−1322.17	−945.6
$ICl(g)$	−210.74	−181.64	−98.438
$IBr(g)$	−177.88	−149.21	−97.040

TABLE A.3   Standard-State Enthalpies, Free Energies, and Entropies of Atom Combination (continued)

Substance	ΔH°_{ac} (kJ/mol)	ΔG°_{ac} (kJ/mol)	ΔS°_{ac} (J/mol-K)
Iron			
Fe(s)	–416.3	–370.7	–153.21
Fe(g)	0	0	0
Fe^{+2}(aq)	–505.4	–449.6	–318.2
Fe^{+3}(aq)	–464.8	–375.4	–496.4
Fe$_2$O$_3$(s)	–2404.3	–2178.8	–756.75
Fe$_3$O$_4$(s)	–3364.0	–3054.4	–1039.3
Fe(OH)$_2$(s)	–1918.9	–1727.2	–644
Fe(OH)$_3$(s)	–2639.8	–2372.1	–901.1
FeCl$_3$(s)	–1180.8	–1021.7	–533.8
FeS$_2$(s)	–1152.1	–1014.1	–463.2
Fe(CO)$_5$(ℓ)	–6019.6	–5590.9	–1438.1
Fe(CO)$_5$(g)	–5979.5	–5582.9	–1330.9
Lead			
Pb(s)	–195.0	–161.9	–110.56
Pb(g)	0	0	0
Pb^{+2}(aq)	–196.7	–186.3	–164.9
PbO(s)	–661.5	–581.5	–267.7
PbO$_2$(s)	–970.7	–842.7	–428.9
PbCl$_2$(s)	–797.8	–687.4	–369.8
PbCl$_4$(ℓ)	–1011.0	-	-
PbS(s)	–574.2	–498.9	–252.0
PbSO$_4$(s)	–2390.4	–2140.2	–838.84
Pb(NO$_3$)$_2$(s)	–3087.3	-	-
PbCO$_3$(s)	–2358.3	–2153.8	–685.6
Lithium			
Li(s)	–159.37	–126.66	–109.65
Li(g)	0	0	0
Li$^+$(aq)	–437.86	–419.97	–125.4
LiH(s)	–467.56	–398.26	–233.40
LiOH(s)	–1111.12	–1000.59	–371.74
LiF(s)	–854.33	–784.28	–261.87
LiCl(s)	–689.66	–616.71	–244.64
LiBr(s)	–622.48	–551.06	–239.52
LiI(s)	–536.62	–467.45	–232.78
LiAlH$_4$(s)	–1472.7	–1270.0	–683.42
LiBH$_4$(s)	–1401.9	–1333.4	–675.21
Magnesium			
Mg(s)	–147.70	–113.10	–115.97
Mg(g)	0	0	0
Mg^{+2}(aq)	–614.55	–567.9	–286.8
MgO(s)	–998.57	–914.26	–282.76
MgH$_2$(s)	–658.3	–555.5	–346.99

(continued)

TABLE A.3   Standard-State Enthalpies, Free Energies, and Entropies of Atom Combination (continued)

Substance	ΔH_{ac}° (kJ/mol)	ΔG_{ac}° (kJ/mol)	ΔS_{ac}° (J/mol-K)
$Mg(OH)_2(s)$	–2005.88	–1816.64	–637.01
$MgCl_2(s)$	–1032.38	–916.25	–389.43
$MgCO_3(s)$	–2707.7	–2491.7	–724.2
$MgSO_4(s)$	–2708.1	–2448.9	–869.1
Manganese			
$Mn(s)$	–280.7	–238.5	–141.69
$Mn(g)$	0	0	0
$Mn^{+2}(aq)$	–501.5	–466.6	–247.3
$MnO(s)$	–915.1	–833.1	–275.05
$MnO_2(s)$	–1299.1	–1167.1	–442.76
$Mn_2O_3(s)$	–2267.9	–2053.3	–720.1
$Mn_3O_4(s)$	–3226.6	–2925.6	–1009.7
$KMnO_4(s)$	–2203.8	–1963.6	–806.50
$MnS(s)$	–773.7	–695.2	–263.3
Mercury			
$Hg(\ell)$	–61.317	–31.820	–98.94
$Hg(g)$	0	0	0
$Hg^{+2}(aq)$	+109.8	+132.58	–207.2
$HgO(s)$	–401.32	–322.090	–265.73
$HgCl_2(s)$	–529.0	–421.8	–359.4
$Hg_2Cl_2(s)$	–631.21	–485.745	–487.8
$HgS(s)$	–398.3	–320.67	–260.4
Nitrogen			
$N_2(g)$	–945.408	–911.26	–114.99
$N(g)$	0	0	0
$NO(g)$	–631.62	–600.81	–103.592
$NO_2(g)$	–937.86	–867.78	–235.35
$N_2O(g)$	–1112.53	–1038.79	–247.80
$N_2O_3(g)$	–1609.20	–1466.99	–477.48
$N_2O_4(g)$	–1932.93	–1740.29	–646.53
$N_2O_5(g)$	–2179.91	–1954.8	–756.2
$NO_3^-(aq)$	–1425.2	–1259.56	–490.1
$NOCl(g)$	–791.84	–726.96	–217.86
$NO_2Cl(g)$	–1080.12	–970.4	–368.46
$HNO_2(aq)$	–1307.9	–1172.9	–454.5
$HNO_3(g)$	–1572.92	–1428.79	–484.80
$HNO_3(aq)$	–1645.22	–1465.32	–604.8
$NH_3(g)$	–1171.76	–1081.82	–304.99
$NH_3(aq)$	–1205.94	–1091.87	–386.1
$NH_4^+(aq)$	–1475.81	–1347.93	–498.8
$NH_4NO_3(s)$	–2929.08	–2603.31	–1097.53
$NH_4NO_3(aq)$	–2903.39	–2610.00	–988.8

TABLE A.3   Standard-State Enthalpies, Free Energies, and Entropies of Atom Combination (continued)

Substance	ΔH_{ac}° (kJ/mol)	ΔG_{ac}° (kJ/mol)	ΔS_{ac}° (J/mol-K)
$NH_4Cl(s)$	−1779.41	−1578.17	−682.7
$N_2H_4(\ell)$	−1765.38	−1574.91	−644.24
$N_2H_4(g)$	−1720.61	−1564.90	−526.98
$HN_3(g)$	−1341.7	−1242.0	−335.37
Oxygen			
$O_2(g)$	−498.340	−463.462	−116.972
$O(g)$	0	0	0
$O_3(g)$	−604.8	−532.0	−244.24
Phosphorus			
P(white)	−314.64	−278.25	−122.10
$P_4(g)$	−1199.65	−1088.6	−372.79
$P_2(g)$	−485.0	−452.8	−108.257
$P(g)$	0	0	0
$PH_3(g)$	−962.2	−874.6	−297.10
$P_4O_6(s)$	−4393.7	-	-
$P_4O_{10}(s)$	−6734.3	−6128.0	−2034.46
$PO_4^{3-}(aq)$	−2588.7	−2223.9	−1029
$PF_3(g)$	−1470.4	−1361.5	−366.22
$PF_5(g)$	−2305.4	-	-
$PCl_3(\ell)$	−999.4	−867.6	−441.7
$PCl_3(g)$	−966.7	−863.1	−347.01
$PCl_5(g)$	−1297.9	−1111.6	−624.60
$H_3PO_4(s)$	−3243.3	−2934.0	−1041.05
$H_3PO_4(aq)$	−3241.7	−2833.6	−1374
Potassium			
K(s)	−89.24	−60.59	−96.16
K(g)	0	0	0
$K^+(aq)$	−341.62	−343.86	−57.8
KOH(s)	−980.82	−874.65	−357.2
KCl(s)	−647.67	−575.41	−242.94
$KNO_3(s)$	−1804.08	−1606.27	−663.75
$K_2Cr_2O_7(s)$	−4777.4	−4328.7	−1505.9
$KMnO_4(s)$	−2203.8	−1963.6	−806.50
Silicon			
Si(s)	−455.6	−411.3	−149.14
Si(g)	0	0	0
$SiO_2(s)$	−1864.9	−1731.4	−448.24
$SiH_4(g)$	−1291.9	−1167.4	−422.20
$SiF_4(g)$	−2386.5	−2231.6	−520.50
$SiCl_4(\ell)$	−1629.3	−1453.9	−589
$SiCl_4(g)$	−1599.3	−1451.0	−498.03

(continued)

TABLE A.3   Standard-State Enthalpies, Free Energies, and Entropies of Atom Combination (continued)

Substance	ΔH_{ac}° (kJ/mol)	ΔG_{ac}° (kJ/mol)	ΔS_{ac}° (J/mol-K)
Silver			
Ag(s)	−284.55	−245.65	−130.42
Ag(g)	0	0	0
Ag^+(aq)	−178.97	−168.54	−100.29
$Ag(NH_3)_2^+$(aq)	−2647.15	−2393.51	−922.6
Ag_2O(s)	−849.32	−734.23	−385.7
AgCl(s)	−533.30	−461.12	−242.0
AgBr(s)	−496.80	−424.95	−240.9
AgI(s)	−453.23	−382.34	−238.3
Sodium			
Na(s)	−107.32	−76.761	−102.50
Na(g)	0	0	0
Na^+(aq)	−374.45	−338.666	−94.7
NaH(s)	−3811.25	−313.47	−228.409
NaOH(s)	−999.75	−891.233	−365.025
NaOH(aq)	−1044.25	−930.889	−381.4
NaCl(s)	−640.15	−566.579	−246.78
NaCl(g)	−405.65	−379.10	−89.10
NaCl(aq)	−636.27	−575.574	−203.4
$NaNO_3$(s)	−1795.38	−1594.58	−673.66
Na_3PO_4(s)	−3550.68	−3224.26	−1094.75
Na_2SO_3(s)	−2363.96	−2115.0	−803
Na_2SO_4(s)	−2877.20	−2588.86	−969.89
Na_2CO_3(s)	−2809.51	−2564.41	−813.70
$NaHCO_3$(s)	−2739.97	−2497.5	−808.0
$NaCH_3CO_2$(s)	−3400.78	−3099.66	−1013.2
Na_2CrO_4(s)	−2950.1	−2667.18	−949.53
$Na_2Cr_2O_7$(s)	−4730.6	-	-
Sulfur			
S_8(s)	−2230.440	−1906.000	−1310.77
S_8(g)	−2128.14	−1856.37	−911.59
S(g)	0	0	0
S^{2-}(aq)	−245.7	−152.4	−182.4
SO_2(g)	−1073.975	−1001.906	−241.71
SO_3(s)	−1480.82	−1307.65	−580.3
SO_3(ℓ)	−1467.36	−1307.19	−537.2
SO_3(g)	−1422.04	−1304.50	−394.23
SO_4^{2-}(aq)	−2184.76	−1909.70	−791.9
$SOCl_2$(g)	−983.8	−879.6	−349.50
SO_2Cl_2(g)	−1384.5	−1233.1	−508.39
H_2S(g)	−734.74	−678.30	−191.46

TABLE A.3   Standard-State Enthalpies, Free Energies, and Entropies of Atom Combination (continued)

Substance	ΔH°_{ac} (kJ/mol)	ΔG°_{ac} (kJ/mol)	ΔS°_{ac} (J/mol-K)
$H_2SO_3(aq)$	−2070.43	−1877.75	−648.2
$H_2SO_4(aq)$	−2620.06	−2316.20	−1021.4
$SF_4(g)$	−1369.66	−1217.2	−510.81
$SF_6(g)$	−1962	−1715.0	−828.53
$SCN^-(aq)$	−1391.75	−1272.43	−334.9
	Tin		
$Sn(s)$	−302.1	−267.3	−124.35
$Sn(g)$	0	0	0
$SnO(s)$	−837.1	−755.9	−273.0
$SnO_2(s)$	−1381.1	−1250.5	−438.3
$SnCl_2(s)$	−870.6	-	-
$SnCl_4(\ell)$	−1300.1	−249.8	−570.7
$SnCl_4(g)$	−1260.3	−1122.2	−463.5
	Titanium		
$Ti(s)$	−469.9	−425.1	−149.6
$Ti(g)$	0	0	0
$TiO(s)$	−1238.8	−1151.8	−306.5
$TiO_2(s)$	−1913.0	−1778.1	−452.0
$TiCl_4(\ell)$	−1760.8	−1585.0	−588.7
$TiCl_4(g)$	−1719.8	−1574.6	−486.2
	Tungsten		
$W(s)$	−849.4	−807.1	−141.31
$W(g)$	0	0	0
$WO_3(s)$	−2439.8	−2266.4	−581.22
	Zinc		
$Zn(s)$	−130.729	−95.145	−119.35
$Zn(g)$	0	0	0
$Zn^{2+}(aq)$	−284.62	−242.21	−273.1
$ZnO(s)$	−728.18	−645.18	−278.40
$ZnCl_2(s)$	−789.14	−675.90	−379.92
$ZnS(s)$	−615.51	−534.69	−271.1
$ZnSO_4(s)$	−2389.0	−2131.8	−862.5

TABLE A.4   Standard Reduction Potentials

Half-reaction	$E°$ (V)
$Li^+ + e^- \rightleftharpoons Li(s)$	−3.045
$Rb^+ + e^- \rightleftharpoons Rb(s)$	−2.925
$K^+ + e^- \rightleftharpoons K(s)$	−2.924
$Cs^+ + e^- \rightleftharpoons Cs(s)$	−2.923
$Ba^{2+} + 2\,e^- \rightleftharpoons Ba(s)$	−2.90
$Sr^{2+} + 2\,e^- \rightleftharpoons Sr(s)$	−2.89
$Ca^{2+} + 2\,e^- \rightleftharpoons Ca(s)$	−2.76
$Na^+ + e^- \rightleftharpoons Na(s)$	−2.7109
$Mg^{2+} + 2\,e^- \rightleftharpoons Mg(s)$	−2.375
$Be^{2+} + 2\,e^- \rightleftharpoons Be(s)$	−1.70
$Ti^{2+} + 2\,e^- \rightleftharpoons Ti(s)$	−1.63
$Mn^{2+} + 2\,e^- \rightleftharpoons Mn(s)$	−1.18
$Cr^{2+} + 2\,e^- \rightleftharpoons Cr(s)$	−0.91
$2\,H_2O + 2\,e^- \rightleftharpoons H_2(g) + 2\,OH^-(aq)$	−0.8277
$Zn^{2+} + 2\,e^- \rightleftharpoons Zn(s)$	−0.7628
$Cr^{3+} + 3\,e^- \rightleftharpoons Cr(s)$	−0.74
$Cr^{3+} + e^- \rightleftharpoons Cr^{2+}$	−0.41
$Fe^{2+} + 2\,e^- \rightleftharpoons Fe(s)$	−0.409
$Cd^{2+} + 2\,e^- \rightleftharpoons Cd(s)$	−0.4026
$Co^{2+} + 2\,e^- \rightleftharpoons Co(s)$	−0.28
$Ni^{2+} + 2\,e^- \rightleftharpoons Ni(s)$	−0.23
$Sn^{2+} + 2\,e^- \rightleftharpoons Sn(s)$	−0.1364
$Pb^{2+} + 2\,e^- \rightleftharpoons Pb(s)$	−0.1263
$Fe^{3+} + 3\,e^- \rightleftharpoons Fe(s)$	−0.036
$2\,H^+ + 2\,e^- \rightleftharpoons H_2(g)$	0 (exactly)
$Sn^{4+} + 4\,e^- \rightleftharpoons Sn^{2+}$	0.15
$Cu^{2+} + e^- \rightleftharpoons Cu^+$	0.158
$Cu^{2+} + 2\,e^- \rightleftharpoons Cu(s)$	0.3402
$O_2(g) + 2\,H_2O + 4\,e^- \rightleftharpoons 4\,OH^-(aq)$	0.401
$Cu^+ + e^- \rightleftharpoons Cu(s)$	0.522
$I_2(s) + 2\,e^- \rightleftharpoons 2\,I^-(aq)$	0.535

TABLE A.4   Standard Reduction Potentials (continued)

Half-reaction	$E°$ (V)
$O_2(g) + 2\,H^+ + 2e^- \rightleftharpoons H_2O_2\;(aq)$	0.682
$Fe^{3+} + e^- \rightleftharpoons Fe^{2+}$	0.770
$Ag^+ + e^- \rightleftharpoons Ag(s)$	0.7996
$Hg^{2+} + 2\,e^- \rightleftharpoons Hg(l)$	0.851
$H_2O_2\;(aq) + 2\,e^- \rightleftharpoons 2\,OH^-(aq)$	0.88
$Pd^{2+} + 2\,e^- \rightleftharpoons Pd(s)$	0.987
$Br_2(aq) + 2\,e^- \rightleftharpoons 2\,Br^-(aq)$	1.087
$Pt^{2+} + 2\,e^- \rightleftharpoons Pt(s)$	1.2
$O_2(g) + 4\,H^+ + 4e^- \rightleftharpoons 2\,H_2O$	1.229
$Cl_2(g) + 2\,e^- \rightleftharpoons 2\,Cl^-(aq)$	1.3583
$Au^{3+} + 3\,e^- \rightleftharpoons Au(s)$	1.42
$Au^+ + e^- \rightleftharpoons Au(s)$	1.68

What Determines a Boiling Point?

WARM-UP

Model 1: Intermolecular Forces in Liquids and Gases.

Molecules attract each other. The forces of attraction between molecules are called **intermolecular forces**. The strength of intermolecular forces increases as the distance between molecules decreases. In a liquid, the molecules are constantly moving and colliding but remain very close to one another. The close distance between molecules results in relatively strong attractions between molecules in a liquid at all times. When a liquid evaporates, molecules in the liquid must overcome these intermolecular attractive forces and break free into the gas phase, where molecules tend to be very far apart. For example, when water evaporates, rapidly moving H_2O molecules at the surface of the liquid pull away from neighboring H_2O molecules and enter the gas phase.

Figure 1. H_2O molecules in the liquid and gas phases.

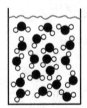   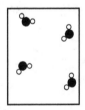

Attractive forces between
water molecules are stronger
in the liquid than the gas
because the molecules are
very close to one another.

On average, gaseous
H_2O molecules
are much further apart
than in the liquid

Critical Thinking Questions

1.   a)   Circle the diagram in Figure 1 that shows H_2O molecules after evaporation.

b)   When water evaporates, are any bonds between H atoms and O atoms within a molecule broken? Use information in Model 1 to explain your reasoning.

2. On average, are the intermolecular forces stronger in $H_2O(\ell)$ or in $H_2O(g)$? Use information in Model 1 to support your conclusion.

END OF WARM-UP

Model 2: Intermolecular Forces and Boiling Points.

To a large extent, the boiling point of a liquid is determined by the strength of the intermolecular interactions in the liquid. These interactions are largely determined by the structure of the individual molecules.

Table 1. Boiling points of selected compounds.

Alkane	MW (g/mole)	bp (°C)	Ketone	MW (g/mole)	bp (°C)
$CH_3CH_2CH_3$ propane	44.1	–42.1	CH_3CCH_3 $\overset{\parallel}{O}$ acetone	58.1	56.2
$CH_3(CH_2)_2CH_3$ butane	58.1	–0.5	$CH_3CCH_2CH_3$ $\overset{\parallel}{O}$ 2-butanone	72.1	79.6
$CH_3(CH_2)_3CH_3$ pentane	72.2	36.1	$CH_3C(CH_2)_2CH_3$ $\overset{\parallel}{O}$ 2-pentanone	86.1	102
$CH_3(CH_2)_4CH_3$ hexane	86.2	69	$CH_3C(CH_2)_3CH_3$ $\overset{\parallel}{O}$ 2-hexanone	100	128
$CH_3(CH_2)_8CH_3$ decane	142	174	$CH_3C(CH_2)_7CH_3$ $\overset{\parallel}{O}$ 2-decanone	156	210

Alcohol	MW (g/mole)	bp (°C)
$CH_3CH_2CH_2OH$ 1-propanol	60.1	97.4
$CH_3(CH_2)_2CH_2OH$ 1-butanol	74.1	117
$CH_3(CH_2)_3CH_2OH$ 1-pentanol	88.2	137
$CH_3(CH_2)_4CH_2OH$ 1-hexanol	102	158
$CH_3(CH_2)_8CH_2OH$ 1-decanol	158	229

MW = Molecular Weight
Alkanes are hydrocarbons containing only C and H with only C– C single bonds.
Ketones contain a C=O group.   Alcohols contain an O–H group.

Critical Thinking Questions

3. Individually, draw the Lewis structure for 1-propanol and then predict which bond will be the shortest and what the C-O-H bond angle will be. When all team members are done, compare answers and reach consensus.

4. Recall that the electronegativity of C and H are roughly the same, but that O has a significantly higher electronegativity. For each type of compound (alkane, ketone, alcohol), discuss and predict whether or not the compound is expected to be polar or nonpolar.

5. For each type of compound below, discuss and indicate how the boiling point changes as the molecular weight of the compound increases:

   a) alkane

   b) ketone

   c) alcohol

6. Based on your team's answers to CTQ 5, describe how the intermolecular forces between molecules change as the molecular weight increases.

7. As a team, find an alkane, a ketone, and an alcohol with roughly the same MW (within 5 g/mole). Rank these compounds in terms of relative boiling points.

8. a) Repeat CTQ 7 with two more sets of compounds.

b)   As a team, describe any general pattern that you can identify about the relative boiling points of alkanes, ketones, and alcohols of roughly equal MW. Use one or two sentences to write your team answer.

9.   Rank the three types of compounds in terms of their relative strength of intermolecular interaction, for molecules of roughly equal MW.

10. Based on the data in Table 1, does the presence of a dipole moment in a molecule tend to increase or decrease the strength of intermolecular interactions? Use evidence from Table 1 to support your team's reasoning.

11. Is the strength of intermolecular forces determined by the bond strengths within the individual molecules? Use evidence from Table 1 to support your team's reasoning.

Model 3: Intermolecular Forces are Weaker than Covalent Bonds.

The intermolecular forces that attract molecules to each other are much weaker than the bonds that hold molecules together. For example, 463 kJ/mole are required to break one mole of O–H bonds in H_2O molecules, but only 44 kJ/mole are needed to separate one mole of water molecules in liquid water.

*Most texts provide an excellent description of the types of interactions that produce attractive forces between molecules. Read about the various types of intermolecular forces present in liquids and solids in your text or as provided by your instructor **before** completing the rest of this ChemActivity.*

Critical Thinking Questions

Discuss and answer CTQs 12 – 18 as a team.

12. Describe the difference between intramolecular bonds and intermolecular forces.

13. Rank these intermolecular forces in terms of their typical relative strengths: hydrogen bonding; dipole-dipole interaction; induced dipole-induced dipole interaction (also known as London dispersion forces).

14. In the alkanes:

    a)   what type(s) of intermolecular force is (are) present?

    b)   what is the strongest intermolecular force present?

15. In the ketones:

    a)   what type(s) of intermolecular force is (are) present?

    b)   what is the strongest intermolecular force present?

16. In the alcohols:

    a)   what type(s) of intermolecular force is (are) present?

    b)   what is the strongest intermolecular force present?

17. In terms of intermolecular forces, why does the boiling point of a particular type of compound (for example, an alkane) increase as the molecular weight increases?

18. In terms of intermolecular forces, explain the general trend that you described in CTQ 8b.

Exercises

1. Based on the data in Table 1, predict the boiling points of each of these molecules and explain your reasoning.

    a) heptane, $CH_3(CH_2)_5CH_3$

    b) ethanol, CH_3CH_2OH

    c) 2-octanone, $CH_3\underset{\underset{O}{\|}}{C}(CH_2)_5CH_3$

2. Both *cis*-1,2,-dichloroethylene and *trans*-1,2,-dichloroethylene have the same molecular formula: $C_2H_2Cl_2$. However, the *cis* compound has a dipole moment, while the *trans* compound does not. One of these species has a boiling point of 60.3 °C and the other has a boiling point of 47.5 °C. Which compound has which boiling point? Explain your reasoning.

3. Rank each of the following groups of substances in order of increasing boiling point, and explain your reasoning:

    a) NH_3, He, CH_3F, CH_4

    b) CH_3Br, Ne, CH_3OH, CH_3CN

    c) CH_4, SiH_4, GeH_4, SnH_4

4. Using sentences, describe the difference between the hydrogen bond between two water molecules and the O–H bond in a particular water molecule.

5. Fluoromethane, CH_3F, and methanol, CH_3OH, have approximately the same molecular weight. However, the boiling point of CH_3OH is 65.15 °C, whereas the boiling point of CH_3F is almost 100 degrees lower, –78.4 °C. Explain.

6. Describe the properties of a molecule that are important in determining its boiling point.

Problems

1. In each of the following groups of substances, indicate which has the highest boiling point and explain your answer.

    a) $CH_3CH_2CH_2CH_3$; $CH_3OCH_2CH_3$; $CH_3CH_2CH_2F$; $N(CH_3)_3$; $CH_3CH_2CH_2NH_2$

    b) HCl ; H_3CCF_3 ; H_2O ; CCl_4 ; NaCl

    c) LiF, O_2 ; H_2O ; CaO; I_2

2. Circle the liquids below that do not exhibit hydrogen bonding. Explain your choice in each case.

H_2O ; $CH_3\underset{\underset{O}{\|}}{C}CH_3$; $CH_3\underset{\underset{O}{\|}}{C}OH$; CH_3OH

3. You are given an unknown liquid to identify. You are told that the molecular formula of the compound is $C_2H_6O_2$. You measure the boiling point of the compound and find it to be 198 °C. Identify this unknown liquid and explain your reasoning. You may wish to consider the following boiling points of various molecules in your analysis:

Molecule	bp (°C)
CH_4 methane	−182
CH_3CH_3 ethane	−89
$CH_3CH_2CH_3$ propane	−42
CH_3OH methanol	65
CH_3CH_2OH ethanol	78.5
$CH_3CH_2CH_2OH$ 1-propanol	97
$CH_3CH_2OCH_2CH_3$ diethyl ether	34.5

4. Which is the hardest to break?

   i)   the H–O bond in water

   ii) the hydrogen bond represented by "·····" in water:

   iii) the H–F bond in hydrogen fluoride
   iv) the H–C bond in methane
   v)   the H–N bond in ammonia

Periodic Table of the Elements*
with average atomic masses to two decimal places

1	2	3	4	5	6	7	8	9	10	11	12	13	14	15	16	17	18
1 H 1.008																	2 He 4.003
3 Li 6.941	4 Be 9.012											5 B 10.81	6 C 12.01	7 N 14.01	8 O 16.00	9 F 19.00	10 Ne 20.18
11 Na 22.99	12 Mg 24.31											13 Al 26.98	14 Si 28.09	15 P 30.97	16 S 32.07	17 Cl 35.45	18 Ar 39.95
19 K 39.10	20 Ca 40.08	21 Sc 44.96	22 Ti 47.88	23 V 50.94	24 Cr 52.00	25 Mn 54.94	26 Fe 55.85	27 Co 58.93	28 Ni 58.69	29 Cu 63.55	30 Zn 65.39	31 Ga 69.72	32 Ge 72.61	33 As 74.92	34 Se 78.96	35 Br 79.90	36 Kr 83.80
37 Rb 85.47	38 Sr 87.62	39 Y 88.91	40 Zr 91.22	41 Nb 92.91	42 Mo 95.94	43 Tc (98)	44 Ru 101.1	45 Rh 102.9	46 Pd 106.4	47 Ag 107.9	48 Cd 112.4	49 In 114.8	50 Sn 118.7	51 Sb 121.8	52 Te 127.6	53 I 126.9	54 Xe 131.3
55 Cs 132.9	56 Ba 137.3	57 La 138.9	72 Hf 178.5	73 Ta 180.9	74 W 183.9	75 Re 186.2	76 Os 190.2	77 Ir 192.2	78 Pt 195.1	79 Au 197.0	80 Hg 200.6	81 Tl 204.4	82 Pb 207.2	83 Bi 209.0	84 Po (209)	85 At (210)	86 Rn (222)
87 Fr (223)	88 Ra 226.0	89 Ac 227.0	104 Rf (265)	105 Db (268)	106 Sg (271)	107 Bh (272)	108 Hs (277)	109 Mt (276)	110 Ds (281)	111 Rg (280)	112 Cn (285)	113 Nh (284)	114 Fl (289)	115 Mc (288)	116 Lv (293)	117 Ts (292)	118 Og (294)

58 Ce 140.1	59 Pr 140.9	60 Nd 144.2	61 Pm (145)	62 Sm 150.4	63 Eu 152.0	64 Gd 157.3	65 Tb 158.9	66 Dy 162.5	67 Ho 164.9	68 Er 167.3	69 Tm 168.9	70 Yb 173.0	71 Lu 175.0
90 Th 232.0	91 Pa 231.0	92 U 238.0	93 Np 237.0	94 Pu (244)	95 Am (243)	96 Cm (247)	97 Bk (247)	98 Cf (251)	99 Es (252)	100 Fm (257)	101 Md (258)	102 No (259)	103 Lr (262)

CPSIA information can be obtained
at www.ICGtesting.com
Printed in the USA
JSHW042148201222
35244JS00003B/12